Praises for
ROCK AND SOUL

BRAVO! Rock and Soul is captivating and awe inspiring.
-RAY PARKER, JR.

Compelling. Heartfelt. Honest.
A resounding testament to the resilience of the force that is Thomas McClary. This book gave pure energy to my soul.
-DR. JULIUS ERVING

An emotion filled memoir of a "Cherished" walk and a "Celebration" of life, through the highs and lows of a natural born star. Thoroughly entertaining and moving.
-ROBERT BELL,
FOUNDER OF KOOL & THE GANG

Printed in the United States of America
First Printing, 2017

ISBN: 978-0-9985210-9-1

Copyright © 2017 by Thomas McClary

All rights reserved. No part of this publication may be reproduced, distributed, or transmitted in any form or by any means, including photocopying, recording, or other electronic or mechanical methods, without the prior written permission of the publisher, except in the case of brief quotations embodied in critical reviews and certain other noncommercial uses permitted by copyright law. For permission requests, write to the publisher, addressed "Attention: Permissions Coordinator," at the address below.

13th & Joan
500 N. Michigan Avenue, Suite #500
Chicago, IL 60611

WWW.13THANDJOAN.COM

ROCK AND SOUL

THOMAS McCLARY

Dedication

*For my wife Beryl and our lovely children.
Each of you will eternally be my greatest legacy.*

Author's Note

THE SENTIMENTS EXPRESSED in this book are my own. I have rendered the events from my keen remembrance. The views are captured in a way that extracted my deepest feelings and the messages of my heart. Timelines and reenactments are written with love. These moments made me who I am and I am grateful to God for allowing me an opportunity to recount them in my lifetime.

Epigraph

*Life is quite profound and complicated,
until we discover that our reason for existence
is anything but.*

CONTENTS

Author's Note 6
Forewords 11

Prologue: Rock... 17
1: This Little Light of Mine 21
2: And Still I Rise 39
3: Life, Liberty and the Pursuit of Restoration................ 59
4: Mustard Seed Faith 77
5: The Sun Never Forgets to Rise 97
6: Experience is A Just Teacher 125
7: Fog on the Glass Ceiling 143
8: Page 217 175
9: Play Another Slow Jam 197
10: Ships in Passing 219
11: The Night Shift... 233
12: A Revolution, Not A Revival........................... 261
13: Bound, Broken and Wrapped in Chains.................. 287
14: The Pursuit of Happiness................................. 307
Epilogue 333

Afterword 341
Acknowledgements 347
Endnotes 350
Bibliography 354
About the Author.. 359

Foreword

THE TRUE CHARACTER of a man is not, nor will it ever be, attached to a price tag. It can be neither bought nor borrowed. The true character of a man rests, rules, and abides in the very elements that make his heart increase in pace. The true character of a man is observed and not spoken, quiet and not boastful, sensible, and not foolish. The true character of a man is held within his heart, that is worn proudly on his sleeve. A man can only be classified as one who embodies integrity and stick-to-itiveness, that transcends boundaries imposed by societal norms and those that contradict the notions of love and kindness.

I've watched over the years, the evolution of the man known to the world as Thomas McClary, founder of the group The Commodores. I've witnessed his might, and the demonstration of pride in the face of injustices that could have destroyed him. I've stood beside him in perpetuity as he left it all on the stage of life. Being a part of the Motown family, Thomas played an intricate role in recruiting Lionel Richie, Ronald

LaPread, Milan Williams, Walter Orange, and William King, to be a part of a group that has sold hundred of millions of records around the world. This illustrates an innate ability to scout talent and intuitively exert business acumen, in ways that many cannot. The difference between success and failure is one's ability to look beyond fault and envision the future. I recognized so many similar qualities in Thomas. Not only was Thomas an instrumental lifeline in the emergence of the career of Lionel Richie, but also a visionary. As a longstanding council and confidant of Lionel, I drew immediate connections between the way in which a career can thrive when surrounded by people who believe in you. Thomas has served as a torch for helping those around him to believe the best of themselves and their talents. And although the business of entertainment can be filled with winding roads, the true character of a man is revealed in how he handles every turn.

Life is peculiar in the way that it turns us upside down, only to bring us back to a starting position, painted with new beginnings. The true character of a man is revealed in moments such as these. They define us and construct us, until we become silhouettes of righteousness. These are the moments that depict grace. Thomas is grace personified. Through moments of peril and moments of prosperity, he has always gifted the world with grace. Even in the midst of hatred, grace prevailed.

Far too often, people fail to realize that the exercise of destructive behaviors and ill will towards others, has adverse effects. Thomas McClary rose to prominence around the world because of his ability to withstand the trials and tribulations that he faced. He is the epitome of dexterity. He embodies a poise that led him towards the creation of legacy and a life well lived. This book details the life and the incredible journey of Thomas McClary, a man and a legend who was able to make, what I like to call, "lots of lemonade out of lemons."

CLARENCE ALEXANDER AVANT
American Music Executive | Film Producer | Entrepreneur

ROCK
and
SOUL

Prologue:
Heart

Being the first to do anything comes with a great deal of grit. The pages of my life reveal a calling that can only be categorized as divine. I have been called to be the first many times. Being the first thrives in the presence of great sacrifice and great accountability.

On this day, I sat in a courtroom as the first Commodore to be sued by his fellow band members. In this moment, I paid a dear price for being the first. The wooden chair, without armrests, wasn't the source of my discomfort, it was the fullness of the tension that filled the room and the powerful memories that became almost too much to bear; records broken, obstacles overcome, and love exchanged. The memories of toil, blood, sweat, tears, and the will to survive that we had all shared so fervently sent sharp pains through my side. My head hurt from the agony of the love that I had shared for each of the men that I had once, and still consider to be my brothers. How had we gotten to this place? How had all that we had accomplished together, driven us so far apart? I was clueless to say the least as to where we went wrong. All that I had ever wanted to do was make music, create, and make a difference. All I had ever wanted was for the sweet melodies, the snarling snares of the drum, and the passionate strum of the guitar to move people with love and cross barriers. You see, music was the universal language of love, and together we changed the world. But today, the gloom and haze from hurt and hatred was too monumental to overcome. Today, we were not united, we stood on separate sides of the battle and I stood alone.

There is something to be said of standing alone. In those moments, I experienced a fusion of humility, neuroticism, and anguish. I was disheartened. I hung my head in horror. The thought of facing the battlefield of contention with no signs of retreat was too profound a concept to grasp. There was no poetic justice, only a haze of melancholy and gloom. In those moments, I was introduced to my greatest instructor — God.

The crossroads of life teach us about who we are deep down inside. Amid turmoil, we learn about our internal motivations. The evidence of our ability to conquer is revealed. In the human mind, we begin to search for answers of why and how God brought us to certain places. In the courtroom, I came face to face with what felt like undeniable defeat. Standing alone can resurrect your greatest fear and stimulates your greatest strength simultaneously.

I closed my eyes in hopes of receiving something to fill the emptiness that my heart had been encapsulated by. A single tear fell, and left remnants of hurt on my hand. As I used the sleeve of my shirt to dry my eyes, I exhaled and began to reflect over the history that we had together. I remembered the joy and the pain. I could hear the muffled sound of the judge reading the deposition and the whispers of the legal teams conferring. In survival mode, my mind wandered towards better days. I began to experience an unexplainable sense of revival as I remembered that I had weathered storms before. Amidst the battlefield of contention, true character emerges. Although the courtroom was bustling with exchange between the legal teams, my mind had blocked it all out. My silent thoughts screamed, in a desperate attempt to remind me that there was a God that ruled over everything, even this courtroom. The gentle touch of wisdom grazed my face, letting me see that our divine assignments very often require us to deny ourselves. I was sitting in the midst of a moment such as this. It had not occurred to me that everything that I was now living through was a part of my spiritual calling. The pain, the rejection, and the deceit proved to be trials of an enemy that I was not equipped to fight. This was spiritual warfare.

It was in that moment that I realized that each of us fight battles that are too big for us and we must learn to give God glory and to uplift the journey that he has slated us to travel. I decided right then that I had a story and a testimony that deserved to be told. My character and my integrity were being questioned, but I serve a God who would not fail me. God favored me and it was time that I recognized just how much He had blessed me. The sweet, sweet smell of hope and destiny amused my senses and guided me towards the recognition of all that had manifested in my life.

You see, standing alone resurrects your greatest fears and stimulates your greatest strength simultaneously. This immeasurable strength is what we need to sustain. Life requires much of us, and in excellence, we must answer the call of duty.

My story was so much more than the chapters that I had written with The Commodores. The book of my life is filled with triumphs and reveals a marvelous legacy of its own. In that moment, I remembered who and whose I was.

My life's story is the embodiment of endurance and resilience in the face of adversity. I've overcome and this same power lies within you. We owe it to ourselves to stand firm and rooted in perseverance. To know a man's story is to know his heart. It is my greatest wish that you will know me for all that I am and all that I have been called to be, and that my life will serve as a light and a beacon of hope at the end of the tunnel. For having lived this life, I want someone to be inspired to never give up. This is my story and my truth.

Allow me to reintroduce myself. My name is Thomas McClary. I am the son of God, the creator of the signature sound — a living legend.

01: *This Little Light of Mine*

And when we look back over our lives, the memories will be the most valuable remnants of our experiences. I remember when I learned how to walk. I was in the midst of the company of my sisters Patricia and Willadean. We were in our living room. There was a coffee table there and I was walking around its perimeter. I remember releasing my hands from the table and taking my first real steps. I was desperately trying to get into my sister Leola's arms.

"Awe man, he did it. He actually walked," they all yelled.

My family was large to say the least. There were eight of us total. With four sisters and three brothers, I never wanted for a best friend. I could always find one in them. I was the second youngest and each of my siblings was two years apart, except for the baby of the family, who was eight years younger than me. It was almost as if my parents had timed everyone perfectly.

During the World War era, my parents were adolescents. Although my mother and father were from two different families, my father bore the name McClary, and my mother was a McAlister, there were many parallels that proved to be true in both of their lives prior to their bond as husband and wife. As youngsters with their families, they had migrated from the Carolinas down to Florida. Both sets of my grandparents owned their own farms. This was unheard of, since most blacks were sharecroppers. They were rare entrepreneurs, who provided jobs for hundreds of workers. Sharecropping was a sustainable way to make a living and they were discerning and wise enough to know that if you worked on a farm, you could avoid being drafted for the war. Both of my parents were true farmers. With a continuous display of drive, determination, and grit, they made a decision to own their own land. This was a tremendous feat during the time. They would eventually find themselves meeting by chance, as they were both the first black kids whose families owned cars in the city in which they grew up.

My mother acquired business acumen after her family made her responsible for paying the salaries of the workers on the farm. She would eventually use those same skills to manage the finances of our home. She was astute and strategic with money. I learned a great deal just by watching her and being in her presence. My father was a laborer on his parents' farm. Due to his vast array of experiences, he would often jokingly refer to himself as the "Jack of all trades and the master of none." My father was beyond charismatic and never seemed to meet a stranger. His ability to charm just about anybody was pretty darn impressive. When my mother and father were married, they decided to take their lives in a different direction and break away from farming. My mother was the first in her family to go to college while my father became a mechanic, a carpenter, and a block mason. Both continued to break barriers of racial discrimination, classism, ageism, and every other ism that existed to set the stage for the ambition of their children.

In 1949, a bouncing baby boy by the name of Thomas McClary was born. My parents had driven thirty minutes to a neighboring city in Florida called Sanford, to ensure that I would be born in a hospital under the care of a physician. Prior to that time, midwives were responsible for delivering babies and the deliveries primarily occurred in homes. Dr. George H. Starke, one of the few black prevalent physicians around, brought me into the world, screaming.

Before, during and after my birth, my parents were a beacon of light for faith and spirituality. Their religious backgrounds had taught them about endurance, love, and kindness. These same sentiments could be found running rampant throughout our home. It was an unspoken priority that my siblings and I be raised with a religious background that would foster our growth and development. Church was never optional. It was understood that on Sundays that is where we would be. It was in church I experienced my first epiphany that music spoke to my soul. The sweet sound of melodies matched the beats of my heart, and the rhythms from the drums were in sync with my breaths. Music ran through my veins.

My mother played the piano and my father sang a little. Music and melodies were a part of our day-to-day life. The first musical leader amongst my siblings was my older brother Samuel. He was so gifted. He played the piano, the organ, the ukulele, the bass, and the trombone. He was so patient and taught my siblings how to play both the piano and the ukulele. Eventually, my siblings Claudest, Charles, Willadean, Samuel, Patricia, Leola, and Karl, who was the youngest, formed a musical group called The McClarys. They would fearlessly compete and sing in different church programs.

It was my personal choice not to be a part of the group at that time. Truth be told, I had very little interest in instruments and more interest in creating ways to generate money. My attention has always seemed to drift towards entrepreneurial endeavors.

Even though I wasn't playing music, I can't think of a time that I was not listening to it. Secular music was not welcomed in our home, but I had such an appreciation for all genres. I loved the blues and of course, I loved the harmonies from the gospel groups like, The Mighty Clouds of Joy, and The Gospelaires, as well as the greats like Shirley Caesar and The Blind Boys. I also loved the blues from epic artists like B.B. King, and Albert King. My ears would later lead me to Chuck Berry, Wes Montgomery and Kenny Burrell. I placed no limits on what my ears grew to appreciate.

There was a radio station out of Nashville, Tennessee that played both blues and gospel music. At around ten o'clock, when our parents were certain that we were tucked in bed and resting, my curiosity would lead me to an old radio that I kept in my room. A disc jockey named John R. would come on and start playing the blues. He was so cold, man. He knew every song and every artist and the sequence he played them in was so sweet. I didn't want to disobey my parents, but my love for the melodies and compositions would not allow me to deny myself the opportunity to simply listen. While most children my age were sound asleep, I was indulging in late night listening sessions. John R. also played a new genre that I had not heard much of prior to then, which was country music. My love for music that was easy on the ears grew at a rapid speed. By day, when not in school, I was a young man in search of an opportunity to make money and by night, an avid appreciator of music.

In the seventh grade, I took the initiative to land my first real job. There was a young man named Alvin Harris, who lived two houses down from me. Alvin was a local newspaper delivery boy. The owner of the paper route, Mr. Paite, was a one armed, white man who was fairly popular within both the black and white communities. In addition to owning the paper route, Mr. Paite also owned the Greyhound bus station. Alvin was Mr. Paite's assistant. He would sit in the back of Mr. Paite's truck and roll the papers before delivering them. I always kept my ears to the ground for an opportunity. I learned from Alvin that he was growing weary of the job and would soon be relinquishing it. I saw it as an opportunity. I asked Alvin if he would mind if I took the job off his hands. I'll never forget the look on his face. It was startling.

"Are you sure you want this job? You have to wake up at 3 a.m. and get dressed for school and be prepared to go straight to school from the job," he said.

What Alvin hadn't realized is that I had paid close attention to the way in which he dressed. He clearly had more resources than most of the other students in our school. I attributed this to Alvin's job. I wanted that for myself. I desired to not be reliant on anyone or anything for additional resources. While I knew that the job might require a great deal of me, I was willing to do the work to achieve my desired end.

"If it will allow me to buy my own clothes and start my own savings account, I don't mind. I want to have my own money," I said convincingly.

I learned a great deal about myself in the process. There was a stick-to-itiveness and resiliency that I possessed that kept me encouraged and motivated. I must admit, the job with Mr. Paite's newspaper route was challenging, but I loved a good challenge. The increased responsibility meant that I had to successfully complete the paper route before school, excel academically in school, and complete my daily chores at home, which consisted of washing dishes, mopping floors, yard-work, and any other odd jobs that my parents deemed necessary. My parents were very adamant in teaching us that no matter what additional roles we took on outside of the home, we must always remain vigilant in the upkeep of our domain. We were taught to take pride in not only our living space, but also our actions and the work that we did. Priceless lessons like those are still with me today. As the paper route became routine, I was intrigued by the fact that I could actually make money and I continued to do so in this role.

Upon the summer following my seventh-grade year, I decided that I wanted to make more money. I had not come to this conclusion without being certain that I was prepared to take on more responsibility. I moved forward with creating another opportunity for myself. My older brother, Charles, had a job packing groceries at a local food chain grocery store named Piggly Wiggly. It was my thought that if he recommended me, they would be interested in hiring me. My strategy worked, and I began working at the grocery store in the afternoons after school. My daily schedule now consisted of waking up at 3 a.m. to complete my tasks with the paper route, then heading over to the grocery store to work. I must admit, I really didn't like the job at the grocer and it became my goal to find another job.

I discovered that there was an opportunity at a clothing store, sweeping floors after the store closed in the evening. By the summer's end, I was ready to attack the new school year with both jobs in the pocket. I went on to manage my paper route before school and the fashion store after. I had always had an appreciation for fashion, which was why I wanted to be able to have my own money in the first place, so this job was a good fit.

As I embarked upon my eighth-grade year, it was evident that my sisters Leola and Patricia were both moving along with their instruments. They were now both playing the piano and the organ and showing many signs of progress. Patricia even began playing the ukulele.

Aside from music, my siblings and I did everything together. I admired the fact that the girls had the same chores as we boys did — yardwork, vacuum, mop floors, etc. You should have heard the melodies coming from our home. We would sing and play music while we did our chores. I'd like to say that together, we sounded amazing. We also found creative ways to spend our leisurely time and enjoyed playing badminton in the big fields near our home.

I realized that I was very much behind my sisters and brothers in terms of musicality. We spent so much time together that I saw how far they were progressing and it made me want to invest a little more of my energy to do the same. Since I was working, I had a little extra money coming in. I made the decision to work in order to purchase my first guitar and an amp. My brothers and I formed and played as an actual group and really began to vibe.

There were two other families in the neighborhood that showed musical acumen. I had the pleasure of meeting Mr. "Zip" Lee Jerry Miller, a most talented blind pianist whose children were also musically talented and had their own neighborhood singing group. There was also the incredibly gifted Steel family. We would all exchange positive energy and were actively competitive. Even so, despite the competitiveness, we all learned from each other and wanted to see each other be successful.

Mr. Miller was an especially important influence in my life. Not only would he show my brother Samuel different chords, but he taught me my first song on the ukulele. The song was called, "Anytime You Feel Lonely." I was astounded that I could actually play a song and it only made me want to work harder to hone my skills.

As a naturally inquisitive adolescent, I began to inquire and strategize on ways to save enough money for the guitar that I truly wanted. I learned that I could establish some credit if I put money away and create a layaway plan for the guitar that I wanted and that's exactly what I did. A few months later, I bought my first guitar, a Silvertone. When I brought it home, my parents were elated, not just about the guitar, but also the way that I had gone about working to establish my credit. I began to feel more powerful with my financial management.

With the hard work that I exerted at my jobs, I got used to having money. It was my own money, which is what made me most proud. I began to put my fashion sense to use and I purchased clothes that I liked and thought were fashionable. I was what some would call "fly." The girls began to notice and that didn't hurt either. It was a little complicated, however, because I didn't have the same interest in them as they did with me. I was more interested in jamming sessions with the band and earning money. I guess I couldn't blame them with those amazing threads that I wore each day. I was told often that I was immaculate like my mom and had my father's charisma. I just loved people and the energy I felt when around them. Even though, I didn't want to date the girls, I maintained a significant interest in making them laugh. As the years progressed, I evolved into a socialite. I was invited to many parties by my peers. Sometimes, I would show up and sometimes I wouldn't. There is a strange side of me that some might refer to as an extroverted introvert. This is when a person really loves people, but they also retreat when in their own domain. This description fits me perfectly. It seemed like I was forced to choose between friends and music on many occasions.

I recall getting in trouble because one of the schoolteacher's daughters invited me to a party. After accepting the invitation to attend, I was also extended an offer to a jam session with some neighborhood guys who I had been wanting to play with. My classmate who had invited me to the party had also gone on to tell all of her friends that I would be attending her party as her guest. It seemed like everyone knew. On the night of the party, I didn't have the heart to tell my classmate that I would rather attend the jam session. My actions spoke louder than my words; I was a no show. I didn't pick her up as planned and that did not sit well with her parents, who were both very popular schoolteachers. The respectable thing to do would have been to decline the invitation with more consideration for her and her family. After that incident, I was in a little trouble as word spread like wildfire about my lack of respect for her invitation. From that point forward, I always remembered how important it was to keep your word. It was a lesson that hit close to home in lieu of all of the lessons of integrity that my parents had worked to instill in us.

There was a continuous stream of strategic thinking that I could not escape. My next venture was to form a band of my own. Joseph Hill, a drummer Eugene Lowe, who played sax and Jimmy Shaw, a bass player became the first official members. Our jam sessions turned into rehearsals. Once I had solidified our membership and commitment, I began to think of venues and events that we could play at. We considered playing at proms. I knew that every band needed an official name, so I came up with the name Matadors and the band members agreed. To fully develop our sound, and to recreate some of those amazing melodies that I had grown to love on the radio, I knew that we needed another member. Samuel Hill joined as our lead singer and just like that, we were an official band, The Matadors.

I maintained a sense of responsibility for the group's success because I had been instrumental in bringing everyone together. Even though we weren't making real money, we were performing our hearts out. I continued to work at my jobs before and after school to earn money. My only goal was to increase my income. The following summer, I strategized to work with the pastor, Everette Brooks, at our church. He owned a lawn service.

When I approached him to inquire about employment, he said, "What can you do?"

"I can do whatever you don't want to do," I replied.

I now had three jobs, the paper route, the fashion store after school, and on Saturdays, lawn service. You could have called me a lot of things, but broke would not have been one of them. These were the best of times. Not only did I have money, but I also had credit and savings. Our parents had always encouraged us to be watchful stewards over our resources and to use our time wisely. Aside from my entrepreneurial drive and musical interests, academic success was at the top of the hierarchy of my aspirations.

I was more competitive academically than in any other aspect of my life. I recognized that education was a means to an end. Especially having grown up in an era where racism was rampant, educational excellence was something that no act of injustice could separate you from. I would venture to say that many blacks felt this way. Our only way out of the oppression that so many pretend is not present was to be educated. I had to be the best. I wanted to be able to provide for myself and for my family. Throughout school, if I was not the top performing student in my class, I was second. There was another young lady who gave me a run for my money each year. Constance Sewell was extremely studious. She and I would go back and forth to determine who would make the best grades. This type of competition was healthy for both of us.

I also developed an interest in student council and the endeavors of the school's inner workings. Students at my school could be nominated for class officers. I often accepted the nomination for president and felt humbled that my peers viewed me in this capacity. Ever ready for the next challenge, I found the need to feed a growing interest in athletics. Grade school was not my first introduction to sports.

Mr. Miller, the blind musician who taught me my first ukulele lesson, was also a phenomenal pitcher. I would often play sandlot with members of my band, The Matadors, Charles Sewell, Lawrence Harris, and Alvin Harris, the young man who had given me the paper route months before. We played basketball, touch football, and any other games that we could think of. These activities became our pastime after school.

An unspoken line of division would separate the geographical area into teams. It would be what we referred to as "cross town" vs. my side of town. My side didn't get in trouble, we made good grades, our parents were God fearing, and we went to church regularly. The perception of character for the guys from cross town, were not as kind. Some of them, but not all, had situations where they had gotten into trouble or had gone to jail. The rivalry was always fueled by the undertone of the perceptions. Sports allowed us to push boundaries and release tension. Like most young men, we all welcomed the attention of the girls. On Sundays, we would routinely play games of touch football after church. When the girls showed up, the dynamics changed and everyone wanted to be noticed. It's pretty amusing to reflect on how touch football often turned into tackle on those days.

There were times when the competition from the neighborhood sports spilled over into our daily routines. My school bus stop was exactly one block from my house. Sometimes, Mr. Paite would drop me off at home after my paper route in the mornings and other times he would drop me off at school. The time we finished the route was always the determining factor.

If the morning route ended early enough, I would run into Jimmy Seal and his crew at the bus stop. Jimmy lived on my side of town, but he acted like he was from cross town and his reputation for being a bully preceded him. He always picked fights and nobody truly wanted to fight him because he was such a brute. My goal was to avoid him at all costs, but I wasn't always so lucky and on one particular morning, I paid a dear price for running into him. I was standing at the bus stop, preparing for the day at school. As I recall it, I was in good spirits. The sun was shining brightly and I could feel the warmth of the rays on my face. Out of nowhere, the light became shadow, but it wasn't a cloud that extinguished the sun, it was Jimmy Seal, standing over me. I looked up and squinted from the slight bit of sun that escaped over Jimmy's shoulder and into my face. I put my hand up to shield my eyes.

"Yes, Jimmy? May I help you?" I stuttered.

Jimmy didn't do a whole lot of talking, he was pretty much results oriented.

"Are you the one that keeps making all of those good grades? People keep talking about you. Quite frankly, I'm sick of hearing your name, man."

He didn't even allow me a chance to respond before he began popping the buttons on my shirt. He roughed me up as everyone stood around and watched. I took the punishment because I was not a fighter; I was a thinker and I wasn't prepared for Jimmy's attack. That day, he beat me up pretty good.

When I returned home, my dad was a little upset with me about what had transpired.

"The next time, Jimmy Seal does that to you and you don't defend yourself, you are going to get two whippings. One from him and one from me," he scolded.

About two weeks later, I saw Jimmy coming towards me again. I could only hear my father's words replaying in the back of my mind. I picked up a big two by four that lay near me on the ground and I hit Jimmy right on the side of his head. I could hear the crowd at the bus stop yelling and making commentary.

"Wooooo, he hit Jimmy Seal," they roared.

I dropped the two by four not far from where Jimmy fell. He sat there, holding his head and appeared to be in shock. I guess he never really thought that I would fight back. Before I knew it, he stood up and picked up the same two by four that I had used to defend myself. My next instinct was to run and I took off. To my dismay, he caught me and clocked me in the back of the head. I still have a scar from that day.

As much as we were divided in the neighborhood, we were compelled to maintain a unified front at school and in the community. Since there wasn't a Negro league in Eustis that we could join, all we had was each other. There was so much racial tension that plagued us as young, black men that the last thing that we needed was to dehumanize and harm each other in ways that could not be resolved. Sports at the school created the unity that we often needed. Baseball was one of the most popular sports and I was a pitcher. During football season, I was the quarterback. There was a tremendous disparity between the funding provided to the white schools and the black schools. Often times, we didn't have the proper equipment to remain safe.

Racism was not just something that we felt at school; we also felt it in our everyday lives. It was so rampant that we often felt helpless. There were huge incidents that would result in stories that made your heart sink down into your shoes. You never truly felt safe, not even in your own home. Stories circulated of the KKK burning men and hanging them from trees on the grassy front lawn that they had worked to make beautiful with their own hands. Black men walking down the street, never to be seen alive again for no apparent reason, and families left without a father to provide for them or tuck their children into bed at night. Racism was the most destructive fiber in the dissolution of the black family that I had ever witnessed. The worst part of it all was that no one felt like they could do anything about it.

Lake County had a Sheriff named Willis McCall. His name alone made black residents shiver. His reputation was synonymous for the death of unarmed black men. The random acts of violence always seemed to be a mystery, but everyone knew the truth in their hearts.

There were countless incidents of black men criminally charged and violently attacked while in police custody. Many times, no crime had been committed. While it was never proven that Sheriff McCall was a member of the KKK, his actions and treatment of the people in our community proved his affinity and sympathy of the clan mentality. (1) Black families were simply afraid to live. There were numerous stories of the KKK showing up at the homes of blacks with torches and burning crosses. Our home was no exception. The legacy of racial terror, which during that era was instilled in me as a young boy, has never really been spoken of. The truth was, you really never slept at night. Instead, you were left to toss and turn and hope for better days.

In addition to all of the mysterious incidents of harm, our city also had the burden of a Peeping Tom. This was yet another factor that added to our fears. The community at large feared leaving their children at home. It was unfortunate that parents had to teach their children strategies to prepare for a most unpleasant visit from the KKK. My parents always told us, "If the Klan ever comes, get down on the floor when they're shining lights. Don't be walking around, stay low." That notion would eventually become an all too familiar reality for us. I recall a light shining in the window, but I didn't know if it was the KKK or a Peeping Tom. I just knew my heart was racing. My nephew, Bryan Johnson, who was about four at the time, was also in my care. I was trying to make sure that he didn't make a sound. I could not remember where the gun that my parents kept was. I kept thinking to myself, that even if I had found the gun, I wasn't sure if I would have the nerve to pull the trigger. Finally, the light and the person shining it went away, but that also meant another night without rest. There were far too many instances of my neighbors and friends mysteriously being killed. Most of the time, you could follow up and find the stories on the news, but they were always filled with lies. The stories would report that those we knew as victims had committed suicide or hung themselves. Honestly, that wasn't the case.

Life, love, liberty, and the pursuit of happiness were all that we were after. We were rich in love and fought tooth and nail to maintain a livelihood that we could one day be proud of. The constant threat to our progression pained me deep in my soul. I often stared out of the window of my room in search of better days and wondered what I could personally do to be the change that I wanted to see in the world. Although there were so many reasons to be divided, we stood tall and together with our heads held high in my small city of Eustis, Florida.

The movements of Dr. King, Malcolm X, and the Black Panthers all gave us hope and courage. Whether you agreed with the approach of a given movement or not, no one could deny that we needed hope, and the promise of the power that was inside of each of us.

My love for music never wavered, but I also knew that education was the most powerful tool that I could use to never become a powerless victim of society imposed standards and systematic racism. I was determined to see what it was like in an environment where books had pages that weren't torn and showed no remnants from the countless names and damage of previous owners. Many of the books at our school were deemed outdated by schools for whites and those with more resources.

I woke up one morning and asked my parents to seriously discuss the idea of me going to an all-white school. It had not been done in Lake County. Although I knew that the opportunity would not be without great sacrifice, I wanted to take my shot at finding a way to triumph, not just for myself, but for the betterment of all blacks. If I could be successful, I knew that I could pave the way for others. I had to know if the quality of education would open more doors of opportunity and ways to solidify my future.

"If that is really what you want to do, we will support you," was the simple, yet powerful response that my parents gave me. The thought of driving past a school baffled me. I set my sights on being the first black student to integrate schools in Eustis, Florida. And so, it began.

02: *And Still I Rise*

I watched on the news as the media threw stones that continued to perpetuate the great social and economic divide and hid their hands, placing the blame on the very victims who remained vigilant in the face of racism and prejudice. The pain was, at times, overwhelming. There was very little value placed on the lives of blacks and I couldn't understand it. I watched as my classmates gained academic success in the classroom. I stood side by side with them in church as we sang Christian hymns. I worked hand in hand with them in our community to practice love and kindness. I played with them in the sandlots. How could there be so much hatred towards a group of people who had done nothing wrong?

The movements of Dr. King continued to resonate with me. In consideration of all of the leadership styles, his was the nearest to my perception of change. Regardless of how many times he was spat on, punched, cut, and even attacked, he always found a way to maintain a dignified front; he always found the strength to get back up again. His disposition brought about so much change. His actions were rooted in love. This inner voice and yearning to make a difference could not be silenced. In fact, it spoke to my heart, even louder. Eustis was not a well know city in the state of Florida, but I was determined to see to it that we made an impact that would be long remembered.

I was invigorated by the prospect of attaining a better quality of education to pursue entrepreneurship. I associated better quality with more resources. My thought process had very little to do with the educators at my then school. They were phenomenal to say the least. Moreover, they did more with less. I still celebrate their efforts today. What I did know for sure was that, entrepreneurship was calling my name. I wanted to own my own resources so that no one could place limitations on what I could or could not achieve. I recognized that the education that my teachers were providing for me at the all black school was the absolute best of what they had. There were deposits that those teachers made in my life that no amount of money could replace. The life lessons, and the way in which they could relate to what each student was experiencing in day to day life, were unparalleled.

Another factor that influenced my decisions during that time was my sightings. There was a great disparity between those who worked in what we called "The Muck," and the whites. The Muck was essentially, working the farmland. People would come from various cities to work in the vegetation areas, to pick fruit, and to perform very basic tasks. Although it was thankless, physically draining work, everyone did what they had to do to feed their families. While blacks were working in The Muck, white teenagers were driving cars and running errands about town. Many of my white counterparts had parents who could afford to buy them cars. They were afforded opportunities to obtain their driver's licenses without hassle. Even the ones that were not entrepreneurs, still seemed to have an edge financially on blacks, and it appeared to me that it was because of the color of their skin. We were separate, but not equal.

I got sick and tired of being sick and tired. By this time, my oldest sister and brother had moved north to make lives for themselves. I began to feel a sense of responsibility for my parents. It was now my goal to see them retire. I could not have sustained the burden of them dying and having worked for whites their entire life. They deserved so much more. Enough was enough. Enough of the unmatched lines and disparity. I knew that someone had to make a difference. I made up my mind to lead the charge for my family.

In my heart, I felt like the first step toward progress was to compete directly with the system that was the culprit of the oppression. There was not one area of my life that I felt was not worthy of working alongside my counterparts, whether academically, socially, or through athletics, I was not less than. I knew that I had the skills to thrive in any environment. I just didn't have the power to make people treat me fairly. I knew what I was up against and I was willing to stand alone on the battlefield of justice to fight for it.

In addition to the work of Dr. King, I had watched Jackie Robinson integrate the Major Baseball League. What he had done was monumental. Although I could not have fathomed the total impact of his integration, he was my hero.

In 1965, I began to spend time alone trying to convince myself that no matter what happened along the journey that I would embark upon, giving up was not an option. I was so fortunate that I could always find strength in the surety of the unyielding support of my parents and God. I stood firmly in the belief that God would be with me through this. All of those days and nights in church had led me up to this point. I needed unwavering faith now more than ever. I continued to mentally prepare for the worst and repeatedly told myself that it would not be easy.

My decision to endeavor to be the first black student to integrate public schools in Eustis, Florida was now public knowledge. There would be no turning back from here. I realized that the restlessness that I had experienced, for fear of a visit from the KKK to our home, paled in comparison to what I now felt. The weight of the world was on my shoulders and I had to find a way to remain vigilant in the face of adversity.

One day, while pacing in the house, the phone rang.

"Hello, McClary residence," I answered.

"Son, it's your principal, Mr. Walter Simmons. Are you sure you want to go through with this?" He inquired.

Not only was Mr. Simmons concerned, but my entire community within the circle of blacks was concerned. Of course, no one more than I, but I couldn't show it. I had to move forward. My dad had taught me the importance of keeping my word. I now felt like the responsibility was not only to my family and me, but also to other young men and women like me. We needed something to believe in. I had to make it through. Although I had no idea what would be on the other side, I knew that there was hope of a better tomorrow.

I'll admit there were moments when I almost changed my mind. As the anticipation mounted, even the press had gotten ahold of the story. There was no turning back. The news was motivation for me to forge ahead.

My family was contacted by the NAACP. The mission of the National Association for the Advancement of Colored People (NAACP) is to ensure the political, educational, social, and economic equality of rights of all persons and to eliminate race-based discrimination. (1)

This was a year of significant triumph in the country. Dr. Martin Luther King Jr. led the march for civil rights from Selma, Alabama to Montgomery, Alabama. The hatred that fueled the resistance of peaceful protest was at an all-time high. The stories of the terrible acts of war and execution of those that marched had traveled and no one in my community turned a deaf ear or a blind eye. People were bludgeoned and attacked ruthlessly. This tumultuous time in history was referred to as "Bloody Sunday." (2)

During this same year, the Voting Rights Act that guaranteed African Americans the right to vote became a law, and there was tremendous backlash because of that. The country seemed to be at war with itself. The race riots that broke out in Watts, California are just one example. (3) People were fed up from oppression, and the absence of equality. The random acts of violence and the shooting, lynching, and death threats to blacks were looming. There was no part of the country that someone like me could feel safe. Amidst all of this, here I was going against the grain and causing a stir.

The leadership of the NAACP expressed their concern to my family for what I was about to embark upon. Their fear was that I didn't have the infrastructure in place to endeavor such a feat. Their lack of confidence scared me even more.

With my head down, I admitted to myself that I felt weak. I had to wonder if they were right. I was weary. I hadn't spent my summer like my classmates, with thoughts of the sun, and the breeze, and girls. I hadn't engaged socially like I once had. Even the music that was still ever present in my heart, took a backseat to my socially driven mission. All of this thinking had truly taken a toll on me. I felt as if I was suffocating. Blacks in my community supported me, but when you decided to take a stand against injustice, it is almost as if you are also making the decision to be alone on a deserted island. I had to grow up real fast. It was my choice to do so. I felt as though this was so much bigger than me. I had been divinely appointed for my assignment and I would fight until the end.

The night before my first day of school was daunting. I tossed and turned relentlessly. It was one of the worst nights of sleep of my entire life. The looming air of the consequences of my actions haunted me. Would I be persecuted? Would I live to see another day? Would I be cornered and beaten? That night, alone in my room, I called on God to be with me. My parents had taught me so much about faith and had immersed us in it. If I ever needed it, it was that night. I needed to know that I would be ok. It was almost as if I was having an out-of-body experience. The over processing of my thoughts allowed me to drift off to sleep and my sleep allowed me to drift off into a sea of nightmares. I sat in my bed, awake and afraid.

When morning came, I prepared for a first school day as any normal high school student would. I made the decision to walk to school without my parents or any escorts. I didn't want to appear afraid. I wanted to embody strength and determination. My parents were waiting for me at the front door and prayed with me before I left. As I placed my hand on the door handle, I closed my eyes, took a deep breath, and exhaled every fear. As I opened the door, I remember being shocked. There was no media, no whites standing in front of their cars with bats, no police yelling racial slurs, nothing. An immediate sense of comfort came over me. I had goosebumps on my arm. I believed that God had answered my prayers and that even though history was being made in the midst of resistance, this would be an uneventful day. I picked up the pace of my stride and I even recall a small smirk. I felt a sense of pride because this was really happening and I was really walking myself to a school that people like me had once been denied acceptance. There was hope after all.

As I turned the corner towards Bay Street, I felt an incredible strike in my back. In my mind, I thought that someone had come out of the bush to attack me. I reached over my shoulder in an attempt to discover the immediate source of pain. I heard roaring laughing as a car passed me. The car was filled with white boys who appeared to be my age. They were throwing oranges at me. In Florida, oranges that are not fully ripe are still a little green and much harder than an orange that is fully ripe. I bent over slightly to weather the pain that I felt. Had I been weak, I would have turned around then, but my mind was made up. Their motives to cause me harm fueled me to press forward. At that moment, I was prepared for whatever the day would bring. I'm not sure why such strength and endurance found me, but I'm glad that it did. I wasn't going to give up under any circumstances. I stood, with my head held high and looked the guys right in their eyes.

THOMAS McCLARY & ARDRE ORIE

Even they could see that I was not backing down. They sped off and one of them yelled a racial slur as the tire screeched on the pavement.

I used that moment as motivation to make me even more determined. I began to walk faster, one foot in front of the other. I could hear the sound of my shoes with every step. I knew my way around the city very well and decided to take a short cut. As I was passing through the community, there was a street that had a significant hill. I had to walk down the hill and then back up to see what was on the other side. As I was coming up the hill, I noticed another car that looked somewhat out of place. I continued walking, but with extreme caution. The car was coming towards me and I began to brace myself. There were four white guys in the car and the closer that they got to me, the louder their voices became. I began to tremble slightly. The driver mashed the gas aggressively and cut across the grass and sidewalk to pull the car in front of me. They cut me off so that I would have to walk around. He stopped the car and they all hopped out. They began to scream, taunt, and throw random objects at me. Two of them were throwing bricks. I ran as fast as I could to get away. They didn't chase me and for that, I was thankful.

Eventually, I made it to the campus. I could see the words Eustis High School at the top of the building. Everyone was standing outside of the campus and no one appeared to want to go inside the school. It was as if I was the plague. Everyone stood, staring at me. No one smiled or even gave so much as a nod of encouragement. What could I have expected, there was no one there who resembled me. I stood for a moment in awe of the severity of what I believed that they felt. All I had wanted was access to the same quality of education as my white counterparts. I stood there in sheer desperation for a simple opportunity. I wasn't asking for special treatment, or for anyone to give me anything. I just wanted equality.

A tear welled up in my eye to think that I was disliked so much that I was not deserving of a fair education. I had never felt that type of hatred in my heart for anyone. I was overcome with sadness. I fought with everything inside of me to not allow the tear to fall. Those standing around me didn't deserve it, nor did those whom I represented. I could see what seemed to be the entire Lake County Police Department, standing next to their parade of cars. There also appeared to be the entire staff and faculty of the school, as well as the entire student body standing outside of the building in stark silence. A single voice, yelled from the student body, "Get that Nigga." His statement was mimicked as many others joined him. That single cry morphed into a roar of many. Repeatedly, they chanted, "Get that Nigga." My dad was in the parking lot amongst many other parents of the community. He came and stood next to me. I needed this action so desperately. I knew that no matter what happened, he would do all that he could to protect me. Most importantly, I knew that I had his support and that was worth more to me than life itself.

A voice came over the PA system, and the chanting began to diminish.

"Student body, this is your principal, Mr. Edmund Weicherz. I want everyone to calm down. We are not going to have any incident here. Everyone is to report to the auditorium immediately." His actions put an end to my standing there in the pit of scrutiny.

My father shook my hand firmly and looked me deep in the eyes. With misty eyes, the edges of his lips curled up into a u-shape and in the midst of a moment that almost became too heavy to bear, he mustered up a smile. I now had the strength to return it to him as I watched him walk back to his car.

The student body slowly began to go inside of the building. I was still shaking from all that had occurred on the journey there. As I started to walk in, everyone stared at me and it became obvious that no one wanted to be in close proximity to me. It was like I was the oil attempting to mix with water. There was a little part of me that somehow thought that it was only older folks who held the idea of racism. To know that students, who looked just like me, with the exception of the color of our skin, felt the same, hurt deeply. What had I ever done, except work hard?

As I approached the door of the auditorium, I had to rub elbows and get closer to the students. Where there is a will, there is a way. That morning, I had already been physically and mentally attacked. I had already encountered oranges thrown at my back and bricks thrown at my head. What else could there be? I wasn't afraid any longer; I just wanted to make it through the day. It was obvious that there was no designated place for me to sit. What I knew was that I was not going to sit in the back for fear of whatever might happen. I deserved to be there. I deserved to have an opportunity to learn and grow just like they did. I knew that blacks were not allowed to swim in the city pool, or drink in the white water fountains, but there was no law that stated that I had to sit in the back, so I didn't.

The principal told the student body that together, we were making history. He also expressed adamantly that he intended to get through the day without incident.

"I assure all that I will remain on top of this situation."

It was more than obvious that the entire student body was not in agreeance with his forward way of thinking. Even while he was speaking, some students disrupted him and the chanting began again, "Get that Nigga. Get that Nigga."

The principal interjected, "Everyone go to your homeroom and get instructions there as to who your teachers will be for the year."

It was apparent that he intended for the day to be without incident. Little did he know about the torment that I had experienced in the simple act of attempting to get there.

As everyone stood up to leave, I realized that I had no idea where homeroom was. I had never set foot in that building and had no point of reference. I attempted to navigate by following the crowd. I was standing in the auditorium and I knew that it would have to be in a location other than where I was standing.

Out of nowhere, I heard a voice say, "Hey, Thomas, right? Well, we are actually in the same class, so if you want to follow me, I can show you where it is."

I was beyond grateful. I would later learn that his name was Duncan Cottrell. I could never forget his kindness. I felt like I had been thrown to the wolves and he was my refuge in that moment.

Walking through the hallways, everyone lined the row of lockers and stared. We had all been taught to be separate. We had all been taught that we were not equal. I couldn't hate them for what they had been taught, I hated that I was a target. I hated the fact that it was hunting season on my life. It was as if I didn't belong, but it didn't make sense. How could a student not belong in a school? I had made it this far, I wasn't turning around. I continued to follow Duncan until we reached the classroom. By the time we got there, it was filled with students. I still couldn't believe what I was actually doing. When we entered the class, I was determined to sit in the middle. I was greeted by the teacher, who was very polite.

"In case, no one knows, this is Thomas McClary and he is from Eustis Vocational High School. From what I know, he is an excellent student and athlete who has made a brave step to join our school and be a part of it. Let's be sure to welcome him."

I hung on her words like hope. Could it be possible that I would be treated with kindness? Were there some white people who did not have the same resentment in their hearts for blacks? This would remain to be seen, but I most certainly had encountered kindness two times on one of the most challenging days of my life and I valued it.

After introducing me, the teacher allowed all of the students to go around and introduce themselves. She then gave us our schedules. As the class was being dismissed and we were leaving the classroom, another student approached me. I was always wary when someone walked near me. I wasn't sure if they wanted to hurt me. I remained on guard.

"I'm Kent Reedy. I'm on the football team here. Are you thinking about coming out?"

"I play football too," I exclaimed.

I later learned that Kent was a junior and the son of the former Mayor of Eustis. It was ironic because my mom had worked as a maid for his uncle, State Representative W. H. "Bill" Reedy. He was very kind and asked me what position I played. I told him that I was going to come out for the team and we bid each other adieu like old pals. The rest of the school day went without incident. I was so thankful to have gotten through. Even though I didn't expect things to be easy, I knew that I could do it and that I would build a stronger resistance to whatever would come my way. I was convinced that I could make it and that was all that I needed to continue on.

That afternoon, I was looking forward to football practice. It was my hope that this would be an opportunity to feel comfortable, in a zone that was familiar to everyone. I wanted it to be known that I would be participating in sports. I was looking for Kent when I arrived at practice. He was obviously nervous when we got into the locker room at how I might be received by the others there.

I overheard a student ask, "Is he going to have a locker in this locker room?" I could see the vacant looks and the same eyes that I had met in the hallway of the school. They did not want me to be there, but I was. I was there and I knew that I had every right to be. I was not only a student that had something to contribute, but also a good athlete who could make a positive impact on the team. I was a hell of a quarterback and I wanted to use my skills and talent.

As I walked out alone to practice, Coach Dub Palmer stopped me before I set foot on the field. He said, "Well

Thomas, we have two quarterbacks, so we don't need a third. We are going to try you out at defensive end."

"Coach, I'm not a defensive player. I'm an offensive player," I said with great concern.

"You are going to play where we tell you to play," he said.

As the play was being setup, I was well aware that I was being set up as well. They did not want to see me succeed and instead aimed to injure me so that I would not be able to play at all. It was almost as if I was being punished for being courageous. As the play began, the guard pulled and the end came and blocked. The play was set up so that three people were coming to block me on a play. Not being a defensive player, I didn't have the skills to engage in that way. They ran over me like a train. I heard the roar of the crowd and the undertone of chanting.

"Kill that Nigga. Kill him."

I recognized immediately what they were trying to do. I did a little better defeating it the next few times that they ran the play.

I got up and I said, "Coach, I'm not a defensive player. I can play running back."

"Nah, you are not a running back."

The rest of the day, they kept banging me. After about five more times, I said to myself, "Enough of this."

The practice seemed like an eternity and in the locker room afterwards everyone was looking at me. One of the players finally spoke up and said, "Well, I know you don't think that you are going to take a shower in here."

I literally had to wait until all of the other players had taken their showers.

"We are not going to ever use that spot that you stood in."

The day was over and it was time to head home, but while all the other guys on the team had cars, or were riding with friends, I was walking. Considering all that had happened that day, I was exhausted and couldn't face any more being thrown at me, literally or figuratively, so I ran. I lived four blocks from downtown and had two choices, the short route I'd taken that morning through the residential area, or the long way down through town. I opted for the same route I'd taken that morning and decided that the run would be good conditioning. No matter what they said, or what position they threw me in, I knew I was going to play football. Since I hadn't had the chance to train with them in the spring, I would use any time that I had to train now. When I got home, everyone was concerned about how my first day had gone. Even as fatigue set in, I did my best to relive the day and share it with my family. My parents told me to stay strong.

"If this is something that you have decided to do, you will not quit because that is not in your blood," proclaimed my dad.

He stood over me with his hand firmly grasping my shoulder. He reminded me of Dr. Martin Luther King, Jr. and the non-violent mentality, as well as Jackie Robinson who had exemplified great courage under similar circumstances. "You will make it through this," he said.

I must admit that I was beyond overwhelmed with everything. There were times, in my private moments that I fought back tears. As the days passed, it didn't get easier. It was an uphill battle. Often, it was the pain from my tears that replenished me. I began to change my way of thinking. I refused to be overcome by the hatred and mean-spirited people that I encountered. Sometimes, I had to give myself a pep talk in the middle of the hallway after an encounter with students who attempted to belittle me, or those that felt I had no place at the school. It probably appeared to onlookers that I was talking to myself, but I didn't care. It was just that hard. Thankfully, my parents and my faith held me up when I was down.

I think that it shocked many people that I didn't give up. I was a lot of things, but a quitter was not one of them. The more resistance I encounter, the harder I fought. Over time, it seemed that some people changed their behaviors towards me, not because they accepted me, but more so because they could only respect my willingness to weather the storm. I would not be labeled an absconder. Not then, not ever.

Amidst everything that was happening around me, I was still responsible for executing academically at the same level. I had something to prove. There was no way that I would fight to attend the school, fight for integration, become a symbol of resistance against injustice, only to fail academically. I studied even harder and applied myself more rigorously.

Andy Hall was the first female that was kind to me. Her parents owned Hall's Nursery and ironically, my pastor, Reverend Jerry Shaw, worked at that nursery. You never know how your character will show up to speak when you can't. Andy and her family were very fond of my pastor. He of course spoke highly of my character and my work ethic because I had worked hard to earn his respect. Furthermore, my family had a great reputation in the community. My parents saw to it that we were actively involved in helping others and that we kept our word when we made a commitment. Andy was very astute. I believe that this also gave us common ground. She valued her education just as much as I did.

My ability to excel academically, also opened doors for more conversation and made me more relatable to some students. Dare I say that we saw a little of each other in ourselves? After our exams, the teachers would announce the grades aloud, which gave insight into how our peers performed. Although this process may have not been favorable for some, it showed that academically, I was a high achiever.

Even as things seemed to go well, there were always more hurdles to overcome. My first real confrontational incident occurred when a young lady at the school accused me of trying to hit on her. This was the farthest thing from my mind because simply attending school and staying alive were my priorities. Her name was Susan Dillard and upon her allegations, we were both called into the principal's office to tell our sides of the story.

Mr. Weicherz began to question us. "Susan said that you tried to approach her sexually," he said.

"What does that mean? What did I do?" I asked.

"Susan, can you explain what Mr. McClary has done towards you?"

"He was looking at me like he wanted to ask something sexual," she murmured.

"How do you look at someone like that? What does that mean?" He inquired. "Did he say anything to you?"

"No, it was how he was looking at me. I don't know, but I think he was going to ask me something sexual."

Even though Mr. Weicherz was white, from my interactions with him, he seemed to be fair. An allegation of this magnitude could mean the life of a black man, especially in the south. Consider the story of Emmett Till, who was brutally attacked and killed for a false accusation that he whistled at a white woman. In that moment, Mr. Weicherz appeared to be reasoning with himself. It was a delicate situation. He proceeded to reprimand me in a way that was harmless. It was almost as if his words were simply to appease Suzy. I knew in that moment that I was in no real trouble. I had not done anything wrong or even questionable and I believe that in his heart, he knew it also. That day, I learned that I must never let my guard down and always be prepared for the unexpected. Character had always been of the utmost importance, and in an instance like that my character preceded me, and I am thankful that it did. Suzanne Hartge, Rita Spears, Faith Zaleski, and Twig Knowles befriended me shortly afterwards. I guess that was God's way of sending angels to reassure me that nobody fell for that stunt.

I had overcome so many obstacles as the first black student to integrate the public school system in Lake County. There was a boldness inside of me that was stubborn enough to deal with whatever came my way. Growing up, I had become so engulfed with fear from the countless stories of neighbors who had died mysteriously, black men slain in public, and talks of Klan meetings that it was overwhelming. There comes a point that you are encompassed with all of these phobias and fears, so much so that you finally must ask yourself, "What do I have to lose?"

At no time during this grueling era in my life did I plan to lose, God had brought me too far, and my parents had worked too hard. The other challenge that became increasingly apparent was the disdain that I encountered from my fellow black peers. Not everyone had agreed with my decision to integrate. I was quickly labeled an "Uncle Tom" and ridiculed in public. This added another layer to the pain of my attempt to make history and make a difference.

It was noticed that I was not going to quit by many public figures and it became apparent that I was going to make history. One evening, I received another call from the NAACP. I was asked to meet with them this time. Up until then, I had not received much support, as it was assumed that the little boy from Eustis would be swept under the rug.

There were still many whites who did not want me at their school and many blacks who did not want me to integrate. I was damned either way. The greatest lesson gleaned was that you couldn't please everyone. When you know your why, you won't have to worry about your how; God will make a way. What I attempted to accomplish was colossal. I knew that there was a purpose greater than me and I would not stop until my mission was completed.

I had taken some time away from music to fight for justice, but the melodies inside of my soul never departed. I would come to realize that to make an impact, you have to step outside of what is safe. You have to be willing to walk alone to get to a destination that sometimes only you can see. Any time there is injustice, someone must hold themselves accountable for being the change that they so seek. I don't regret anything about my journey to integrate the school in Eustis and it is my hope that it becomes a part of a legacy that teaches young people that you are never too young to make a difference.

03: *Life, Liberty, and the Pursuit of Restoration*

I've heard it said many times that the road less traveled bears clear lanes. In some instances that can be a good thing. For one year, I was traveling a lonely journey towards completing my education as the only black student at Eustis High School. In my senior year, I found great joy in no longer having to travel unaccompanied. Robert Evans, a dear friend, scholar and athlete, joined me in continuing the pursuit of integration. Robert and I played on the baseball and football teams together and exchanged a sense of pride in familiarity. It was a great pleasure to be in the presence of someone else who understood exactly what I had been going through.

Over time, the noise among the blacks in the community also began to settle. The Uncle Tom slurs and many of the condescending overtones were not as prevalent. I guess they realized that the hands of time could not be turned back. There was even an emergence of discussion regarding my old high school and the possibility of turning it into a ninth-grade center and integrating it to include white students.

In retrospect, I know that I would never have been prepared, nor capable of accomplishing such a tremendous feat without the unyielding support of my community. My family and friends, who laughed, played badminton, football, basketball, table tennis, and swam in the lake, and shot bb guns with me, were my source of strength. Without these precious moments, my childhood would have vanished due to the never ending battle with injustice.

With the great effort to make a difference behind me, the time came for me to begin thinking about the next phase of my life and my learning — college. College was not optional in my family. My older siblings had already been enrolled in college for several years and their having done so gave me the opportunity to explore my options.

After the laborious battle in the fight for integration at Eustis High School, and the unimaginable treatment that I had endured over the years there, I yearned to share time and space with those who were more like me and could relate to the ongoing struggles that I faced in the world as a black man. I felt like I had been away at war and needed desperately to return home.

I asked my parents to take me for a visit to Tuskegee University. I had heard so many positive things about the school's academic strides and their cultivation of people of color, but being on the campus allowed me an opportunity to experience it for myself. While I had made plans to visit Bethune Cookman College, which is now Bethune Cookman University, and Michigan State, it seemed unnecessary after visiting Tuskegee.

When I returned to Eustis, I applied immediately and not long after I received a letter of acceptance. I couldn't have been more proud. My family was overjoyed and the celebration prior to my departure was triumphant. It is safe to say that I could have been one of any number of black men who never made it out of Eustis alive — but I did — and for my faith, family, and future I was thankful.

    I caught the bus from Eustis to Alabama with all of my belongings. When I arrived, it was a major shock to me. It was pouring down rain and the atmosphere had no resemblance to the Florida sun that I had been accustomed to all my life. As my feet hit the ground, I realized the tremendous responsibility that I had assumed by no longer being under the care of my parents. I spent some time wandering about the campus, organizing my thoughts and learning my way. Emory I, Emory II, and Emory III signs labeled the dorms and made it easier to locate my room. After sorting through the buzz of the hall and finding my dorm room, I met my roommate who was from South Carolina. He spoke very little as I entered the room, but that didn't matter. I was far more concerned with getting registered for classes and settling in. Unlike my new peers, I had not arrived on campus early and therefore had less time to prepare for the upcoming semester.

    On the first night, I sat quietly reminiscing about Eustis. I was elated to have achieved my goals, but I must admit that there was a part of me that felt like something was missing. My mind wandered and I recalled the countless hours of learning to play music with my siblings. From there, my thoughts drifted and I lingered over the memories of the amazing jam session I'd had with the band that I had assembled back home. The Matadors had become a part of who I was. The music was in my soul, but I couldn't seem to find the melodies at my fingertips. I resolved right then, that I would not only attain academic success, but I would also find the people and resources that I needed to put together a new band while at Tuskegee.

Relatively speaking, I was starting at a disadvantage. My parents did not think that it was a good idea for me to bring all of my musical equipment to college, so I left that part of my life behind, or so I thought. I knew that it would be a challenge for me to locate instruments and equipment but I didn't care. I was determined to see this through.

The next morning when I woke up, my mind, actions, and attitude were harnessed together towards executing my musical plan. I was accustomed to working and having my own money. Now, I found myself at Tuskegee with no band, no job, and no money and that was not going to work.

As I stood in a long line waiting to register for classes and trying to work out in my head how to achieve my new goals, I overheard a guy whistling a song called, "Listen Here," by Eddie Harris. His whistling was very distinct as he carefully formed the intricate licks and nuances of the song. I remember thinking to myself that there was no way that he was not a musician. He was positioned about six people behind me, but the line was moving very slowly. I could no longer hold back.

"Aye man, are you a musician?"

The gentleman was very shy and he looked down, "No, not really."

"I am looking to put a band together. We are going to be the Black Beatles," I exclaimed. I was standing on my toes and I spoke with so much enthusiasm that my passion for music was obvious to anyone standing near.

He was noticeably rattled and replied, "Oh God, man. I'm not a musician, but you sound really intense about this. I live here and I know some musicians. If you are serious, I can round up the guys that I know and have them audition for you." I was beyond excited; it was as if the stars had aligned. Throughout my life, it seems like music and I have always had a funny way of finding each other.

Before my turn in the registration line, he gave me the address of where I could connect with some of the musicians that he spoke of. 521 Old Montgomery Road would become a place where more magic than I could have ever imagined would happen. We said our goodbyes and returned focus to the reason that we were there, registering for college courses.

There was so much to be done and so much to learn as a new student that I didn't follow up with the information that the gentleman in the registration line had given me until the end of the week. I tried to temper my high hopes, as I didn't know what would come out of meeting these so-called musicians.

The Saturday following registration, I set out in search of 521 Old Montgomery Road and discovered that the home was right across the street from Tuskegee. During those times, it wasn't seen as impolite to visit someone's home unannounced, especially if you had good reason for doing so. As I walked up the steps, I noticed that the front door was open and I could hear the sound of young men speaking and laughing. I knocked on the door and one of them walked over.

"Hey man, how are you?" He asked.

"Hello, my name is Thomas McClary and I met a guy in the registration line at Tuskegee who told me that I could find some musicians here. I'm working on putting together a band and I know that it's going to be amazing. I just need to add some musicians to the team."

"Oh yeah, sure man, that sounds good. I'd love to hear more. Why don't you come and join us in the basement." He stepped aside and invited me in. "My name is William Smith, but everyone calls me 'Smitty'. I play the saxophone. That's Andre Callahan," he said, pointing. "He's a drummer."

"Real nice to meet you guys. I can dig it," I replied. I heard a beautiful melody coming down the stairs. It was a sax and man it sounded so nice. I recognized the player as the gentleman I'd met in the registration line.

"Oh, hey man. Say, I thought you said you weren't a musician?"

"I'm not really. This is my uncle's sax. I just jam a little with these cats."

"Well it sounds pretty darn good to me. You've got some real talent man."

"Awe, thanks man. I'm Lionel Richie, what's your name?"

"I'm Thomas. Thomas McClary. It's nice to meet you."

After meeting all the guys, Smitty invited me to sit and listen to them play. Andre Callahan didn't really have any drums and truth be told, I didn't have anything to play either. After some time exchanging energy with the fellas, I restated my intentions of assembling a band. I knew that I could do it because I had done it with The Matadors. I assured everyone that I could find the resources that we needed to make the band a reality. We all vibed and they put faith in me to make it happen. That day, we all decided that we would move forward together.

As I walked away from 521, I could feel the hole in my heart closing. I couldn't stop smiling because I knew that I could count on myself. I was going to make this band happen, come hell or high water. I had so many reasons for reigniting the music that lived inside of me.

The next day, I returned to meet the guys to share my findings from research that I had done. There was a freshman talent show at Tuskegee and I thought that it would be a great opportunity to get in front of some real people. I told them that if nothing else, this would help us meet some girls and make new connections at the school. The guys agreed and I began to strategize on what we would need to be successful. I knew that I would have to find a bass player, and more importantly an amp and a guitar so that I could finally prove to the guys that I was who I said I was. I wanted them to know that I was a man of my word and that I could make things happen.

Although I did not know anyone at Tuskegee, it did not deter me. I had been taught by my parents to use what I had in front of me to create what I needed. As I sat in my dorm room, I began looking through an old Tuskegee yearbook that had been left by a previous resident. I came across a photograph of another band called, The Jays. That photo sparked an idea. I knew that if I could find the members of that band, I could potentially borrow a guitar. It was a priority for me not to return empty handed at my next meeting with the guys. At the very least, I would have an instrument. I sat and continued to assemble a plan to find the guys in the photo. Although not small, Tuskegee was a close-knit college community and I knew I would meet someone who would help me find these bandmates.

I started my search at the rec center the next day. It was a nuclear hangout for many and my hope was that I could find one of The Jays members — if not one of them directly, then maybe someone who knew them or knew where they lived and could point me in the right direction.

With my borrowed yearbook in hand, I began asking around. "Excuse me, can you help me find any of the guys in this band?" I inquired, while pointing to the picture. The first twenty minutes or so, I came up short. Many students there were freshman like me and just trying to learn the ropes. I heard a voice amidst a group of guys speak up.

"One of the guys lives in Residence E. I think he plays the keyboard in that group you're talking about, man."

It was a start. I thanked him and left the rec center hopeful that I was one step closer to finding the resources that I needed to get the band up and running.

Two days later, I decided to pick up where I had left off, this time taking my search to Residence E. As I got closer, my eyes set on a young man holding a briefcase and walking with haste. As I got closer, I could feel goosebumps on my arm as I realized that he was exactly who I had been in search of. I walked faster to catch up to him. As I got within arm's reach, I wasted no time. "Hey man, are you one of The Jays?" I had the biggest smile on my face. There was no way that he could not have talked to me.

"Yes," he replied. "My name is Milan Williams."

"Say man, I'm putting this band together and we are going to be the Black Beatles." There was nothing that anyone could say to me to convince me otherwise. I had set my mind towards the notion that the band that I would assemble would be epic.

"We are trying to put something together for the talent show, but I don't have an instrument. My parents made me leave all of my equipment back in my hometown of Eustis, Florida."

He interjected almost immediately. "Hey, I play keyboard, but I'm also a guitarist. In fact, I have a guitar in my dorm room. I'd be willing to let you use it if you really can play."

Honestly, I must admit that I wasn't nearly as skilled with the guitar as I would have liked, since I had spent most of my time learning to play the ukulele. It didn't matter much though because my enthusiasm to assemble a group could not be denied. What some fail to understand is that real music lives in your soul. No matter how much classical training one engages in, if the music isn't in your heart, you will never witness the magic in the melodies. I wasn't going to let the differences between the instruments hurt my chances. I had every intention of leveraging my knowledge and skill of the ukulele on the guitar to show him that I was worthy of borrowing his instrument.

I agreed to his offer and we walked to his room. I had such a good feeling about everything. There are moments in life that God prepares you for before you even realize that you needed the preparation. This was one of those moments for me. After arriving in his room, I noticed the guitar laying on the floor near the window. It was a beautiful red Gibson SG.

"Here it is man. Let's see what you can do," he said.

I walked over towards the window and I could feel the warmth of the sun beaming into the room. It was confirmation from God that everything would be OK. I kneeled down to remove the guitar from the case and as I picked it up, I could feel the strings on my fingers. They felt like home. I stood there in silence for about thirty seconds. I could tell that he was waiting to see if I could do what I claimed. He wanted to ensure that my actions spoke louder than my words.

I took a deep breath, closed my eyes, and began to play. I incorporated methods and rhythms that I had used when playing the ukulele. My casual strumming turned into licks and the licks turned into melodies. Before I knew it, I was in the midst of my own groove session. Thankfully, he was into it too.

"Wow, that's really good, man. You ain't no joke. I'd like to see what else you come up with for your band. Go ahead and borrow my guitar. You have to play."

I was elated to hear his words. Things were slowly coming together. "Say, man, do you have an amp?" I asked.

"I don't, just the guitar, but honestly, with talent like that -- that's all you'll need to succeed."

I was humbled by his encouragement and willingness to help me. He didn't have to, but he did. That was the way that it was when I was growing up. It wasn't considered going out of your way to help your fellow man. Even though technically he and I played the same instrument, there was no competition. That was a beautiful thing back then. I was so excited when I laid eyes on the guitar that I hadn't even noticed that the case it was perched upon wasn't in fact a guitar case. It was more like something he had put together to have a place to store the guitar. It was all good though. I had what I needed and now it was time to show the guys that I could yield results.

I thanked Milan again and promised to return the guitar in the same condition as I had received it.

I was more excited than ever about the prospect of the talent show. When I returned to meet with the guys, I not only shared my extraordinary news, I also began to strategize to recruit more members. I did not want us to step on that stage unless we were working with a full band. I wanted to knock the audience's socks off.

I heard through the grapevine that there was a student named Offrey Hines, who had won second place in the talent show the year before. He was a bass player from South Carolina. My thought was that if I could convince him to play with us, not only would he add to the sound, but he could also give us some insight as to the inner workings of the show so that we would be successful. It became my mission to find him. I returned to the rec and began my usual antics of asking around.

This time, I ran into a group of students who would prove to be insightful.

"Hi, excuse me. Does anyone here know Offrey Hines? He plays the bass."

One of the guys replied, "Oh, yes. You can probably find him at one of the dorms."

Other students mentioned that he might not have arrived back on campus from his hometown. "You know what, he actually is coming in on the bus tonight," said another student who knew him personally.

"Thank you. That is a big help. Thank you so much." I departed the rec center, thinking as hard as I could about the best way to connect with Offrey. I had to get him to agree to be in the band for the talent show.

After about an hour of pacing back and forth in my dorm room, it occurred to me that since I already knew where Offrey would be, what I needed to do was get myself to the bus station to meet him.

When Offrey stepped off the bus, I recognized him immediately from the photos. You would think that I would have been nervous approaching a stranger to ask a favor of them, but I wasn't. When you are walking in purpose, you get this astounding sense of boldness.

I walked up to him and introduced myself "Hello. My name is Thomas McClary. I'm a freshman at Tuskegee and I'm putting this band together and we are going to be the Black Beatles." To my surprise, he smiled as if to say, 'count me in,' from the moment I uttered those words. His friend, who was there to pick him up, offered me a ride back to campus and on the way I learned that not only did Offrey have a bass, but he also had an amp. If you are willing to be faithful and work hard, God will match your efforts. He had sent me what I needed to get the band up and running.

"We have a place that we can rehearse right across from the campus," I informed him. I wanted to let him know that I was organized and not going to waste his time. I meant what I said when I proclaimed that we were going to be the next Black Beatles.

The following day, I informed the rest of the guys that I had not only located a guitar, but also a bass, an amp, and new talent. The guys were impressed with my work ethic. It was meaningful that they had put their trust in me and I had no intention of doing anything except keeping good on my promises.

I organized our first rehearsal and doing so was monumental. Our roles in the group began to take shape and my resourcefulness would come in handy. I used the one amp that we had to power my guitar and Offrey's bass. Andre Callahan was on the drums and Lionel Richie and Smitty were both on sax. From the moment that we began playing, I knew that there was something special about our sound, but it would require a lot of molding.

"Let's see if we can play 'Cold Sweat,' by James Brown," I exclaimed. It was the first song we attempted to play together. I can still hear the rawness of the music in my ears now. For me, the moment was nostalgic. It was my first time connecting with the melodies, aside from my short-lived play in Milan's room to prove myself worthy of borrowing his guitar. Our chemistry was undeniable. I sat and watched as some of the guys closed their eyes and soaked up the moment, while others played in a trance to the vibe of the music. We jammed that day, man.

The good chemistry would prove to be valuable as we also had a limited amount of time to put together an act for the talent show. There was only one major problem standing in our way -- we had no lead singer. The guys looked to me to find a solution and it was my plan to deliver. I began asking around the campus to find out who could potentially fill the role. My roommate disclosed that he had a female friend who could sing. She lived at James Hall and I decided that same day to walk over and convince her to join us. Her agreement made it official and just like that we had a full ensemble, complete with a lead singer. Our rehearsals were structured and we focused on learning the Lou Rawls rendition of a song entitled, "Tobacco Road," as well as practicing and preparing "Tighten Up," by Archie Bell & The Drells.

Our next order of business was to come up with a name for the group. I offered the name The Matadors, as the group back in Eustis had disbanded, but the group didn't care for it. Offrey Hines, who we also called "Railroad," suggested the name The Mystics. The group liked it, as did I, and with a unanimous agreement, we officially became The Mystics.

The show date was getting closer and the anticipation was mounting. I listened with intent to the music. There was still something missing in the depths of the sound. We were on point with the performance and the execution of the music, but the sound needed something more. It took me a while to figure it out, but eventually I recognized the missing sound to be the trumpet. I told the group that I believed that it would be nice if we had a trumpet and I set out in search of a player to join us. I discovered a gentleman from Birmingham, who played trumpet in the college band. We recruited him and he was an amazing fit. Although it might seem difficult to get all of these seemingly random people to gel, that wasn't the case. It goes back to the love of music. In this scenario, we were all at Tuskegee to pursue higher learning, but that also meant that for many of us, our love for music took a back seat. Being empowered to do what we love and create music together was a dream come true and it showed in our playing. We now had three horns, a bass, a guitar, drums, and a singer.

As our rehearsals got longer and the time till the showcase got shorter, I tried to think of every factor that could affect our success. We worked through musical mishaps and choreography until we were ready, but even so, I couldn't predict everything.

The night of the showcase arrived and we were ready. I was so proud of the work that had gone into assembling the band and my vision of creating the Black Beatles was not as distant as I had once thought. As we stood backstage and peeked from behind the curtain, we noticed the packed house. The sight of the audience made me even more excited. I knew that the preparation we had put into our performance would pay off.

The Tuskegee Freshman Talent Showcase was like a rite of passage. The audience was notorious for being honest about the performances. If an act did not do well, the crowd did not hold back on letting them know accordingly. They would even go so far as to throw peanuts. It is my belief that as a performer, you need to find common ground in the midst of a tough audience. When you can win a crowd like that over, you are in a sweet spot. Should you stand before an audience to perform, there are two things you must have, first, a tough layer of skin and second, be confident in your preparation. We had done the work and now it was our time to shine. We received the notice that we would be up next and I informed all of the members and made sure that everyone had what they needed. Everyone looked confident and it was my hope that the confidence that I felt inside had transferred to everyone else. After the act prior to us ended, there was a small break and we positioned ourselves behind the curtains.

When the curtains opened and we were revealed to the audience, I could not have prepared for what happened next. Every one of our group members, apart from Andre Callahan and me, took off running behind the safety of the curtains. As I stood there staring at the audience and them staring back at me, I was composed; I was in shock, but I was composed. I had never stopped to think about the fact that I had played before live audiences back at home with The Matadors, but many of the members of The Mystics that I had assembled had never played in front of an audience. They had only ever played in the privacy of our respective rehearsals.

During my days of playing with The Matadors, I idolized Chuck Berry because of his showmanship abilities. He moved, danced, and engaged his audience while playing his instrument. I remember being mesmerized by his capacity to capture the audience's attention and keep it. As I stood there on stage, his image popped into my mind and I imagined that I was him in that moment. I could feel a bead of sweat rolling down from my forehead, as the spotlight in that moment felt like I was on a much larger stage rather than in the auditorium of Tuskegee College. I closed my eyes and I channeled Chuck Berry. I played with intensity, passion, and confidence and the audience was into it. I learned in that moment how to build from the interaction and energy of the crowd. At the end of my performance of James Brown's "Cold Sweat," I stood there alone on the stage in the midst of applause. Even though I had worked hard to win them over, I still remembered my purpose — the band. I was determined for this showcase to be the first of many. I spoke into the mic and introduced my bandmates.

"Thank you guys so much. Now, this is what you've been waiting for. Allow me to introduce the band." I could see the rest of the members staring at me. In that moment, I needed to lead as I had always done. I made eye contact with a few who were directly in my view and reassured them that it was ok. When they heard the cheers of the audience, they began to come out from behind the curtains. There we were, in the thick of our first performance as The Mystics. That night, we won the crowd and the talent show.

Although the melodies of our dreams sang a sweet tune, they were quickly drowned out by the darkness of the looming oppression of blacks amidst the civil rights movement. No matter how much our souls wanted to live for the music, our hearts and minds were forced to live in the trenches of the fight for equality. Things would get worse before they got better, and we would all become casualties of the war raging right in front of our faces on the campus of Tuskegee.

04: *Mustard Seed Faith*

When the showers of life pour, the prospect of drowning evolves into certainty. On April 4, 1968, we witnessed a nation paralyzed and begrudgingly observant of the cold-blooded assassination of Dr. Martin Luther King, Jr. I sat in horror as I watched the one, small, black and white TV in the dorm. The series of events displayed were crippling. The room was filled with students, just like me, who felt the weight of the world and the burden of hatred. We must have sat there in shock for hours watching in disbelief. We were perplexed and dumbfounded and overcome with anguish. Some wept in solitude, while others sought desperately to find some type of release or comfort from friends, but there was nothing. I searched in desperation to find something to eclipse the desperate pain in our hearts. We were all bound in the first stage of grief — disbelief.

I longed for a false reality. I wanted to believe that the hatred projected towards black citizens was not real. I dreamed of days when the color of my skin wasn't a constant factor in the establishment of glass ceilings and the tension levels didn't amount to the death of those who looked like me. To no avail. The violence was real and inescapable. The war zone that I had so desperately tried to leave behind was ever present, even in my new place of higher learning. Dare I describe the Civil Rights Movement as melancholy? All that it meant and all that it stood for, was a true testament to the endurance, strength, and might of a people. The beauty in that can't be denied. Even so, recognizing it as the backdrop for our existence was pensive. How harrowing it was to associate your life and every breath that you took with a fight for dignity and respect. There we were on a college campus, in pursuit of excellence and the good old American Dream, and it was unequivocally overshadowed by hostility, strife, contention, and warfare because of the color of our skin and what America had decided our fate would be.

Around the same time that I arrived at Tuskegee as a freshman, the student body began to organize a march to protest the unprecedented killing of Samuel Younge, Jr., a Navy veteran, and a political science major at Tuskegee. His murder was another layer of blatant disrespect for our lives and equality. Sammy, as he was affectionately called, was much like the rest of us; he knew that his life's meaning would be rooted in remaining faithful and vigilant as a soldier in the fight for justice. As an active leader in the non-violent Civil Rights Movement, he took great pride in sparking an initiative that would register black students to vote. His main objective was to realize equality through education and the use of all facilities. Upon a visit to downtown Macon County, where he hoped to increase registration, Sammy was gunned down for attempting to use a whites-only restroom at a gas station. The lacerations of discrimination were further agitated when

Sammy's murderer, Marvin Segrest, was acquitted by a jury of his peers. Under no circumstances, should Sammy's life have been a casualty of a racially inequitable war.

Like the many lives whose names never saw the light of day, there was no justice for Sammy; his untimely loss was senseless. I had heard a little about the story prior to enrolling at Tuskegee, but to live in the thick of it was enough to create unrest within my spirit.

Although, my head had been nestled in the melodies of assembling the band, I was never in danger of ignoring the revolution. I had fought so hard in Eustis and felt weary, but I was no different from my peers. We didn't have the luxury of despondency, because we knew that our lives, and the lives of those who would come after us, depended on the actions that we took amidst those moments. There was no difference between the fight at Tuskegee and the fight at Eustis High School. I wasn't alone in either. The support systems were just aligned differently. I assembled with the rest of the students and we fought together in solidarity. It was empowering to see everyone using their God given gifts and talents to raise awareness and become vocal in the fight for justice.

Many students, including myself, emerged as leaders and acquired new levels of professional training. One gentleman, in particular, used his voice to galvanize and empower the student body. He came on the speakers in the dorms and played music that reminded us to be proud of who we were and that injustice would not prevail. He also used his platform to discuss the case of Sammy Younge. He recognized the importance of keeping us all informed. As they say, knowledge is power.

I would eventually learn that the man who continued to inspire and motivate us was Tom Joyner. (1) Joyner went on to become one of the most prominent minority radio hosts in American history, and is a continued testament to the power of information and those who control the messaging that we give and receive.

As I learned more about the various movements and efforts to take a stand on campus, I immersed myself once again into assuming roles of fearless leadership. A group of students, including myself, made the decision to pay a visit to the official radio station in the city of Tuskegee. We were represented in numbers and prepared to lift our voices. The owner of the station believed that we were there to burn it down, but our methods of protest were not hostile. It was sad that the automatic assumption was that we would meet violence with violence. Even after all the torment that we had experienced, we used our minds to fight, not our fists. As we approached the station, the owner came out pleading, "Please don't burn the building down, please.

Tom, spoke out on behalf of the group, "We won't do any damage to the station if you allow us to go on the air and talk about our cause." That day was Tom's first time on the radio and his monologue was powerful, moving, and ardent. He became a champion in the peaceful protest of Sammy's untimely death — so did we all.

There were so many fires to put out in the world and Tuskegee reflected only a microcosm of what was going on in society at large. With Sammy's death at the forefront, we would have been remiss if we hadn't also acknowledged the fact that we were witnessing the absence of equality on our own campus.

The student body was fighting, what also appeared to be a losing battle, for a quality education. There were significant concerns regarding the educational offerings and opportunities for students to excel. These issues were imperative to the students of Tuskegee because everyone knew the value in the quality of their education. We were not just attending school to say that we had done so. We were attending school with the prospect of a better life, and for most of us, our lives depended on it. Students much like myself, had taken leadership positions and one group of students in particular confronted the institution's board of trustees directly, as they felt that their mounting concerns were not being heard. The students were known as the ACASE or Ad Hoc Committee for the Advancement of the School of Engineering.

The board of trustees was made up of mostly white individuals, with the exception of the president. For us, race was not an issue, but the lack of acknowledgement for our very valid and most pressing issues was.

There were eight significant points of contention outlined by the student body. The requests were straightforward: An extension of library hours, revision of the guest speaker's policy, clarity on the grading system, explanation and clarification on the electives and pre-elective selection process, decision as to the authority of the Dean of Students, revision of the ROTC program requirements, research into scholarships for athletics, academics and leadership, and finally an overhaul of the engineering department's instructors.

Although all of the concerns affected me, as a student at Tuskegee, the final issue was paramount as I was a student at the School of Engineering, which was commanded by an Indian gentleman by the name of Dean Zbigniew W. Dybczak. It was believed that he showed favoritism in who he hired. Many of the professors, who were responsible for educating us were Indian and we felt as though we were not reaching our full potential because we could not understand what our teachers were saying. The professors, although well versed in engineering, spoke very poor English.

I cannot stress enough, that we took our education and the opportunity to be present at an institution of higher learning very seriously. The upperclassmen that were close to graduation had even more concern than new students like me. The students, who were very bright, were not progressing accordingly and their grades reflected as such.

As with every important movement, there arises a leader. I met and befriended William F. Robinson, a senior at Tuskegee. He brought me up to speed regarding the students' educational concerns. In early April of 1968, only days after the assassination of Dr. King, I became a witness to the notion that things get worse before they get better. Led by Robinson and another student named Jacqueline Deveaux, the ACASE decided that a peaceful yet impetuous demonstration was in order. The engineering students wanted to get the attention of the school's president, Dr. Luther Foster, and have him do something about their unanswered concerns.

The Student Nonviolent Coordinating Committee or SNCC was emerging during this time. The SNCC believed in nonviolent protest, however, unlike Dr. King, the committee wasn't opposed to violence when confronted. Malcolm X's movement was gaining momentum as well and the appeal of the peaceful protest was often muted. Blacks were at the height of an intensified yearning for social and political reform. These views, with the help of the Student Government Association, became the prominent beliefs across campus.

It all came to a head on the day Dr. Foster was hosting eleven members of the board of trustees on campus to discuss the upcoming Founders Day Program, which was a celebration of the legendary activist Booker T. Washington, founder of Tuskegee. Taking advantage of the situation, the exasperated group of engineers made the drastic decision to hold the trustees hostage in Dorothy Hall. Tension on the campus was high and the climate was dismal as the hostages were held for over thirteen hours behind chained and padlocked doors. The severity of the actions taken was inconceivable. At the same time, it was ironic that the laurels and principles on which the school was founded upon, were now in question as we were all suddenly thrust into a hostile environment.

Lucius Amerson, the first African American sheriff to be elected in the south since the Reconstruction was the presiding sheriff of Tuskegee and during the hostage event, made an effort to reach out to the students to try and find a resolution, but it was to no avail. (2) The students in protest had taken control of the phones and no one was able to communicate in or out of the area where the hostages were being held.

The pressure the students felt spread throughout the campus and into the city at large. Everyone heard about the hostages and the desperate measures commanded by the ACASE.

Teachers and staff, together in their own posture of protest, stated that those who did not attend class would receive a zero grade. No one wanted to leave their rooms during this time, so a number of students chained the classroom doors closed, deciding that if class couldn't be held, then the teachers wouldn't be able to pass out terrible grades.

Negotiations were at a standstill, so Sheriff Amerson personally arrived at the school and began passing notes underneath the doors of Dorothy Hall in a desperate attempt to communicate. During the negotiation process with the sheriff, the students allowed one of the trustees to make a phone call, but they didn't realize the important connections this young man held with the then Governor Lurleen Wallace. That one call, ignited 300 National Guardsmen and 70 state troopers to assemble in town, armed with tear gas and combat gear, ready to bring an end to the mounting war inside the college hall, by any means necessary. (3) A standoff ensued, but the hostages were eventually released unharmed.

Even though the hostage situation had ended, tension on the campus and in the city was still high. Many questions arose in relation to those thirteen pressing hours. The National Guard remained on campus, but we questioned if that was in an effort to keep the peace and make everyone feel safe? It looked like that from the outside, but to the students, it felt like we were being held captive. What about Sheriff Amerson, could we trust him? Being black didn't automatically make him an ally. If another situation occurred on campus, could we guarantee we would be treated fairly? In many ways, our race had been pitted against one another and survival was just that, survival. Had the hostage situation done more harm than good? Would the students' efforts bring about the changes needed at the school?

Amidst the troubled waters, students and staff members at Tuskegee worked tirelessly to put back together the pieces of the puzzle that had seemingly been demolished. Despite these efforts, all students were informed that their admittance to the college was not guaranteed the following semester. They were now in jeopardy of not attaining the education desperately needed to better their lives. Those who had been part of the hostage situation, had even more to worry about as a lawsuit was announced and none of the students had the money to hire attorneys to defend the mounting charges. For those students, after a turbulent period of deliberations and counter arguments, the judge decided that they could be reinstated to Tuskegee under the conditions that they pursue their education and no longer form any political stances or takeovers. For the rest of us, we were forced to await our fate in the form of an acceptance letter and we each waited with bated breath to see if we would be welcomed back to the school. Everyone felt like they were in the thick of it and no one felt secure in their futures.

At the beginning of May, we received a newsletter from the president addressing some of the issues that had been points of contention. The letter was favorable and moved to get some of our main complaints resolved. We were granted extended hours at the library. The teachers provided a more comprehensive outline of the grading system and we were able to have more freedom in terms of speakers that could come and address the student body as it related to civil and political activities. There was also clarification on the electives and the role of the Dean of Students was defined. The ROTC program was now only required of freshmen and not mandatory for all four years and appropriations for athletes, students with dramatic leadership and other constructive talents would be looked into. Overall, the students received the answers they had long looked for, but true validation of their concerns came with the resignation of Dean Dybczak and the school's decision to begin accepting applications for new teachers.

As time passed, things began to calm down and there was a oneness about the campus. I have always tried to help others by fighting against any injustice that threatens hope and equality, not only in the African American community, but all people. I felt very comfortable diving in and doing whatever was deemed necessary to make a difference. I would venture to say that hope is one of the most powerful factors in the succession and progress of the human race. We hang on to hope as if our lives depend on it and they do. We wait in the wings for hope, patiently wishing that it would grace our presence. Hope is what faith is made of. Its absence ushers in the presence of disparity. Without hope, there can be no forward movement.

As days passed, the quiet on campus allowed the death of Dr. Martin Luther King, Jr. to further penetrate our hearts. We wondered how to fight in unison in the absence of our vigilant leader? Many remained silent. The hostage situation and the stress of the aftermath had allowed us a brief reprieve, a distraction if you would, from the loss that stole our hope like a thief in the night. Dr. King had given so many a reason to simply stand and fight in the face of injustice. We worked for equal opportunities with no real end in sight because we witnessed real examples of those leading the charge. Dr. King was hope personified. They, whoever they could be classified as; the powers that wanted to keep systematic racism intact and those who wished to continually perpetuate the degradation of the black race had won, or at least it felt like it. You could see the signs of defeat on every student face, in every image on TV, in each article in the newspapers, and even amongst the leadership of those who continued to fight at the national level for equality. The assassination of Dr. King was responsible for our greatest loss, the ability to hope.

The climate was so somber that I almost lost the melodies. The imagery portrayed in mass media did not stop, nor did the countless stories of violent hate crimes. We were all sick and tired of being sick and tired. Everyone needed something to believe in again, including me. In some of my darkest moments, I found myself humming a tune. Often times while sitting in class, my foot would begin to tap the floor in a rhythmic pattern. Even as I stood talking to a group of my fellow classmates, I could feel a throbbing in my fingertips. I hadn't quite put the pieces of the puzzle together, but as the days passed, I felt a sense of peace that I hadn't felt before. I continued to remain prayerful and to ask God to deliver us all from the hatred that we had all been tormented and victimized by. I also asked God to send me a sign of what to do next. I needed divine direction.

I had received my second acceptance letter to Tuskegee, giving me permission to attend the fall semester. After reviewing my financial statements for school, it became abundantly clear that while I had enough to cover my tuition, I had nothing extra. I had never been in this position, having worked as many jobs as humanly possible back in Eustis to avoid this very scenario. I sat on the edge of my bed while pondering and I began to tap my foot on the floor and my fingertips began to tingle. Out of nowhere, I stood up and began mimicking playing the guitar. I could hear music. It almost felt like a new thing was stirring in me. A light bulb went off and I recognized in that moment that God had sent the music to save me. I knew then that I needed to make the band a priority. I needed to create a way for all of us to save ourselves from the black hole of oppression and to ensure that our musical gifts and talents did not go to waste simply because we lived in a society that did not value us. I needed to create something that could never be erased. That night in my room, I resolved that no matter what happened, I would not stop until I had created the Black Beatles that I had always dreamed of.

The next day, I began to strategize. I recognized that our one amp was not going to be sufficient to give us the sound that we needed. Furthermore, we did not have a sound system, microphones, or any equipment for that matter. Although Andre Callahan had a drum set, it was not adequate for the level of play that I envisioned for us. The guitar that I had borrowed the previous semester had been returned. Beyond that, I also needed to find additional band members, as some of the members, Bill Winston and Abram Brown, had graduated and were no longer in the band.

Jimmy Johnson and Michael Gilbert were the leaders of a band called the Jays. I knew that they had some of the equipment that we needed and I resolved to borrow some from them until I could find the resources to get us more of what we needed.

Clearly, I wasn't the only one who God had spoken to about allowing the music to resurrect hope. On the same day that I went to the Jay's rehearsal house to meet with them about borrowing some equipment, I learned that Michael Gilbert was trying to recruit members from my horn section as well as my drummer for The Jays. "Oh man, this is ironic, I've got some of your guys downstairs. Maybe we just need to all come together. The other half of our guys, drummer Arthur Lawrence and guitarist, Bobby Owens, are pursuing jazz and you guys don't have any equipment, maybe we can merge," he said.

I thought about the vision that God had given me for the band and I realized that I was willing to do whatever it took to achieve significant growth for us all. We merged and man, it was powerful. The first song that we worked to perfect was, "Tighten Up," by Archie Bell & The Drells. The chemistry was unreal. I would have expected nothing less as we were all concrete roses, fighting to rise above the surface.

Now that the merger was solidified, another official matter that needed to be resolved was a name for the group. We needed something new that would represent our progression. Nobody wanted The Matadors or The Mystics, so one evening at rehearsal, we literally sat together to brainstorm potential selections. Out of nowhere, Michael Gilbert said, "Let's do this. Y'all blindfold me and I'm going to open a dictionary.

Wherever my fingers stop, that is going to be the name." We were so desperate to find a name, that we all agreed upon the suggestion. His finger stopped on the word "commode."

"Ladies and gentleman. . . The Commodes," I said in an extremely sarcastic manner. Everyone around the room was shaking their heads in disgust. That was not going to work. His fingers searched again and it stopped on the word "Commodore." "The Commodores," I said out loud. It rolled off the tongue smoothly and I could see the settlement on the faces of the group members. We all felt at ease. That night, we became The Commodores.

The band now had seven members. Jimmy Johnson played sax and sang lead vocals. He also represented the group for many bookings as he had the most connections. Michael Gilbert played bass and was also on vocals with Jimmy. Andre Callahan was on drums. Milan Williams played keyboard and guitar. Lionel Richie played the sax while William King was on trumpet and I was the final member on guitar. On special occasions, we enlisted another college singing group called, The Duponts, to join us. The members were Tom Joyner, Howard Kenny, and Killer Craig. We marketed this package as, "The Commodores Duponts Review."

We landed a gig in Montgomery and it became a solid commitment for Tuesday nights. We received $500 per show. I must admit that by the time we divided the money seven ways and subtracted our expenses, we each had what some would refer to as chicken coup money, but being able to play and pursue our dreams while simultaneously getting an education made it all worth it.

Performing became our ultimate side hustle as we worked to achieve excellence academically. We kept performing until the end of the 1968 school year. The melodies in my heart were less somber than they had been and I can honestly say that my hope was restored. I truly believed that the music would allow us to transcend all of the barriers that we had encountered and I was hopeful about the possibilities for what would be on the journey ahead.

While the gig was nice, I was determined to establish connections that could help us meet more people and get us in front of more audiences than just our collegiate cohorts. To my surprise, Michael and Jimmy had connections with the Dean that opened some doors.

Back in 1966, The Jays had been granted access to contacts in New York. A gentleman by the name of Benny Ashburn had arranged a few gigs for them and when that run ended, the Dean told them that if they were ever in New York again, to contact Ashburn for further performances. The opportunity to go to New York, using the connections that Dean Phillips had orchestrated, was still on the table. We set our sights on making that happen for all of us and even with very little resources in place, there was only one obstacle standing in our way. Lionel Richie's parents were not on board with allowing him to go. During the times that Lionel's grandmother had allowed me to sleep in her bedroom in the basement, I had proven myself to be reputable and trustworthy. By gaining her confidence, Michael Gilbert and I resolved one afternoon to talk to her in hopes of convincing her that the trip was a good idea. We knew that if we could attain the approval of Lionel's grandmother, she would advise his mother and father accordingly. It worked, but we had to assure her that we would not be doing drugs or using any alcohol and that we would remain enrolled in school. We also informed her of our plans to stay at the YMCA and other locations that would be safe while in New York. At this time, William King decided that he stood a better chance of pursuing his interests as a lifeguard in his hometown of Birmingham. He left the band, though he would later change his mind. This would prove to be the first of two exits and re-entries into the band for him.

Collectively, the rest of us saved enough money from our gigs to purchase a used van. We didn't have enough money to purchase a trailer so we packed all of our instruments and luggage into the van. We headed to New York with a vengeance. The fact that this trip was materializing gave us a sense of hope that we had not felt before collectively. Our plan was to take New York City by storm. We learned so many valuable lessons along the way. In retrospect, it was this trip that taught us that you don't have to have everything that you need in order to chase a dream, you only need to be willing to chase it with your whole heart. Furthermore, you must surround yourself with those who are just as hungry or very close to being as hungry as you are. Together, we arrived at many conclusions together, some good and some developmental, but we were together and ready for the world.

We made it all the way from Tuskegee, Alabama to the turnpike in New Jersey only to realize that we had run completely out of money. We didn't' even have enough money to pay the toll. The gentleman who was there collecting the money looked in the van and saw all of us and the equipment in the back.

"Where are you gentlemen headed?" he asked.

"Say man, we are trying to get to New York. We're a band and we have some major gigs planned. We just need to get there," I said in desperation.

"You guys don't have enough money?"

"No, sir, but we will after we play these gigs." I spoke those words in the most humble way possible. We were delighted when he let us through.

As soon as we arrived in New York, we began looking for a place to stay. No one wanted to call any relatives because there were so many of us, we didn't want to be inconsiderate of someone else's living quarters. With no other options in mind, I was forced to call my brother, Charles, and he agreed to allow us to stay at his place for the night. Night turned into morning and we agreed that it didn't feel right staying there. There were simply too many of us. Our next best option was to go to the YMCA to see if we could perhaps work in exchange for room and board. When we pulled up in the van, Lionel and I went in to speak with the manager. We nominated Andre Callahan to watch the equipment. We became a little disheartened when we were informed that the YMCA did not have any rooms available for us. When we arrived back at the van we discovered that all of our equipment had been stolen. There we stood, after driving an insurmountable number of miles, with no money, no equipment, and no prospect of locating the gigs that we had come to play. To make matters worse, we never even had the phone number of Benny Ashburn, who we were in search of to set up the gigs. In that moment, the wind was taken from beneath our wings.

In disbelief, we ventured our way down the street toward a club called Small's Paradise. As we stood there, helpless, and admittedly concerned, pondering what our next move should be, we noticed a gentleman walking down the street with tons of equipment. As he got closer, we all recognized that the items looked familiar. All of the equipment belonged to us. He was bold enough to be walking past us, right in front of the club, with what he had stolen. You wouldn't believe that he was vying to sell it.

"Hey man, that stuff belongs to us. We're here to play and that's our equipment," I said.

In what will go down as one of the most memorable moments that we experienced together, the thief said, "If you give me fifty dollars I'll give it back to you." Andre said, "Why don't we just take our stuff back, cause we don't have the money."

Unbelievable! Out of nowhere, a stranger who had overheard the exchange stepped forward. "I'll loan you guys the money."

"Awe man, thank you. We'll figure out how to pay you somehow," I vowed. "We've just got to get these gigs together."

"Well, maybe I can help you with that. My name is Benny Ashburn."

It was one of those moments that taught us an invaluable lesson about the exercise of faith. The best of what is to come in life does not come when you want it to come. There must be moments of agony that occur. There must be trials and tribulations that play out for any real revelation of triumph.

In a single moment and a twist of certitude, we had found Benny Ashburn, recovered our equipment, and been booked to play even bigger gigs than we had imagined. This was a significant juncture for the group and a resounding testament to the power in the exercise of mustard seed faith.

05: *The Sun Never Forgets to Rise*

The sweltering hot summer of 1968 in New York proved to be a notable era for the group in many ways. Benny Ashburn whom we had come to New York to find had not only helped us to retrieve all our equipment, but also managed to convince the management of the infamous nightclub, Smalls Paradise, to give us a chance on stage. I was told that the famous basketball player Wilt Chamberlain was the financier and a gentleman by the name of Peter Smalls was the manager of the club. Smalls Paradise was heavily frequented by celebrities, as it provided them with moments of lavish indulgence, without the fanfare interfering. The nightclub was immaculately appointed and it proved to be nostalgic for us as we were in the midst of doing what we had only dreamed of — playing music for sold out audiences. It was paradise indeed.

We were named a resident band for a few weeks and during that time Benny Ashburn provided us with lodging in his apartment. The staff at Small's Paradise allowed us to practice during the daytime and we worked hard while enjoying the beautiful scenery. Just think, if we hadn't convinced Lionel's grandmother to let him come to New York, he would have been working in a bomb factory in Joliet, Illinois with his dad during that summer. Knowing what could have been our fate, kept us honest and we were very adamant about keeping our promises to Lionel's grandmother. Our image and actions remained clean as we were still students and representatives of Tuskegee University. Not one of us felt safe enough with our side hustle as musicians to forfeit our status as students. Even so, we aspired to be the best and it showed during our rehearsals. We were focused on continuing to develop our signature sound. I knew that we needed to set ourselves apart from the other talent that was also enlisted to play at Smalls Paradise. It was the goal of the club to keep the party going by maintaining a robust offering of bands and entertainers to keep their clients happy.

We also worked to consolidate ourselves as a band and further determine what each member's role would be and how we could become the best versions of ourselves.

Michael Gilbert and Jimmy Johnson were our two lead singers and even though we were performing songs by other artists, we would put our own twist on the way in which we delivered the song. We called it "Commodorizing." We would take a Glen Campbell song that had more of a pop or country flavor and essentially, give the song some soul. Our ability to transform songs became increasingly popular with the guests at Smalls Paradise, because we would often select songs that were popular on the radio but mainly from white artists. The songs were familiar, but appealing in a new way because of the soul that we sprinkled on it.

As the days passed, we continued to procure the trust of Benny Ashburn. We had taken over his apartment, but we kept things in order and were meticulous about not damaging anything. We weren't oblivious to our luck and remained ever cautious and courteous, so our good fortune wouldn't change.

While performing at Smalls Paradise, we received the opportunity to participate in a Battle of the Bands. Other groups included Kool & the Gang, a very popular R&B band out of New Jersey, (pre-recording artist days) The Brooklyn Bridge, Jimmy Castor Bunch, and Willie & the Mighty Magnificents, who had won most of the competitions in the past. That summer, they won again, but we came in second. Second place may not have been considered a win for some, but we were beyond inspired to share the stage with acts of that caliber and even further honored to be considered on the same level. We were just a few guys from Alabama who literally arrived with next to nothing. That stage and magnitude of performance gave me the glimmer in my eyes that I so desperately needed. I had motivated the guys often from an empty place. This time, my cup was full. God had shown me the possibilities of what could be and proven that he would further wow us with his wondrous grace and opportunity. I wasn't the only one who saw it, we all felt the miracle that we were so blessed to be a part of and ambition set in on a larger scale for all of us.

To utilize our time wisely while in Benny Ashburn's apartment, we devised a number of marketing tactics that we could use when we returned to Tuskegee. We devised slogans and strategies to share what we had done during our time in

New York. We wanted to make sure we capitalized on the fact that we had performed as a band among celebrities who celebrated our work. We all agreed that our angle would be to present ourselves back in Tuskegee as celebrities who had taken New York City by storm — "Straight from New York City's, Smalls Paradise." All of our promotional items and efforts back at Tuskegee would now be produced from this angle to book more gigs.

Using contacts that Michael and Jimmy had already established, we introduced ourselves to a gentleman by the name of Bobby Jackson. He was responsible for booking the acts at the Elks Club and another club in Union Springs on the weekend. Our New York fame helped us become the house band at the Elks club in Montgomery backing up Jerry Butler, Ike and Tina Turner and eventually opening for Pigmeat Markham, Peggy Scott, Jo Jo Benson, and Billy Stewart. We were bracing ourselves to explore new opportunities and it was clear that we were on target for success. William King would also make a decision to return to the group around this same time.

Returning to Tuskegee before the new school year began, left me with no true home for the rest of the summer. I didn't have enough money to return home to Eustis or pay to live elsewhere. I spent my nights squatting in the dorms with Milan Williams until we were caught by the Dean, and from then on spent my time jumping from couch to couch until Lionel Richie and his grandmother took pity on me once again and invited me to stay in the basement apartment of their home.

When school reopened I was disappointed to discover that some of the same instructors, who had been hired by the now resigned Dean Dybczak, were still teaching at the school. I didn't want my time with the band restricted because the curriculum demanded many hours beyond the call of duty, simply because the instructors couldn't be understood. As such, I decided to change my major from engineering to business administration. I was not willing to compromise my education, or the future of the band. I began making plans to map out a blueprint to anticipate what would be needed next for the band. I knew that there were still some components that were missing.

Sometimes, you don't even realize that you already have the very things that you are searching for. One day as we were preparing for a performance, I heard a voice emerge from the shower, singing a Jerry Butler song. The voice had this distinct ability to capture the essence of the song, but with a very different sound. It was something that I hadn't heard before, but it was out of sight. I had to find out who the vessel of this magnificent voice was.
"Wow man, you sound good."
"Oh, I was just pretending," he said.
I gasped with the excitement of my new discovery. "You need to pretend more. We are going to need to lean on you man," I said. Lionel or "Richie" as I called him, had been the one singing. From that day forward, I realized that his voice would emerge as a recognizable talent on a much larger stage.

Traveling the road paved with perseverance, we continued to build our fan base and momentum for the band grew in both New York and Tuskegee. We capitalized on every opportunity that we could, to steal away to New York to perform. During the Christmas holidays of 1968, we returned to Smalls Paradise as we had a vacation from school. Richie's talent began gaining notoriety amongst our fans. He was an undeniable rising star. The consensus was that we wanted Richie to sing lead after hearing what he could do in rehearsals. We needed this type of energy and persona to be recognized as the face of the brand. This decision would prove to be climactic for the group.

Our sets consisted of the Wilson Pickett song "I'm a Midnight Mover," and a vast array of artists that allowed the depth of the talent within our group to shine. Jimmy Johnson played saxophone and he would sing a lot of Junior Walker songs. Michael Gilbert led all of the songs that we performed by James Brown. The sheer musical aptitude within our group was impressive to say the least. For the first time in my efforts to assemble the band, I felt like we had the right equation that could skyrocket us to stardom.

One particular night while playing at Smalls Paradise, we were in the middle of performing a James Brown set. The song was "Cold Sweat" and we were grooving. As we were getting close to the bridge, in walked James Brown's drummer, a man well-known for his stupendous talent. His name was Nate. Upon noticing him enter the building, Michael Gilbert turned around and said to Callahan, "Man, you have to hit that snare. You've got to hit it like Nate."

We turned the energy up another notch. The levels kept jumping and the crowd was going absolutely wild. The groove was so hard that Nate hopped on stage and jammed with us. The set was filled with rhythmic beats and fast paced tempos. Man, if you were in that room, all you could do was dance. The vibe would not have allowed you to escape. That's the beauty of music, it transcends so many boundaries and frees your mind. In the midst of music, you forget about your worries and the ills of the world. To feel something so unexplainable in the depths of your soul is to me, magic. That night, we felt something together. I looked at the spirit in the eyes of each of the band members and it gave me a sense of satisfaction. I knew that night that we were going to make it.

During the set, Wilson Pickett walked into the club. With chart topping hits like "Mustang Sally" and "Hey Jude," he was a household name and a major celebrity. We had another set to go and we were already on fire. Our energy captured Wilson and he became so excited that he too came up on stage and started singing with us.

The room was filled to capacity. There was no longer any standing room. We were all on a high from this mesmerizing set and the audience was in a state of shock. They had only paid to see The Commodores, but they had been granted access to an experience that no price tag would have been worthy of. We benefited as much as the audience. That high was one that cannot be described. We were now feeding off the energy of a drummer who had played with James Brown. He had this ability to break down the sound, rhythm, and music from one extreme to the next. I had never met anyone who could make a drum whisper. It was effortless and eloquent at the same time. The music that we made on the stage that night was fascinating. I mean, if you were standing there, you could feel the heartbeat of each of the players on the stage. The energy that was exchanged elevated everyone's performance to the next level. Moreover, we had idolized Wilson Pickett for so many years and now we were playing in a dream that we had never believed would come true.

It was magical for me because as a musician, you are not only listening with your ears, but you are listening with your heart and your soul. All of this was translated to an audience who was sitting there in anticipation. That night, I zoned out and my body was elevated. I can honestly say that besides the trying times back in Eustis and the scares of the hostile environment at Tuskegee, this was my first out of body experience. The rhythm of the band became fluid, we were now moving as one. This is the crux of what a band does. The music penetrated the room and shifted the atmosphere. We ended the set with me playing "Summertime" as if I was Jimi Hendrix himself. Nobody could believe their ears. Some were standing with their mouths open. We were all on a high from the sounds that no one wanted to come down from. It was bliss.

When we returned to campus, we had a few coins. During our marketing talks, we had discussed the prospect of adapting our overall look to reflect our growth and newfound stardom. During this era, suede was a popular look and since I had always loved fashion, I saw this as another opportunity to appeal to the ladies. We decided to have suede outfits custom made. I opted for a pink and green suede pants set. The inside of the pants were pink and the outside green. I also had a pink and green vest and a pink and green suede hat made. I believed that I was the male mascot for the ladies of Alpha Kappa Alpha Sorority, Inc.

Despite all the positive things happening for us at that time, the horrors going on beyond our borders couldn't be ignored and eventually they began knocking at our doors. The Vietnam War's draft system was thriving and black men were being recruited at alarming rates. If you were eligible for the draft, chances were that you would be selected. One of the criteria for staying out of the system was being enrolled in school. No matter how hard we wanted to pursue music, many of us refused to leave school because we had no desires to go to war or become a casualty of a system that didn't even deem us equal.

The year was 1970. I was putting all of my efforts into the band, which made it all the more disheartening when the news came to us that Michael Gilbert, who had decided to drop out of school and pursue music full time, was drafted. This was a tremendous shock to the group, both emotionally and logistically. Michael's roommate, Jimmy Johnson became leery of moving forward with the group as he and Michael were a one two punch combination. He was truly uncomfortable without Michael, and so we lost two band members at one time.

I could feel us losing hope and momentum again, despite how well we had done in New York. The overarching theme was that we should revert back to being students only. We knew how to do that well and it didn't come with all of the baggage that being in the band did. What I knew above everything else was that God had given me a vision for what could be. Beyond that, we all needed to keep making money. I was determined to make the band a source of income for us all.

Collectively, we took another blow when Andre Callahan decided that he would volunteer for the Navy. He no longer wanted to go to college and his parents were putting pressure on him to pursue something other than music. The Navy had benefits and he found comfort knowing that he could pursue a career doing something positive. To him it was a logical decision because we had not attained our big break.

All that had happened was a testament to the gumption that we needed to stay the course. I now knew how to strategically weather the storm of the process of losing and gaining new members for the group. I saw it as an opportunity for advancement and learned to not attach emotions to the process. I loved all the guys whom I had shared time, energy, and space with. We were like brothers, but life had proven to have many layers. I immediately began looking for new members to replace Andre Callahan and Michael Gilbert, which wasn't as challenging as before because we now had established a name for ourselves based on what we had done in New York and what we had accomplished closer to home.

Lionel Richie knew of another local band that police officer, Richard Pinkard was the leader of. This is where we discovered Ronald LaPread, who replaced Michael Gilbert on bass. With that position filled, I searched for a replacement for Callahan. I had heard of a gentleman by the name of Walter Orange who attended Alabama State. Orange was involved with another band singing and playing the drums. Despite his involvement with another group, I contacted him and was surprised by his excitement to come aboard with us. We had built a reputation for excellence and creativity that others wanted to be a part of. I was working to construct a signature sound and was well aware of all of the music that was out and the importance of finding a style that would be unique to us. It would take years of blood, sweat, and tears to achieve, but so does anything truly worth having.

With our new band mates in place, our rehearsals took off the ground in Tuskegee, and we embraced every moment together because we recognized that they were not promised. Our band now consisted of only six members as we had decided not to replace Jimmy Johnson. We had Walter Orange on drums and vocals, Ronald LaPread on bass, Milan Williams on keyboard and guitar, Lionel Richie on sax and lead vocals, and myself remaining on guitar.

I was in a constant state of strategizing to determine the needs of the group and making necessary decisions in order to progress further. We had a show coming up at the Wonder Gardens in Atlantic City that Benny Ashburn had booked on our behalf. It would be our first big gig with the new members. Harold Melvin & the Blue Notes had just come out with their first song "I Miss You," and we were the opening act. While in Atlantic City we also opened for jazz pianist and band leader, Count Basie at the Steel Pier, a historic amusement park.

With Lionel Richie and Walter Orange as singers, I believed that I had assembled a group that could really become the vision that I had so vividly dreamed of. Now, it was time to get Ronald LaPread and Walter Orange indoctrinated into the concept of how we were able to produce such a big rich sound. How was it possible for a four piece rhythm section to sound bigger than a fifteen piece band? How in the world could we make our audiences shed tears and scream as we sang music that wasn't ours but we made it our own with the signature sound?

I had visions of new goals for the band. It was my thought that the way in which we interacted could be critical to our success. We were all married to the music, but I knew that relationships were built on far more than love of the music. I often wondered what it would take to ensure that we had a solid foundation of friendship in place before reaching the levels that we would eventually realize. I began to evaluate the personalities in the group and our respective strengths and weaknesses. I wanted to understand the group's dynamics and how we could elevate our performances and celebrity. We were now all on the same playing field musically. I was no longer the only one with the experience of having been in a band. We were also notably, still young. I felt as though my job was to maintain the focus of us becoming the Black Beatles. I encouraged everyone to continue to play and keep defining our signature sound.

I had an idea to form a group within The Commodores with the intent to play offset gigs and practice intently as a core of the band. I approached Milan Williams, who was now a part-time student, as well as Ronald LaPread and Walter Orange, who had decided to leave school, to see if they would join me.

It was not an uncommon practice, as many large-scale bands collaborate with emphasis on segments of the band to fine tune sound and cohesiveness. Our segmentation was a rhythm section and we called ourselves The Mark IV. In certain instances, we didn't want to market The Commodores and having additional gigs worked for the members selected and myself because we all needed spending money.

The Black Forest, a nightclub nestled way out in the woods of Tuskegee, Alabama, would become a recurring gig for The Mark IV. It was a place for the students to get away and hear some live music and enjoy the art of fellowship. The owner, Bill Carr, who was just opening up, thought it to be a good idea for us to be regular performers there as we had an ability to draw a crowd. The students would pay fifty cents each to come in and hear us. Now all we had to do was determine what songs we would play.

I found the project of selecting songs exciting. My ears and my heart led me to the sounds of Jimi Hendrix and Carlos Santana. No one could question their musical talent. We started to play a lot of songs from their collections and the student's reactions were priceless. Not only did they love our sound, but they also showed an adoration for the evolution that was happening right before their eyes. Who would have known that twenty years later, Carlos himself would be backstage at Madison Square Garden watching my performance and afterwards congratulating me for my signature sound.

We went on to play songs from Sly Stone, James Taylor, and Crosby, Still, Nash & Young. We had really diversified our sound, our music, and our technique as we began to supersede cultural boundaries. Cover songs by Three Dog Night, Chicago, Blood, Sweat & Tears, and Glen Campbell were also added to our repertoire. My thought process and vision unfolded in ways that would demonstrate our ability to appeal to a wider audience, without losing the integrity of the soul. I knew that in order for us to be different, we had to illustrate visuals and a sound that the world had not yet seen. The proof was in our variety.

Lionel Richie and William King were not playing with us during these times. If they would have, we would have had to call ourselves The Commodores and we wanted to reserve that for the bigger stages and performances.

Not only did The Mark IV expand, but as a full entity The Commodores band and brand began to expand. New York was now our solidified base of operation. We would find ourselves spending less time in Tuskegee. We also began to see financial reward for our work. We had raised enough money to purchase a van and we could now afford to rent a trailer for our equipment. Benny Ashburn made arrangements through bookings, for us to come back and forth to New York regularly. There was one constant factor that kept us as we traveled extensively, God. We had so many close calls amidst our road trips, that revealed the grace that encircled us.

Although Ronald LaPread was our best driver, we all shared the responsibility. I can recall a time when we were driving from Tuskegee to New York. After we arrived in New York, we learned that our assignment was actually in Toronto. We would be tasked with driving to Canada for the performance and driving back after. The trip was somewhat gruesome and after performing, all we desired to do was rest. That night, all the guys were asleep in the van, including me and I was the driver. I awoke to the terror of the van going down a hill. We were destined for destruction. The hill was curvy and snow was everywhere. I was speeding, but I also knew that if I hit the brakes, it could be even more disastrous. The trepidation from the van racing down the hill woke everyone. By the grace of God, there was not an accident or an injury. God kept us all.

On another occasion, Milan Williams was driving and everyone was asleep. That seemed to always be the case. I'm not even sure what woke us all up, but I do recall a tremendous feeling of dismay as we discovered that we were sitting on a train track. "Man, we are on a track," I yelled. Milan panicked and backed up and then he pulled forward again and stopped.

"I don't know what to do," said Milan. He was shaking with his hands on the steering wheel.

"Man, get off the track," everybody yelled with horror. He gained an ounce of composure and pulled off just before the train came. That marked yet another moment in which God showed us that he had a greater purpose and calling for all of our lives. In those moments, although stricken with fear, I realized that we still had work to do and that we were meant to continue to climb higher.

Another testament to our faith occurred when we were on Braniff Airlines flight. It was considered a prop job airline and we were flying from Tulsa, Oklahoma to Memphis. The pilot began addressing everyone over the speaker, "Please fasten your seatbelts at this time. We may have to execute an emergency landing," he warned. It became apparent that the pilot was doing all that he could to avoid an accident. Something wasn't right. The plane was now flying sideways and as I was sitting next to the window, I could see that the propeller on my side of the plane had stopped moving. I was sitting next to a woman who was headed to a funeral and her anxiety was almost overwhelming.

"Oh my God, I am on the way to a funeral and now they are going to be coming to mine," she said.

I worked earnestly to keep her calm, which also proved to be the only way to maintain my own composure. Just before the plane prepared for a crash landing in a nearby cornfield, the pilot straightened the plane out and we were all seated just as we had been before our flight took off. We all knew that we were much lower to the ground and unsure of what would happen next. We were all startled as we began to hear a series of loud noises. Bam, Bam, Bam. The plane sounded like it was coming apart. We plummeted into the cornfield and the shrieks, screams, and wailing of the other passengers could be heard throughout the plane. When we hit the ground, my first instinct was to shake my arms and legs to see if everything was still working. I realized in that moment, just as my life had flashed before my eyes, that God had yet again kept me. We were evacuated from the plane and an emergency bus came to pick us up. I walked away unscathed and after being dropped off by the bus, I turned to look back at the wrecked plane and I could feel the tears welling up in my eyes, but I did not allow one to drop because of the joy that I was suddenly overcome by. I began to walk forward, as that was the only direction that was of concern to me. My vision for my life with the band had become even clearer. I was eager to work harder and life had new meaning for me.

With a replenished gratitude for life itself, I knew that God had not spared my life for me to not walk in destiny. That moment, I resolved to be the absolute best version of myself and to do all that I could to help others do the same. I had a new melody in my heart and this time, the tune reflected harmonious ambition that would fuel me and the group for years to come.

Our rehearsals became ever more intense and our abilities truly developed. Our song collection was so diverse that we could play for anyone. Any audience of any ethnicity could be entertained by our show. Even though racism continued to rear its ugly face and cause lines of division in the country, our music knew no boundaries. It was all in the groove, man. That was one of the characteristics that set The Commodores apart from many of the other groups who were equally amazing during that era. Together, we recognized the increased marketability in a diversified sound and we worked with everything inside of us to continue to develop something so special and so rare that it couldn't be denied. I would coin the term "the signature sound" and I harnessed all of my energy to ensure that we perfected our abilities to deliver in every way.

We would eventually be introduced to a magnificent lady named Suzanne de Passe. She was a cohort of Benny Ashburn and had been hired by Motown to run the A&R Department. In this role, she was tasked with cultivating The Jackson Five, a group consisting of five talented brothers who would go on to be recognized as one of the world's largest musical acts to date.

The Jackson Five had made an appearance on the Ed Sullivan Show and had catapulted to acquire large scale success. They were in such high demand that they were enlisted to go on a major tour.

We later learned that Suzanne de Passe contacted Benny Ashburn about allowing us the opportunity to audition as the opening act for The Jackson Five. She needed to determine if we would be a good fit to accompany them on their tour. We were all in agreeance that our rehearsals needed to be uninterrupted and that we needed to be laser focused on executing a strong audition. This was the opportunity of a lifetime.

Benny Ashburn's mother owned a rental home in Oak Bluffs, a town located on the island of Martha's Vineyard, Massachusetts. Benny saw fit for us to stay there and rehearse in order to prepare for the audition. When the day of the audition arrived, we felt prepared. One thing that we knew about success was that it was not going to simply be handed to us. We were out to get everything that we knew we deserved because of our desire and ability to work for it. This was our day to show the decision makers what we already knew.

The audition was held at a nightclub called Turntable, which was owned by an American R&B vocalist named, Lloyd Price or "Mr. Personality" as he was more commonly known. High energy, intense, spontaneous, and funky described the vibe in the room. We went through the Three Dog Night song, "Liar," a number by Blood, Sweat & Tears, a few James Taylor and James Brown hits, and ended with a song by Sly & the Family Stone. We "Commodorized" everything. We were singing and dancing so much that I honestly believe that we forgot we were auditioning. We were simply performing as if we were in front of a packed house. Leaving it all on the stage was not something we did, but more so who we were.

"You guys are in. You are going to be a part of history," said Benny Ashburn. Suzanne de Passe had selected us to be the opening act for The Jackson Five. The moment was surreal. We stood there on the stage in silence, looking at one another before falling into a web of relentless laughter. We cheered with joy and excitement for what would be.

I was blown away by the opportunity. The first person that I told was my sister, Leola, who was two years older than me. We were still so close and sharing it with her meant everything to me. "Have you told Mom and Dad?" She inquired.

"If it actually happens, I will tell them," I replied. They had always taught us not to count our chickens before they hatched. I knew that we would see this moment come to pass, but I wanted to be careful about not adding any additional stress, anxiety, or worry to my parent's plate. They were getting older and I'd much rather present them with facts.

The news of the tour began to break before we even began to speak about it. Suddenly, there were noticeable differences in our social lives. As the tour began to manifest, we began acquiring friends that we hadn't had before. New found fame also meant meeting women that we would not have otherwise been in the presence of. Prior to attending Tuskegee, family and music were my first loves, and after becoming a college student, academics became my second love.

When we arrived back to the campus, there was a girl in my dormitory, who was "waiting for me," she said. She introduced herself and began staring at me. From that moment, it seemed as if she followed me around everywhere. It was peculiar behavior to me because I had never been exposed to actions of this nature. "I can't do this. I have classes," I said.

Eventually, I found myself amid my very first intimate encounter, with a young lady. Whoa, that was a time! It seemed as though the ladies were coming from all angles. At the time, I can't say that any one of us minded either. Even the girls who had been assigned to tutor us academically made advances towards tutoring us socially. The courses that we were enrolled in were not easy and we were still very serious about excelling academically. The element of the lady friend had now become a factor for everyone in the group. This was not something that we would have known to account for because we were all so naive.

The first major incident that occurred to this end was when Lionel and his first girlfriend broke up. It was his first heartbreak and it took a major toll on him. It hurt so badly that he actually missed a performance. As guys who had never been in love, many of the group members didn't understand and extended very little compassion. Lionel received a great deal of pressure and backlash from the members. They pestered him with comments such as, "You have to man up, this is the band," and "What are you doing? How can you do this?" In those moments, I found myself reaching out to Lionel, not because I understood the heartbreak, but because I understood pain. It was a pivotal moment for my role in the group as I suddenly found myself emerging as a mediator.

"Hey now, come on everybody, it will be OK. This sort of thing happens, you know?" I tried to be encouraging. What I knew was that not one of us was exempt from heartbreak and if girls were going to be a part of the equation, then heartbreak would be sure to follow. We didn't know that we would all experience heartbreak down the road and in many different ways as life unfolded.

I casually enjoyed the company of the ladies, but was very reluctant to get too serious. My idea of a whirlwind romance was very different from most. I was married to my studies and in love with the music. We continued playing in Birmingham, and returning to New York in between. There was one young lady from Birmingham who made her interest in me known. After the shows, she would approach me and ask the same question, "Where are you playing in between?" Our next stop was New York and I disclosed that information to her. I had assumed that similar to all of the other instances, the conversation would end and I would bid her a good night. After we traveled to New York, I got word that she had followed us there. That day, the weather was harrowing and she was stranded. She had only planned to visit New York for the day and return home that night. The next thing I knew, we were getting phone calls from the newspaper and our now manager, Benny Ashburn, implying that this girl was missing and assumed to have been kidnaped. The real kicker was that the last time she had been documented as being seen, she was with me. I was alarmed, concerned for the band, and of course concerned for the safety of everyone, but I was certain that she was not with me. I had never invited her to travel with us, as we took the band and our business very seriously and had no desire for that kind of distraction. We were later informed that this same young lady was not only married, but married to an airline pilot. This explained how she was able to travel so quickly to meet us in New York. She was trying to come up with an excuse to give her husband as she had originally thought to be home before he even noticed her missing. As the weather didn't cooperate, she decided in a desperate attempt to not get caught or reprimanded by her husband, to have someone put out that word that she had been kidnapped. I couldn't believe that someone would go to such extremes. It was a rude awakening for me as far as fans, girls, and the associated behaviors. It taught us all to keep a healthy distance and that we were targets for the unwarranted behaviors of others. We resolved to keep an even tighter circle and keep the lines of communication open amongst each other so that we could truly support one another.

 The transitions didn't stop. We were all coming of age and the responsibilities and experiences associated with real life continued to grow. During this time, we also experienced a paradigm shift within the group. We wanted for all of the members to take an overall interest in growing, not only musically but also as entrepreneurs. Some members had more of an interest in the business than others.

Walter Orange became displaced after he left Alabama State. The distance to performances in Montgomery with The Mark IV led him to leave school and we became roommates. This gave me the opportunity to learn more about him and we became friends. We were just two young guys, hustling and trying to keep it together as the band grew. As we reached higher levels of success, it was imperative for Walter to stabilize his living situation, as it was for all of us.

Up until this point, Walter had only been a salaried member of The Commodores. We decided to make him an equal member and though he didn't appear to have a genuine interest in learning about the business aspects of our careers, I felt obligated to bring him up to speed and acclimated. The theme of entrepreneur versus musician would continue to weave itself through the inner workings of our lives and eventually become a point of contention as the group realized higher levels of success.

Life as we knew it was no longer the same. In more ways than one, we were blessed; we were young and in the midst of monumental success. In retrospect, I must say, there were at times a few hints of half-witted behavior that accompanied our youth. We continued to travel and play gigs wherever Benny booked us. He worked hard to ensure that we were exposed and always working.

Upon a visit to Canada, where we had been requested to perform, we drove towards the designated customs area. As we approached customs, Lionel threw out a bag and whispered to us, "If they come up to us and ask us about a bag, let's say this is a group bag." Not one of us committed to Lionel's plan.

"Nah, this ain't no group bag," I replied. Sitting in the customs office was rather frightening because we were not completely sure of why we were there but we had a pretty good idea. Approximately half way through the approval process, we were stopped and detained. We were informed that there were some marijuana seeds in the bag that Lionel had thrown out and as a result, we were all being held. They were very kind to us.

"Look, you guys are college students, right? We are going to have you go to a judge's house here in Canada and whatever the judge says, that is what is going to happen." We had no choice but to accept their judgement.

We were loaded into a van and driven down an extremely dark, country road. We were understandably nervous and could only fathom the possibilities of what could happen if we had been back in the states. To make matters worse, many blacks were moving illegally to Canada in order to avoid being drafted. We were gravely concerned.

As we got to the judge's home, however, we were pleasantly surprised by his treatment of us, as it was nothing like what we would have experienced back at home. "You guys seem like nice guys and I see that you are college kids. What I am going to demand is that you each tell your parents what happened and have them write me a letter stating that you have disclosed this incident to them and that you won't do it again," he reprimanded.

We were all in agreement with what he rendered because we knew precisely how much worse things could have been.

After that, Lionel resolved to put the weed down and Ronald LaPread and I resolved to pick it up. No one ever really knew about it because we had such a squeaky-clean image and we fought hard to maintain it.

From the outside looking in, the whirlwind of a ride that we were on, would be a dream come true. The truth is that it was scary. The entertainment industry is not for the faint of heart. The bottom can be snatched from under you at any time. Only the strong can survive and remain level headed in the midst of ascension to success.

There were times when some members straddled the fence between being fully committed to the group and continuing to pursue their other interests. During this time, William King maintained his pursuit of tennis and there were times when the sport took precedence over the group. Milan Williams, who was extremely astute, was also in pursuit of becoming a pilot. To make light of it all, while addressing the issue, his nickname became "Left Field."

A solid bond of brotherhood would soon materialize for those group members who were consistently together. It is very hard to be around people for so many important moments of your life, with the privilege to do what you love together, and not connect through a bond or friendship.

Each member of the group had their own defining personality. Lionel for instance, was known to be extremely frugal. We all were, but Lionel's exercise of his right to save his money was phenomenal. He came up with the nickname, Jack Benny, for himself, in lieu of the way he squeezed his pockets. He was sharp, I had to give him that. He would even go so far as to store his money under the mattress and count it often.

The relationship between Lionel and myself continued to grow. He and I spent the most time together and I truly believed he was my friend. After Lionel's experience with heartbreak and my notion to not get too deeply involved with a woman, we were the perfect pair of bachelors. Lionel and I were our own force and while we enjoyed the company of ladies, music became the absolute priority. It was my belief that Lionel and I saw the same possibilities for what The Commodores could become. Our dreams were much bigger than what the naked eye could see or the small mind could conceptualize.

While my friendship with Lionel was unquestionable, we also valued the relationships with the group members as a whole. I would venture to say that The Commodores was a brotherhood. We were always looking for ways to become even closer as a band and liked to come up with alternate ways to communicate with one another. CB Radio helped us do just that. CB Radio was a platform to keep the lines of communication open and to have fun outside of music. We all came up with handles to identify ourselves.

I struggled with trying to find a name for myself, but Milan Williams came up with a handle for me; I became known as Adam Ant. Shaggy Dog was Ronald LaPread's nickname because he owned a dog with long fur. Walter Orange was Silver Dollar, Milan Williams was Captain Quick Draw because he could tap in quickly on his opponent. The goal was to have powerful communications that could overpower the opponent. If you could shut someone down quickly, it was a big deal. William King was Red Baron and Richie was of course Jack Benny. Notions like CB Radio helped to maintain the integrity, oneness, and spirit of the band.

We were gelling and more importantly, we were optimistic. We had all individually experienced the struggles and strife of life in general, but now more than ever, our eyes focused on the ultimate prize of stardom. We knew that our success would allow us to cross barriers that had never been crossed and ultimately improve the quality of life for our loved ones. While many were considering athletics as their "way out," we knew another lane that was to some a best kept secret. Not one of us doubted that we were in the presence of the greatest opportunity of our lifetimes. Unlike many of the stories that we had once been told of oppression and struggle, the stars were now aligned so that we could see the world differently. We were becoming invisible in the face of oppression.

I now know that the most rewarding gift for having lived this life was the opportunity to walk in purpose. There is no greater feeling or opportunity afforded to a human being.

06: *Experience is a Plentiful Teacher*

The Commodore brand was now a recognizable entity. We knew that embarking upon a US tour as the opening act for The Jackson Five would change our lives forever. We felt eager and more ready than ever musically. For so long, we had taken care of all our business affairs and managed to make great strides with the assistance of Benny Ashburn. We now recognized that no matter how much we wanted to be in control, there were logistically some areas that we would have to get support in and inevitably, there would be issues of trust the moment we transferred the balance of power from one hand and heart to the next.

Benny Ashburn quit his job, as an executive at Coca Cola, to manage us full time. Anytime that someone transfers roles and becomes responsible for your welfare, you scrutinize them differently. Wanting to keep busy, Benny expanded his client roster early in his new-found career and it did not sit well with us. We weren't quite ready to share our manager with three other groups — Sun from Dayton, Ohio, Platinum Hook from Newark, New Jersey, and Three Ounces of Love, a female group from Detroit.

Benny was now unavoidably under the microscope. Prior to his tenure as our manager, we had been somewhat responsible for ourselves. To now have Benny completely responsible for us was different. It is my belief that we often missed the fatherly role that he played originally in our lives within the industry. His obligations in that realm dissolved as he was tasked with looking out for our best interests in many other ways. No longer was he just the guy who booked gigs for us on good merit and his reputation. He was now on salary and employed by us. We depended on his knowledge and we respected him, not only because he was older and wiser than us, but he had stood up for us countless times.

Benny Ashburn's evolution from mentor to manager now meant that he would be tasked more with contractual obligations, finding business managers and lawyers, and of course managing our public relations and bookings. As with any shifts and changes of this magnitude, there lies an accompaniment of discord. He would often have individual meetings or pull aside certain guys for specific reasons. It left those of us not invited feeling unsettled. This also meant that when we did meet with him as a group, the tension between the six of us also became a factor. There were times when tempers flared during meetings due to a lack of understanding.

Upon our visit and performance one evening, I became very upset with Ashburn during a group team meeting because he was simply not answering the questions that were being asked of him. We were all educated and smart enough to understand the ins and outs of the business that we were now deeply immersed in. Everything from royalties and marketing information to branding strategies, we deserved access to.

Benny felt as though it was his responsibility to handle our affairs, and that we did not need to be intricately involved. That night, I lost it. I remember picking up a Coca-Cola bottle and I charged at him. In haste, I threw the bottle and he ducked. The bottle crashed against the wall. "In case you don't think that we are serious, we are very serious. Disclose all of the details or this will be World War III," I said in a rage. We were chartering new and very unfamiliar territory and it was unnerving for some of the members, including me, to feel as though we were being left in the dark about any developments regarding The Commodores.

The truth is that no one can prepare you for the rise to stardom, not even those who have been there and experienced it firsthand. Every artist or group has a different path and a different set of dynamics from which to operate. We had so many people offering to manage us, pitching their ideas, and making promises about what they could do for us that it was often hazy. However, none of them could match the fatherly love of Ashburn.

We also knew that it was now imperative that we position ourselves to become recording artists. We could not just keep playing other people's songs. That would not get us to the level of success that we aspired to.

Benny's personal ties to Suzanne de Passe had officially landed us the role as the opening act for The Jackson Five tour.

We received the details of the tour and were elated to learn that it was to be hosted in all fifty states. This would be their first national tour of all the states and ours as well. The strategy outlined by management was that the tour would begin in smaller markets to iron out the kinks before reaching the larger markets. Needless to say, we were surprised to learn that the first stop was listed as Miami, Florida. This was not exactly a small market, so we had to hit the ground running.

Just before the tour with The Jackson Five, Benny Ashburn pulled us aside and spoke with us in depth about our mannerisms and how we needed to stay in our lane. He wanted us to be self-contained and do what was asked of us while on the road. He also wanted us to be role models when necessary because the Jacksons were much younger than we were. We also believed that character had played a huge role in the extension of the opportunity to embark upon the tour. We were still very much clean cut and recognized as young musicians in pursuit of academic excellence.

We had one gig left to fulfill at Smalls Paradise, before our departure. The club opened at ten o'clock and we were scheduled to hit the stage twenty minutes later. We had a hot set that night and the energy was elevated because we were all feeling like real rock stars. Man, we were on cloud nine. We knew our value and that we had something amazing that the world would now see. As we played, we could always see everything that happened out in the audience, although most often, it had no effect on our performance. As long as the guests were grooving, we were in tune with our music and giving all that we had.

That night, a gentleman named Frank, who we easily recognized, walked in flanked by an entourage. We had made his acquaintance on several occasions and we knew that he spoke very highly of us. He too was from the south, but had taken residence in New York. Frank took us for breakfast and lunch a few times to a restaurant called Sylvia's and another place called Wells Supper Club. Wells Supper Club was located in Harlem and was a great spot to socialize and immerse yourself into the culture of the city.

Frank was also a regular at Small's Paradise and a big spender. He enjoyed seeing those in his presence happy. On this night, we could see from the stage that another gentleman was sitting in Frank's reserved section. The gentleman was accompanied by several women who followed his directive. It appeared that he was their pimp.

Although discreetly, our eyes began to connect with each other on stage as we questioned how everything would play out. I remember thinking to myself, "Whoa. This guy and his girls are sitting at Frank's table." We knew that Frank was known as a tough guy, but that night would prove just how tough he was. Frank's bodyguard walked over to the man who was in Frank's seat, and without hesitation picked him up. All we could see from the stage was the man's feet, dangling over the crowd. Frank's bodyguard took the guy out of Small's Paradise and no one saw him again that night. The girls were still seated at the table and appeared to be frightened and awaiting direction. Frank walked over and back-handed the girl closest to him. He slapped her so hard that her wig was suspended in the air. It wasn't funny in the slightest; I felt more surreal. We couldn't believe that all of this was unfolding before our eyes. For all of the clubs that we had played in, we had never been involved in any incidents of this nature. We were still the naive college guys who just wanted to play music. We later learned that the gentleman who had been abruptly escorted out of the club by Frank's bodyguard was placed in the dumpster and told not to come out until after we were finished performing.

What we did not know was that Frank was a bona fide gangster and not just any gangster, but the notorious and influential crime boss Frank Lucas, who had made millions of dollars during the 1960's and 70's from the sale of heroin. (1) Up until that night, we had only seen the best in Frank. In retrospect, I now know that everyone else knew not to cross Frank which allowed him to be the amazing gentleman that we had shared time and space with. Benny Ashburn grew up in Harlem and we had met Frank through him so we never questioned anything about him, there was no need to.

The irony was that this major incident occurred after Benny had delivered that impactful speech about how to not get involved in drugs and the wrong crowd. Yet, there we were, in the company of one of the most notorious gangsters of our era and trouble was the last thing on our minds. Thank God, we survived that night and every other force over the years that could have threatened the image and legacy that we had worked so hard to build. We left Smalls Paradise with an appreciation for life and the naive disposition that had kept us along the way. We transitioned the energy and prepared to hit the road with The Jackson Five.

Our first show was somewhat intimidating, not because we had never performed before, but because we were unsure of what to expect. We had prepared our entire lives for that moment. We all felt solid about our dance moves and could perform them with ease. When we hit the stage, the flair that we were becoming known for grabbed the audience's attention. For me, the influence of rock and roll was at an all-time high. I was so inspired by Jimi Hendrix. In an effort to bring my own flair to all that I had seen and been influenced by from Hendrix, I had all of these pedals which created a variety of different sounds. (2) I didn't want to be limited to what I could do musically while on the stage. I also felt a sense of uneasiness because I knew that some of the steps that we were doing, could alter some of the connections on the equipment. We were responsible for setting up our own backline equipment and our own instruments. We were not yet a large enough act for someone else to do that for us. That night during our sound check, we discovered some kinks that still needed to be worked out. Overall, I didn't feel like we were ready. In the middle of one of the songs, one of my effects came disconnected. There was an important part in the music coming up that I needed to use that effect for. The dance moves were coming up and I wasn't sure if I would have time to fix it. As I stood there playing, I pondered whether to bend down to reconnect the effect or not. In a move of haste, I stooped down to connect the effect and all the guys ran over me. It was terrible. I was distraught and beating myself up so badly. As a perfectionist, this was a huge calamity to me. In my mind, our first night had been ruined.

As I was standing in the wings of the stage, I heard a voice speak to me over my shoulder, "It would have been better for you to keep the entertainment going than to musically play the part that you were trying to get. In the scheme of things, these are kids and their parents were with them. They were enjoying the show. You were more of a distraction than entertainment." The gentleman speaking was Marvin Gaye's music director. This was a huge learning experience for me. What I knew for sure was that I had learned a hard lesson, one that I would never make again.

After both acts performed, we were escorted into a dressing room. The backstage area was incredibly busy. We did not know how to distinguish all of the people that were in the crowd. Some were staff members assisting with the tour, some were management, and others were professionals whom we had no knowledge of. Amid the crowds, we noticed that an influx of parents and their children whom they had brought to attend the concert began filling up the backstage area. It was apparent that security was one of the glitches that would need to be ironed out as we prepared to take the tour to larger markets.

The members of The Jackson Five were rushed into our dressing room to take cover. There we stood, face to face for the first time with Michael, Jermaine, Marlon, Jackie, Tito and their cousin, Johnny Jackson, who played drums, and another cousin, Ronnie Rancifer, who played the keyboard. That night while trapped in the dressing room, we also met Joe Jackson, their father. Suzanne de Passe and her assistant,

Tony Jones had also made their way into the one dressing room that offered reprieve from the crowds. (3)

The pandemonium just outside the door, led to a discussion on logistics and how to avoid scenarios like this on future dates. After all, we had forty-nine shows remaining.

"This can't happen in every city," said a member of their management. Bill Bray, the security guard who had been hired to escort The Jackson Five seemed to be perplexed.

From nowhere, a small, yet certain voice arose and began to speak. "I've got an idea. Why don't we let The Commodores ride in our limousines and all they have to do is squat down in the seats and not let anyone see their faces and the people will think that it is us." That bold idea was voiced by a young Michael Jackson.

"Man, that's a great idea," someone yelled out. Their team began strategizing and the idea that Michael presented was set in motion.

"We can use them as a decoy and we can get another truck and go the opposite direction," said Michael. Man, was this kid young to have been so witty. I was amazed at how the adults listened to what he had to say, not because of who he was, but because he spoke with substance.

The fact that we all wore afros made Michael's suggestion even more practical. The team called for an armored truck to escort The Jackson Five, while we were led to the limo. Just as Michael had predicted, the crowd thought that we were the Jacksons and they began to follow us. When we got to the hotel, the fans were lined along the sidewalks and walkways to the front entrance. They were disappointed to find out that we were not the Jacksons, but we were asked to sign some autographs because of our affiliation with them. This was a defining moment for us because we had now gained another set of fans and a new audience.

The tour progressed and so did our stardom. Our reviews were going through the roof. We were something different that the world had not yet seen. From the way that we performed to the musical offering that we gave the audience, we had secured our own lane. Even Joe Jackson became concerned about the popularity that we were gaining. As an astute businessman, he would see to it that our reviews did not surpass his act. As we prepared for our San Francisco stop, we were instructed that the tour would go from San Fran to Los Angeles and Los Angeles to the Hollywood Bowl. These were all major media markets and everyone involved knew that the fruits of labor in these markets would yield sweet returns in dividends and reviews.

Joe didn't want us to upstage The Jackson Five and his antics became apparent. In retrospect, there was no way for us to upstage them, as we didn't even have any records that had been released. We had not formally recorded any of our own music yet. During the tour, we had been using the same tractor-trailer as the Jacksons to transport our equipment. After we played in San Fran, we loaded our equipment like we had done after all of the previous shows and set our eyes on the next and last show at the Hollywood bowl. When we arrived for sound check, neither our equipment nor our uniforms were present. Our suspicions were valid because The

Jackson Five had all their equipment in place. How could ours be missing if it was transported in the same method that theirs had been. With time constraints before the show, it seemed unlikely that we would be able to rent equipment so quickly. We had only arrived hours before we were set to be on stage.

"For forty-nine shows, our equipment has been on point, how is this possible?" Benny questioned. Joe gave it away when he came around the corner as we were in the midst of a heated discussion.

"Oh, hey guys. Is everything good?"

"Nah Joe. Our equipment was left in San Fran," I said.

"Too bad," he said. "The show must go on." His smirk was worth a million dollars in torment.

We were forced to think quickly on our feet. I reverted to my instinctive moments from the talent show back at Tuskegee. Although he hadn't come from a sincere place, Joe was right. The show had to go on. We now had a name to uphold and a reputation to grow. In true Commodore fashion, we didn't back down. We owned everything that happened to us just as much as we owned the fact that we were responsible for what would happen next.

"Ok, guys, we are going to make lemonade out of these lemons," I said. We were able to quickly rent some guitars and we convinced Joe to let us play on the Jackson's basic equipment. Lionel didn't have any horns available to him for that show. The only garments that we had from our wardrobe were our tops. We carried them with us, which allowed them to dry after each of the performances. They were custom fitted so that so that they would stay tucked even during our dance movements. Thankfully, we also had our boots. They were knee high, very colorful and matched the tops.

With our outfits set, I told Richie and King that when it came to the horn parts, they should simply sing. We decided in that moment to do what we had always done and use exactly what we had in front of us. The spirit of the group was increased and what had been meant to harm us fueled us in ways that were indescribable. When you are that close to your destiny, you become equipped to weather tremendous storms. As we stood there backstage, preparing to leave it all on the stage, my mind flashed back to us standing on the sidewalk after having made it from Alabama to New York with not a penny to spare and having had our equipment stolen. If we had survived that moment, surely, we were destined for success in this one. I smiled to myself and at each of the guys. I wanted them to know that we were going to be OK.

"You guys are up now," a voice announced. We went out onto the stage with incredible enthusiasm and did what we do best. We sang our hearts out and the lights seemed to have a different effect that night. As opposed to the audience laughing at the costumes that we had assembled, we become trendsetters. Instead of being defeated, we were victorious. That night at the Hollywood Bowl, we were taught a great lesson on survival and life in general. Under no circumstances can you allow things that happen to stop you. You may have to adjust your path or move at a slower pace, but while in pursuit of your goals and your purpose, you must remain in motion at all costs. This lesson would prove to be prodigious in the years to come.

The next morning, we witnessed with our own eyes, the reviews that we longed for. I could hardly believe my eyes. I must admit that I had to pinch myself, we all did. This was really our lives. The words were printed in black and white and seeing them further confirmed that, we had done the right thing and we deserved a seat at the table. The headlines read something to the effect of "The Commodores Come Out in Boldly Dressed Attire, Perform an Incredible Show." That was such an exciting time for us.

With new levels of success came the extension of new opportunities for The Commodores. Our last stop on the tour was in Hawaii. While on the plane, a gentleman began speaking to us and sharing that he was en route to get married. He told us that he loved The Jackson Five music and was happy to be in our presence. He extended an opportunity for us to play at his wedding while in Hawaii.

"Have you ever seen a million dollars in cash?" He asked. Still naive, not one of us had seen a million dollars, but we were eager to do so and most certainly interested in this gentleman's offer. I left the seating area to go back to where Benny was seated and share the offer with him, as I knew that he would be responsible for closing the deal.

"There is a guy who wants to pay us a million dollars to play at his wedding while we are in Hawaii."

"No, we aren't doing that. It looks to me as if he might be involved with organized crime," said Benny. His instincts to protect us at all costs had kicked in and I could see it written all over his face. It was not worth my arguing. I knew that Benny was serious. As I made my way back to the guys, my mind drifted back to the Frank Lucas situation and I determined that the gig would not be in the best interest for the Commodore brand. We bowed out gracefully and remained focused on the reason that we were on the flight to begin with, which was to close out a monumental tour with The Jackson Five. The tour had been a massive success. We now looked ahead to the future and felt empowered because we had our first tour under our belts.

As always, I stole away for quiet moments of reflection. I had always believed that every experience could yield a valuable lesson. What had all of this meant? What could we take away from our experiences that would help us reach the next level? What were we missing and what should our next move be? These were all questions that I asked myself. I wanted to continue to add value to the group by returning to the table with strategies, solutions, and a vision for what could be. This had always been what I felt the guys looked to me for. I had produced the vision to bring us all together, but I always felt equally responsible for the vision to keep us together. The tour was much more than a time to perform songs and garner new attention; it also served as a sufficient teacher. As a musician, no matter how much you practice or how prepared you believe yourself to be, there are certain things that you cannot truly learn without experiencing it with your own senses. You have to taste doubt and touch triumph to know that the two exist.

The valuable lessons gleaned could be applied to not only our lives as musicians but life in general. I had always been a student of experience and this moment was no different. Life is always about learning and the minute that we forget to do so, we offset the balance of growth. Every chance that was offered to me, I turned around and shared with the group. It was important to divulge the valuable lessons that I learned during the tour with others. What good is it to be better and not share with others how you arrived at that destination? During the tour, I learned the importance of hit songs. Both The Jackson Five and The Commodores had good live shows. The difference was that The Jackson Five had a bevy of hit songs that got enormous airplay on radio and TV. When they performed their hits, the crowd went crazy, which also sent record sales through the roof.

It was imperative for us to write some hit songs with our unique sound. This was the missing element since we knew how to give a great performance. In life, you have to have some hit songs or talents that you recognize and capitalize on to add value to who you are and what you can bring to the table. We are each valuable based on our ability to contribute to society.

I also learned the importance of a set list for the way that the show flows. The opening and closing of the show are just as vital to your set list as maintaining the momentum during the show with equal highs and lows. Every monologue, every grunt, groan, choreographed dance step, and moment to peak the audience's interest, must be thought out.

In life, we may not always have the plan, but we should always be thinking of how to prepare for what we want to have happen and harness our energies towards that end. Everything that we do matters. Sometimes we take life for granted, but large moments are composed of a multitude of small actions. Everything counts.

Time management and the ability to multi-task also became leading strategies for successful execution. While on tour Michael Jackson had a tutor, and could often be seen engaging academically when not performing. This was validation that we could stay in school and still pursue our music career. We learned that we could be great musicians and great students in a world that sent messages otherwise. This applied to our lives so genuinely because although we had every intention of taking music as far as possible, we also knew that an education was something that could never be taken away from us. If music did not work out, we would always have the option to utilize our education to the fullest.

I had also learned a great deal of business acumen by observing the brilliant mind of Suzanne de Passe. Not only was she a skilled leader, but she implemented an unprecedented strategy with her staff. To be responsible for masterminding the early career of The Jackson Five was priceless. She demonstrated the importance of creating an element of mystique and exclusivity around a band in a way that the industry had not seen. She was responsible for creating the superstars that The Jackson Five evolved into. She could turn an everyday person into a bona fide star. She was witty and brilliant in her role.

Taking the time to reflect proved to be mind-blowing. The tour had taught me so much. It encouraged me to continue my higher education and to learn more about the entertainment business and specifically marketing. This time also validated that the squeaky clean, collegiate image was a good thing for us in the music business. It made us different.

I can honestly say that The Jackson Five tour elevated our success. Upon returning to campus, our visibility soared. We now had more access to students and faculty who wanted to see us excel academically. We received a great deal of support from tutors and from professors demonstrating a willingness to ensure that we passed some of our more challenging courses.

During the tour with The Jackson Five, we had worked extremely hard and earned every accomplishment. Nothing had been given to us. From the moments of despair in the thick of racism and the battle that produced the clouds of destruction from oppression to standing in the middle of the streets of New York, hopeless after having our instruments stolen with no promise for opportunity to sold out audiences who had been converted to new believers in our music; we had proven ourselves. We were The Commodores and there was no turning back. We stood atop a mountain of greatness. Even so, we could not realize our conceivable potential if we kept playing other people's songs. I knew that we would now need to position ourselves to become recording artists. The following year, we were invited back to do a second tour with The Jackson Five. The next chapter would prove to be an uphill climb and the next level would prove to worth every struggle.

07: *Fog on the Glass Ceiling*

After the success of the second tour with The Jackson Five, we came to a fork in the road. We could either go down in history as an amazing performance act or we could solidify our legacy by recording songs of our own. As we saw it, the latter was the only option. Our intent was to ascend. We would be forced to lock ourselves away to write and to try to come up with a concept to define our signature sound. There was no other option.

In 1971, we signed a contract with the incomparable Motown Records. An entire book could be written on their monumental accomplishments. Motown's standard for excellence and the titanic talent that was produced under its auspices was undeniable. It was an honor to be in the company of so many artists that we had admired over the years and many whose music we had covered.

Motown Records was embellished by a spirit of hustle and excellence. Their creator, Berry Gordy began the company with an $800 loan from his family's savings. He was determined to create a sustainable company that would benefit artists and music through its offering of countless hits. Home to musical greats like Mary Wells, Marvin Gaye, The Miracles, The Supremes, Stevie Wonder, Diana Ross and The Jackson Five; Motown was an industry trailblazer. It was as if everything that was released from Motown was a guaranteed success. (1) We were now tasked with the decision of determining if Motown records was a good fit for The Commodores.

With a group consisting of as many members as we had, making a decision that everyone agreed upon was challenging, but it wasn't impossible. We had a strong sense of who we were musically, but being given the job of developing the signature sound that belonged only to us was no easy feat. What we never wanted to do was take the money, go into the studio, and just sing pre-record tracks like everyone else during that era had done, but that was the Motown formula and who were we to challenge a dynamic that had churned out so many stars and quality music. Thankfully, Benny Ashburn allowed us to make the decisions as to how we wanted to proceed both creatively and financially. We had no interest in taking any money up front and were smart enough to know the prized advances were fool's gold and that it would eventually have to be paid back through profits.

There we were at the crux of an opportunity that most could only dream about and one that even we had not been certain would be realized and we were hesitant. We had signed the contract, but we didn't activate it because we didn't take any money. And although that sounds crazy, we would later garner a great deal of respect in the industry for our business acumen.

Berry Gordy was baffled to say the least. I'm almost certain that he hadn't come across any other artists who refused to accept an advance. Let's face it, most artists, including us had put their hearts and souls into their careers and their musicality, which also meant that the funds were low and the debts were high. We had lived for so long, so frugal that we knew how to do so and still flourish. Berry Gordy sent for us and allowed us an opportunity to visit the studios, which we had never been in. As I reflect, I now know that God always had a plan for us. How had we risen to such large-scale levels of success without ever having truly been in a studio? Only God can orchestrate a career of that magnitude.

Arriving in Los Angeles was surreal. We had never seen so much diversity in one place. People were sporting everything from long hair to afros. Everyone seemed to be wearing sunglasses and the vibe was very laid back. We had toured many places by now, so it wasn't as if we hadn't seen something different than Tuskegee, but to consider living on another coast was definitely something that made us ponder. An ongoing conversation amongst the guys was that we needed to be careful and not get "too Hollywood". That was a term that we created which meant not getting caught up in the lights. LA had it all, but we had heard the horror stories of entertainers losing their footing to drugs or even addiction to fame that cost them their careers. Subliminally, using the term also meant that we were referring to remaining humble and not feeling that any one of us was better than the group as a whole.

When we arrived, we learned that we would be staying at The Tropicana, the same hotel The Jackson Five, Buddy Miles, Carlos Santana, Stevie Wonder and several other artist had stayed at when they came to LA initially. Suzanne de Passe assigned Tony Jones and Eddie Langford the task of indoctrinating us into the Motown family. It wasn't long before we move into the same apartment building as Stevie Wonder, who immediately befriended us. He was a true testament to what hard work could garner as he was always writing songs, singing and humming. He was cool to be around and his undeniable talent was magic. As he worked on new songs, he would occasionally invite us to come and preview what he had assembled. We would get a taste and then he'd say, "Nah, nah, nah, you can't hear anymore," and he'd be done sharing his creative process. Stevie went on to achieve worldwide success and his music would not only prove to be entertaining, but was a lifeline of social messages sent to empower the black community. With his musical genius, he found a way to be pro black without being anti anyone else.

We began to strategize on the best method to attack the process of creating our signature sound. Just getting into the studio proved to be a process. The legendary Smokey Robinson, and the uber talented Norman Whitfield had both produced massive hits and they were both interested in helping us if we would allow them to. One could deduce that we were seen as a little difficult because we did not make an immediate decision as to our process, but quite to the contrary, it was because of our decision to not dive in head first that there was a mystique about us that appealed to other artists. Everyone was now waiting to see what our strategy would be and what results it would yield. The talk was that maybe we hadn't received the right combination to create what we wanted, which made producers, songwriters and arrangers hungry to work with us. It placed us in a winning scenario because many artists have to request to work with certain professionals in the industry and that doesn't always lead to the request being honored. We were lucky enough to have them all offering their services to us before we even needed to ask. We had gotten so much publicity from both tours with The Jackson Five and all of our hard work that we were a hot commodity and everyone wanted to stake claim to our first release.

While our strategy remained elusive, what we did know was that we were not tech savvy and in fact quite clueless in the studio. Years prior to The Jackson Five tour, we recorded a song with a producer by the name of "Swamp Dogg" Jerry Williams, Jr., but the record didn't get much publicity and we didn't learn anything during the process. After much thought and consideration, we came to the conclusion that in order to prepare for the studio we needed a talented arranger and a great engineer. Along came James Carmichael, a highly acclaimed arranger. We scheduled a meeting with him to determine if there was synergy and eventually, we made a deal. If he co-produce with us, it would give him a promotion and he would be eligible for residuals and royalties and not just a salary for arranging. This proved to be a win win combination and we were all eager to get down to business.

It seemed as though we designed a method for everything. The one thing that we all agreed upon was that if order was present, there would be no room for chaos. No one had an interest in anything that would disrupt or dissolve the creative process. We even came up with a procedure for how we would select songs for the album once they were created. We all had something to contribute to the music and we all had the ability to generate a concept, but only some of us could create entire songs together.

Fairness was a priority and we opted to run things as democratically as possible. We decided that everyone would get an opportunity to pitch their songs for the album and we would allow Carmichael to be the mediator as he was the only non-member. We figured he was in the best position to make objective decisions on which songs would be best received by our fans, the music critics, and the radio. It was only later in years to come that we would learn democracy wouldn't work in our favor.

The members of Mark IV had an existing chemistry because we had worked so closely in the clubs back in Tuskegee. As we sat together to compose, we often found ourselves flowing in the same space and time without any written music or charts as a guide, and it was beautiful. Quite often, I would initiate a riff and then Milan or Ronald would join that riff, complementing it with Walter's creative contribution. Of course, there were times that it would go in the opposite direction, but the chemistry remained the same. Over time we became astute at coming up with riffs and licks. If it was funk, we would try to make it as funky as we could. If it was beautiful, we aimed for it to be as melodic and tear jerking as possible. Whatever the mood of the music was, we were going to strike it. The reservoir of our musical stores was deep and well-rounded and the creative process allowed us to channel all of the styles that we had acquired. From a bird's eye view, you would have witnessed an innocent group of guys who were simply romantically tied to the God given talents they had been given and waking up each day to cherish those gifts. In those moments, we made the most of everything that was inside of us. We would find ourselves exhausted from creating and it was one of the best feelings in the world. This work would pay off in many ways and the world would eventually come to know The Commodores as recording artists and not just talented musicians who covered the music of others.

By 1972 the world and my outlook looked somewhat different from my lenses. Things were changing. People were dyeing their hair and the various nationalities in LA were more prevalent than ever. It was almost as if you didn't have to acknowledge color or race. I was learning every day that the music could cross boundaries where the color of my skin could not. We were laser focused on becoming a household name and creating a hit that would result in a rise in our popularity and to show what we were really made of.

One day, I was walking down the street on my way from the hotel to the studio when I heard someone yell my name, "Hey Peewee!" Peewee was a name that was given to me by my former classmates. I thought that I was mistaken because it was unfathomable that someone from there would be in LA. The gentleman called out again, "Peewee!" and I turn around to see Howard Sewell. He was indeed a former classmate that I had not seen in years. He was in LA visiting and had heard about us getting a recording contract with Motown. He was so excited and expressed intently his joy for us. We stood there for a while catching up and laughing as we reminisced over old times. He treated me the same as he always had, but I felt something different. It was as if he felt that I had "arrived." After my brief exchange with Howard I knew that The Commodores were going to be famous. That was my first moment. I had always known that I had assembled something special. I never questioned our talent or our work ethic. What I did not know was the plan that God had for us and how it would all play out. From that day forward, the magnitude of my vision for The Commodores and what I believed would evolve for us was the largest that it had ever been. Even though we had not released any records, I had divine reassurance that we would conquer the world and I created with that notion in mind.

After sitting in on listening sessions with the likes of Marvin Gaye and many other talented artists, we were exposed to the vast possibilities of the recording process. We were now hanging a "Do Not Disturb" sign outside of our sessions because we didn't want the creativity obstructed in any way. It also helped to enhance and cultivate the mystique that surrounded us, what we were recording, and the strategy behind our process. The other ugly truth was that we did not want others to witness how much we didn't know about the recording process. We needed time to learn and an environment that would foster the training. I was thankful that we allowed ourselves time to grow as it cultivated our sound even more. What I can say is that it didn't sound like anything else that I had heard and I had heard it all. When you fuse that many influences and sounds together, it can only be unique.

"Gentlemen, I am going to be honest with y'all, quiet as kept, but some of this stuff . . . I don't understand it. It is different," said Carmichael. Although he was co-producing the music, he never once stifled the fruits that were produced when we were creating. He let the music flow.

In the sessions, there was a down to earth sentiment about Carmichael. He was originally from Alabama and he too understood our southern roots. His nickname became Reverend because he would have ready these monologues that mimicked preachers. He used these moments to teach us valuable lessons and to give us diplomatic insight into what he observed throughout the process.

"Now gentlemen, we need to stay on page 217. And if you open up your hymnal to page 217, that's where all the hit records are. If you find yourself wondering, and dare I say . . . we're not talking about you Ronald, and if you find yourself distracted by phone calls . . . we are talking about you Lionel . . . ." He had this way of leading without interjecting, intimidating, or intruding. Page 217 was a phrase that he used to keep us focused. It became the go to reference when we needed to re-center or get back on track for the music.

Carmichael had the ability to keep things light and always had us laughing. He loved chess and he encouraged us to play in between recording. He remained vigilant during the recording process and was always on top of what was going on. We became dependent on his wealth of wisdom and his experience in life and the music world. He was an honest, God fearing, straight up guy, who told the truth and would go on to become an irreplaceable fiber in the Commodore sound and legacy.

Another source of inspiration in the studio came in the form of women. The Reverend knew best and would often invite them in. The girls were instrumental in terms of giving us feedback. If we were writing a song that was designed to make you cry and no one was crying, we knew that the song should not go on the album. Carmichael never disclosed to our guests that we were using their feedback because he wanted to keep the opinions pure and get real reactions from those who listened.

As we evaluated what was popular and much of what was being released, we determined that we did not have a lead singer. While on tour, my interpretation of Jimi Hendrix's, "Summertime" and a song called, "Wichita Lineman," by Glen Campbell were our big hits, but we still needed a song of our own.

I kept bringing up the Black Beatles dream that I still clung to. Lionel and my friendship continued to evolve and we found a resurgence of musical collaboration. We fed off of each other and our vibe was truly phenomenal. We began to call ourselves Paul McCartney and John Lennon.

"Since you have a clean slate, you could opt for an instrumental song to be the first release," said Carmichael. "If you start with an instrumental song and it's not a big hit, you don't lose your opportunity to come back with a vocal song. If it is a hit, it can be a great stepping stone to say, 'not only do we play our own instruments but we sing

too,'" he said.

"Outer Space" was an instrumental piece by Billy Preston. Milan Williams wrote our first hit "Machine Gun" and you can hear how "Outer Space" influenced it, if you listen carefully. When Carmichael asked for a bridge for "Machine Gun," it was an excellent time for The Mark IV to stamp the signature sound. So I came up with the idea of using the bass as if it was a lead vocal with the other instruments answering and building with counter licks which was innovative at the time.

We were now full throttle in selecting and determining which songs, that we had composed, would make it onto the album. In addition, we were tasked with creating the vocals for the songs. It was hard work, but we were diligent in creating our best products. I created the main lick for a song that made the album called, "I Feel Sanctified." Once the composition of the music was completed, thanks to Jeffrey Bowen, the group came in and we wrote the lyrics together. We were harmonious at creating together. We had what we thought were at least two records for our first album that would be strong possibilities of hits. As artists, you know that the goal is to create an entire album that will make waves on the charts and be loved by your fans, but you also recognize that there are some winners that right from the start will be hits. For our first effort, we felt certain about two.

It took just under a year of constant toil, but we were now done with recording the album and looking forward to it being mixed. Carmichael, who had already expressed to us on several occasions that he did not understand what we were going for, said he would ensure that it was technically correct. Our last step was to strategically leak by word of mouth, that we had in fact created an album

Our intent was to get Berry Gordy to come in and hear it because he had to approve the budget for promotions. If it turned out to be a project that he was excited about, then we would get a sufficient budget to market the music that we had worked so hard to create. Marketing is just as important as the music itself. We requested the assistance of the great Norman Whitfield, who was an incredible producer and songwriter to mix "Machine Gun." A great deal of gratitude was owed to Norman because he had actually come into the studio and saw us struggling to mix the song. "Would you allow me to give it a shot?" He inquired. We agreed and took a seat to watch him work. I followed his efforts closely because I was ever the student. I never felt comfortable not knowing anything that I needed to know, especially if my success depended upon it. Fifteen minutes later, he had mixed "Machine Gun" and his finishing touches turned out to be the final mix.

That day, Berry Gordy entered the studio while "Machine Gun" was playing and the atmosphere was vibrant. The groove was funky, but it had a rich feel to it. Hints of rock and roll, the blues, and even a little country, infiltrated your system when you heard it. You couldn't stay still when "Machine Gun" played. It just wasn't possible.

"This sounds like a hit. What's the name of it?" Asked Gordy.

"The Ram," Milan replied.

"It sounds like it should be called 'Machine Gun,'" Gordy said with certainty. Not one of us had any intention of disagreeing with him. If that's what it took to get his blessing, we were down to commit to naming the song "Machine Gun." That evening, we all felt victorious. We had finally overcome the hurdle of becoming recording artists. No matter what reviews the song would receive, I knew that we all felt a sense of accomplishment that we had not yet been privy to.

When Motown released *Machine Gun* the album, it went gold. It was the first in their illustrious history. Neither The Temptations nor Marvin Gaye, could claim that honor, not even The Jackson Five or Tammi Terrell. Many had sold gold singles, but never an entire album.

In 1974, the album broke records worldwide. In Nigeria, it became the largest selling album in the history of the country. We continued to break records in Japan, and the Philippines. During a performance date in the Philippines, we broke The Beatles attendance record with 272,000 at the Araneta Coliseum. Ferdinand Marcos was the president at that time and he sent the military to escort us from the airport because the crowd was so large. They lined the roads with signs that said, "Commodores, We Love You." We were humbled and grateful for the love shown from the fans and it was another testament to the fact that the music made the colors disappear and the melodies more prevalent. As we rode past all of the people, I reflected back to my tumultuous walk to school that was paved with hatred. Now, here I was riding along a road paved with love. I was overcome as I sat in silence.

When we arrived at the hotel there must have been 100,000 people following us. As the military led us to the entrance we noticed a gentleman on the balcony. "Hey, who are you guys?" He interrogated. "I'm the greatest, who are y'all?" He yelled. Unbeknownst to us, the reigning heavyweight champion of the world, Muhammad Ali was staying at the same hotel. (2) We weren't nearly as big in the states as we had become in the Philippines and he was not familiar with our work. It was a hilarious interaction. The performance was something that I will never forget. To look out into a crowd and see people moved emotionally and singing songs that you created despite the fact that it is not their native tongue is something that I will never be able to put into words.

When we returned to the states, it was time to get back down to business. We had only been locked in for a one album deal with Motown. We had fulfilled that obligation, which left us open for other opportunities. Other record companies were eyeing our irrefutable success. We entered into an incredible negotiating period. After proving our value, we had absolutely no interest in re-signing a contract under the same terms and conditions that we had previously signed. I would tell any artist at any given moment that times like these, you most certainly will benefit from an education and an understanding of sound business practices. As a part of our deal, we determined that we wanted to own our publishing. Nobody with Motown had done this, not Stevie, Marvin, Diana, Nora, Smokey, nobody. We knew that Motown would agree to most of the terms that we offered in order to retain us as clients. I have to note that Stevie Wonder had an extremely savvy lawyer Johanan Vigoda. He had written a clause in Stevie's contract that would come to be known as the "Favorite Nation Clause." This clause stated that if there were a negotiated contract higher than what Stevie had in place, that his contract would also have to be amended to that dollar amount. Stevie got his publishing as a result of us getting ours — so did Marvin, Smokey and Norma. From that point forward, The Commodores would go down in history, not just for records but also business acumen.

With so many decisions on the table, the prospect of growth can also be scary. We were more hungry than ever because we saw with our eyes what was at our disposal. God was ever present and active in all of our affairs. We had so many new bold and courageous ideas, and I'd like to believe that I played a large role in the manifestation of them for The Commodores. I was in a continuous state of encouraging and working to realize a larger vision. I didn't question my talent either. I knew the gifts that God had given me. I don't speak from a place of conceit, but more certainty. I think that sometimes we lose our way in life when we are uncertain of what our contributions are worth. It behooves us to remember our worth and our value. Now confident in myself as a young man and musician, had the heart of a lion and believed myself as good as Jimi Hendrix. By the grace of God, and my parent's prayers I kept humble, grounded, and ready to learn.

From this place of confidence, I also challenged everyone. If someone had an idea that was great then I encouraged them to share their thoughts on execution and build support amongst the group for the idea. I demanded excellence from everyone, but my goal was to harness the most impactful energy that could be produced. The truth is that I also loved just as hard as I challenged. Even as I had thrown that coke bottle at Benny Ashburn, I loved him just as hard as I threw that bottle. I was passionate. It was almost like a basketball player on the court. The fuel from competition and the desire to win kept the fight for our absolute best at the forefront.

Even with all that we had achieved, some group members seemed unfulfilled with our level of success and set out in search of further gratification. Milan, had earned the name "Left Fielder" because he was often out in left field in pursuit of other interests and William King made the decision to leave the band to focus more intently on tennis and pursue his education. He was not there as we recorded our first album, and his leaving was a great disappointment to me as I wanted us to see things through as a complete band. It was difficult constantly wondering who had the wherewithal and faith to see this success through to the end, but success is not for the faint of heart. I strove harder to find ways to bring the remaining five members closer together. We were now adults and real life brings about more than just music. I would often wonder how I could find ways to discover my weaknesses and work on them as well as discover the weaknesses of the guys in the group and build them up. They were my brothers.

The added attention forced us to hire more staff to ensure that we left no stone unturned. We enlisted the help of a booking agency and sought ways to maximize the fact that we were newsworthy. Radio personalities were becoming interested in us and were able to open further doors. IBM, a major software company, approached us to learn about our story. They had heard about these college guys who were now pursuing music and how we were structuring ourselves in a corporate manner. This was particularly different for black artists and we were hailed as trailblazers from a business perspective. We set up a corporation and established Commodore Entertainment Corporation as the parent company. This company would house our other businesses that we set our sights on building, including a merchandising company that housed the products that we were developing.

We were now receiving countless requests to perform as the opening act for other performers in the US. The largest breakthrough was when we were invited to open for The Rolling Stones in Philadelphia. That was huge! Performing in this manner increased our visibility and allowed the audiences of the other artists to become our fans as well. Promoters were booking us with The O'Jays, Stevie Wonder, Kool & the Gang, The Beach Boys, and the list went on and on.

Even through all of the new-found fame, we still maintained humility and did our best to be vigilant over our finances. Prior to this time, none of us had really purchased anything for ourselves with the money that we had earned. This time, we decided to enjoy the fruits of our labor and make our first major purchases together.

My first vehicle was a convertible super beetle and my first housing purchase was a trailer located in Tuskegee and when I bought it, I felt that it was a solid investment that could be rented or sold, however, after I witnessed the damaging effects of hurricanes on trailers, I saw it as the liability it was and got rid of it. Walter Orange and I had also shared the rent of a house for a short stint. This gave us both the courage that we individually needed to purchase a more permanent residence. I believe that we connected and understood each other because we both recognized what it meant to come from humble beginnings. Neither of us wanted to return to those financial constraints, so we moved in the absence of haste. I decided that instead of purchasing a huge house for myself, I wanted to pay my parents' home off first and I did.

"This little group you got, may not be such a little group after all. You are talking about wiping out my mortgage," my father said. My father had always been supportive of my efforts and my work. His words gave me the ultimate seal of approval. Our philosophy was simple; we would not fall into debt to the point of not being able to afford what we were doing. We were very conservative and this was another reason why IBM was so impressed with us. They gave us $50,000 to use our story as a motivational piece for their employees.

Being in this space financially made me feel that everything had been worth it. Even the days that I wanted to give up or those moments that I felt like nothing was working, led me to this point. The joy that I felt in my heart was not about the money, it was the fact that I had the ability to use my God given talents to improve the quality of life for those whom I loved. That was the ultimate reward.

We were celebrities and we were treated as such. The then mayor of Tuskegee, Johnny Ford hosted a Commodore Day and named a street after us. More girls were showing interest and we had a crowd of bona fide groupies. We were growing in popularity both at home and internationally and it felt surreal.

Prior to this time, we had had no need for an accountant. We were all very engaged and in the loop with our finances, but the money was moving so fast, we wanted to ensure that we could remain on top of everything. With more money, however, came more worries. We began taking note of other groups and the financial tragedies that had occurred. We did not want our legacy to end that way and we never wanted to be in a position where we couldn't count on our own money.

After the IBM deal, we began receiving phone calls from other businesses and brands who wished to extend business opportunities to us. Schlitz Malt Liquor contracted us to do a TV commercial and Mercedes Benz gave us cars to market as giveaways for our show in Houston and the offers just kept coming. It was surprising because at that time, corporations were not using entertainers in that manner, especially not black entertainers.

Our schedules picked up and it became virtually impossible to meet the requirements to maintain full time enrollment at Tuskegee. We began exploring the option of taking a sabbatical from school. There are some moments that you cannot let pass you by. The growth of our musical careers would be considered one such moment. We needed to pursue the dream full time. In doing so, we had to be very careful to not get caught up in the Hollywood scene. There were too many distractions to count and our time away from school needed to be focused on our aspirations and not be our downfall.

Even though we were a part of Motown, we still maintained a certain level of autonomy. To date, we had not been to Berry Gordy's home. This was a huge thing for Motown artists. It was a treat to be invited, but it was also a demonstration of respect to attend. We hadn't been because we hadn't quite aligned ourselves as Motown artists. It was almost as if we drove in our own lane. To some extent, that was OK, but you also had to be a part of the subliminal culture of the Motown brand if you wanted the company to back you. That was true of any company, not just with Motown. There is always an unspoken culture that drives agendas and ultimately executes them that can't be ignored.

In order to get promotional and marketing dollars spent on us, we knew that there were certain marketing efforts that we needed to engage in in order to remain in good graces. Even though we had danced to the beats of our own drums, we recognized that it was time to get in the game in a way that we hadn't before. Moreover, there was no way that you could not respect what Mr. Gordy had assembled. He was iconic and will forever stand as one of history's great moguls.

Benny Ashburn asked us to attend Berry Gordy's birthday party hosted at his Bel Air home and we committed to go. When we got there, it was a peculiar feeling for all of us. We were just not Hollywood enough, it seemed. We wanted to blend in but we were also reluctant because we didn't want to be swallowed by the black hole of fame that so many had fallen victim to. During the party, everyone prepared to sing happy birthday to Mr. Gordy and he insisted that everyone do it in unison. It was like one big choir. At the time, it was rumored that Ms. Ross and Mr. Gordy had an ongoing romance. Ms. Ross arrived late and there was tremendous tension in the atmosphere. It was blatantly clear that Mr. Gordy was not happy with her tardiness. If I hadn't known before, I now knew that Mr. Gordy meant business.

Aside from attending the party, we were attempting to become more immersed in the Motown world and develop our own individual personalities. We were still growing as men and there was a lot of room for other individuals to get into our heads. We started to listen to other people's advice about their success and their journeys in the Motown family. This was helpful in many ways and somewhat disruptive in others.

We all had the opportunity to exchange time and energy with the legendary Marvin Gaye and we were grateful when he took us under his wing. His guidance was sound and his leadership was very important to us. He told us that we were smart to stay out of Hollywood and that our returning back to Tuskegee regularly was a strategy that would keep us out of a lot of unnecessary drama. He spoke of doing things differently in his career and divulged to us that everything that we saw was not as it appeared. In detail, he spoke of how some of the cars that the artist drove, did not belong to them and that they were leased by Motown. He also spoke of how lives of musicians could be impacted if they stepped outside of the ring of favor. He explained how that sometimes meant the risk of losing those amenities granted by the label. "Don't be deceived by everything that you see," he said. This was the unspoken culture that I recognized within the infrastructure. Our goal was to have a better understanding not only of ourselves, but also of Motown so that we could remain in good graces but also grow as artists.

We began to ponder if Benny Ashburn was still the best manager to take us where we needed to go. We had come so far together. On the one hand, we didn't want to lose him because he was exclusively ours. On the other hand, he wanted to grow his business and brand. He began to look at other artists to consider managing them. Rightfully so. How could he grow as a manager in his profession with only one group under his belt? Many managers handled the responsibilities of several artists or groups simultaneously. Even so, there was still an undertone of dither and apprehension that we felt.

We had to take into consideration that Benny had quit his job to manage us. "I'm not collecting what other managers collect. Some managers collect up to 20%, I'm only collecting 15%." This was often his response when we came to cross roads such as these. "You guys don't want me to manage other groups. It makes it harder for me," he would say with disdain in his voice. These were tough conversations that had to be engaged in and resolved. Eventually, we elected Benny Ashburn to be a seventh Commodore. This strategy allowed him to receive royalties as we did, which was an incentive for him to stay on and be exclusive to us. However, trust issues became an ongoing undercurrent in the group.

At that time, we all had one manager and one lawyer. Lionel began to receive outside guidance and so did we all. We sensed that Walter was being led and influenced by others. Walter thought, if Lionel could do it, so could he. It appeared to some that Walter Orange began to trust his outside information more than the internal information. It also appeared that as a result of the outside guidance, he became leery of the business within the group. I reflected back to the time when Lionel and I drafted him into the band. He had only wanted a weekly salary, nothing more. Both Lionel and I had to convince him that we wanted to make him an equal partner back then and that he should be compensated accordingly. Now, the tides had turned and it was believed that the advisement was coming from other sources besides Lionel and me.

Lionel's talent was undeniable. I was thankful that I'd had the vision and seen his potential long before anyone else had — including him. He was proof that I had the ability to scout untapped genius and these actions proved to be fruitful in many ways for The Commodores. The world had not yet been fully introduced to the magnitude of his greatness, but it was plain to see that he had a gift and many took an interest in helping him cultivate it. He began receiving more mentorship and interest from Suzanne de Passe. Even our left fielder, Milan Williams, who had been waffling on his dedication appeared to be getting individual advice. I was no different as I too sought the wisdom of those who had come before us.

Ronald LaPread and I attempted to make sense and consolidate all of the outside advice we had been given in order to present it at our group meetings. We wanted to be true to what we started, but we also wanted to bring more info into the arena to sow bigger seeds. I'd be lying if I said that we were not all in a state of skepticism. Benny Ashburn remained our cheerleader during these complicated times and tried to keep everything and everyone centered. He wanted to put a little more fire into our enthusiasm for the music.

The glass ceiling of our dreams had not been shattered, it was just a little foggier than it had once been. Some people think that to hold a dream in your hands and have it change is a loss. I believe that the beauty of the dream is in the ability to stand before it and look out across all of the might that it took to accomplish it. When we learn to fall in love with the journey, nothing can ever be a loss. Life is a constant motion to dig your nails into the side of the mountain and climb. Ascension is what dreams are made of. No matter what was happening in the wings, the music never hid behind the curtains. The music that was in our hearts never stopped performing, it was our muse and the fuel that kept us burning. The music connected us in ways that words could not. We continued to allow ourselves to be used by the music and to build a foundation that would withstand the test of time.

Beryl McClary, Berry Gordy, and Thomas McClary in Santa Monica, CA, honoring Clarence Avant at a fundraiser for cancer.

Carlos Santana and Thomas McClary, after a concert at UCF.

The Commodores and Bob Marley in 1980 at Madison Square Garden.

The Commodores and The Jackson Five for the first time playing at Madison Square Garden on July 16, 1971.

The Commodores and Marvin Gaye, March 25, 1983.

First artists to acquire publishing rights at Motown.

Granddaddy Europe McAlister, Entrepreneur/Hero.

Grandmother Eva McCray McAlister, Prayer Warrior/ Visionary.

Thomas McClary, the late Benny Ashburn and the late Milan Williams on "The Nightshift".

The McClarys, the first musical group of Thomas McClary.

*The McClarys and the Shaws with
Pastor Jerry Shaw started their first church in 1957.*

Live at the Superdome, Lionel Richie, Thomas McClary and Ronald LaPread perform "Easy".

08: *Page 217*

The music had led the way along a journey that could only be described as magical. We began again to create and assemble our next album. Our process became so structured that it was almost like clockwork. I would assemble the basic music and the group would fire off with contributions, but we all still took the initiative to create on our own as well. As musicians, we had to move when the groove made its presence known. We kept our original system for voting songs on the album intact.

As we continued to learn the business, we also started to understand how the money for the songs was divided. The fact was that there was a separate check for writing and publishing. That meant that if someone received a writing credit, they would receive a larger payout for the song. With this knowledge, the undercurrent of distrust reared its ugly head as we voted for the songs for the second album. I began to sense that the integrity of the music was not the only factor for picking songs. The pay that could result was now being considered when the voting took place. It was as if the monstrous levels of animosity were being foreshadowed. When you compound this mindset with the growing intensity of outside whispers, it becomes a recipe for a cataclysmic disaster. Benny could sense the faint smell of dissention and his whole objective seemed to become a way to maintain the sentiment that had made us so powerful to begin with.

In the studio, we began to lean more heavily on James Carmichael for the selection of the songs that would be placed on the album. He was neutral because he sincerely wanted our best work. Just like Benny, Carmichael worked to remind us that we needed to continue to reach new levels in our sound, but not venture so far away that our fans and listeners could not recognize us. Carmichael was so charismatic that our turmoil could not live in his presence. As always, he kept his chess board and his pseudo pulpit intact, which kept the environment light.

The imaginary book and page number, 217 became a universal symbol of hope and redirection for The Commodores. This invented book of rules was what he would refer to when things became disruptive or got out of hand. "Ok, gentlemen, let's get back on page 217," Carmichael would say when we started to stray afield. If there was a particular take that we were doing that was on point, he would say, "Ok, now that's on page 217." If someone was off task, they would say, "I'm sorry, I need to get on page 217."

Page 217 was where the genius was unlocked. It encompassed the integrity of the music and reminded us of the love that the group had been built on. Outsiders and those who would visit the studio would be unaware of what we were speaking about, but no one needed to know except us. It was the underground railroad for our communication. In this space, we creatively discovered musical phenomena that broke barriers and resembled innovation at its finest. There were studio musicians who had played the same music, but we were able to play it our own way. The way that the music sounded and the way that it felt is what mattered most to us.

Due to the overwhelming success of *Machine Gun*, we discovered that William King wanted to rejoin The Commodores. Just like when he left to become a lifeguard before our first trip to New York, we allowed him to return. I couldn't imagine anyone not wanting to be a part of the success that we had managed to achieve with that record. We were making history.

"The Bump," a song from the first album, inspired the dance craze bearing the same name. In another instance, my riff from "I Feel Sanctified," was used in a song called "Standing on Shaky Ground," by The Temptations. I didn't receive credit for it and it angered me because we had used the exact same producer. The song was a big hit for them and in hindsight just knowing I had anything to do with the song should have been satisfying. However, my frustration at the point, motivated me to work harder and learn more about the business, so that I would not be a victim of this relatively consistent occurrence in the industry again. I knew that I had a lot of riffs inside of my creative storage and it was time to unleash some of them.

Even though our first album was performing well and we were gaining a continuous flood of fans, we still had not established ourselves as a group with a true lead singer. Up until now, Lionel and Walter Orange had shared the position with the rest of the band as backup. For our second album, Carmichael was sticking to the initial game plan, which had worked so well previously. We decided that if we could score a hit with the instrumental album, we would then move to the phase of a hit record with a true lead singer intact, which we hoped would help make a bigger impact.

Our second album would be called *Caught in the Act*. We wrote and created at home just as much as we did outside of the studio. One evening, Stevie Wonder came down to my apartment and allowed me to hear a sample of a new song that he was working on. The sound was so funky that it inspired me to go deeper in my own music. That was the beauty of being around other artists.

From the inspiration garnered from Stevie Wonder, I wrote a song entitled "Slippery When Wet." The song was so good, that it was selected to be the first release without us having made all of the final selections for the album. I was honored that the song was chosen, but even more than that, I was eager to continue because I had surpassed the notions that even I had set for my capabilities. You never really know how much greatness is inside of you until you are pushed to bring it all out.

In the creative process, I analyzed the music that was produced by how it would be received by our fans and I pondered how other artists would approach it. All of these thoughts collectively led me to the continuous development of a sound. I tried to imagine what it would sound like if Albert King and Stevie Wonder were asked to play something funky in a song. The guitar would be raw and raunchy with a bold sassy attitude, accompanied with a foot stomping clarinet, which Stevie Wonder had made so famous in "Superstition." If you added some classic Memphis horns then you would have the formula of the signature sound for this trendsetting song. The evolution of our artistry had been so powerful and I was now calling upon it to give us even more ammunition in the midst of producing the second album. Another revelation became apparent to me during the process. We were all listening to Lionel sing, "Slippery When Wet" and in his voice you could honestly hear remnants and interpretations of so many of the greats that we had listened to growing up, but the mixture and fusion were all his own. It was not just The Ohio Players, or Sly & the Family Stone, or Earth, Wind & Fire, it was all of them. What others had been speculating about regarding his talent, we now knew to be undeniable. Lionel's voice was amazing and different; it was iconic.

We were all emerging. Milan Williams had a hit and I had made my mark with "Slippery When Wet." Other members were diligently working on hits that would materialize. We were on page 217. We decided to go back to Tuskegee to recharge the essence of our creative juices. We invited Carmichael to come with us to help during rehearsal. Lionel and I lived not far from each other and we continued with our John Lennon and Paul McCartney antics. Lionel was valiant in his ability to sing and after we nailed our rehearsals in preparation for promotion of the album, we returned to LA for the selection process of songs that would indeed make the album. Everyone would submit their songs to see if we had enough strong material to dictate the signature sound. "Gentlemen, we need to be a little more pop but at the same time, we can't lose our base of what we initially started," Carmichael said.

While still trying to develop as writers, we were also attentive members in the James Carmichael school of learning. He would always say "Everybody is inspired by everybody and nothing is new under the sun. The key is how to use the inspiration in a way that does not imitate." There was so much beauty in his words. I never let that statement leave my heart. To me, life was about inspiring and being inspired. I wanted to bring about a sound with the impact of Jimi Hendrix, but with the funk of Sly Stone. I knew that the intricacy of the sound at the intro of a song, coupled with the lick was something that was different. High energy and funky were the two characteristics that I was after. It was also important to be able to be creative in the present vibe and not allow it to pass.

The singles, "Machine Gun" and "I Feel Sanctified," established us as a funk band and gave Lionel and Walter the first small roles as lead singers. The verses of the songs were very short and although the songs were successful, they did not give them the opportunity to showcase their full range of abilities.

This was a time of transformation in my musical relationship with Lionel. Our collaborations gained momentum and we came to recognize our chemistry and the excitement ensued. Lionel created a song called, "This is Your Life." It was Lionel's debut of a song with a moderate tempo. Lionel had written the song alone and I helped him to arrange the music, along with James Carmichael. The entire group received credit for the co-production of the song as we believed that to be fair at the time. There were several instances in which the group received co-production credits and co-arranging credits, but only the individual writer or writers and James Carmichael would actually be doing the work.

In 1975, our third album was released. We were successful in meeting our goal of emerging as a group with a lead singer. "Sweet Love" was the first song that Lionel sang and harmonized with himself. The song was indescribable. It was so crisp, new, gentle, and refreshing. I honestly felt that Lionel's voice coupled with the music, created a sound that had the ability to penetrate your skin and get into your soul. "Wow, man, you're not a soulful singer like Aretha Franklin but Nat King Cole wasn't either. He was a stylist. There is a difference between someone who is just a singer and someone who is a stylist," said Carmichael, who took that moment to educate us on what had evolved amidst our creativity.

The sound of music was ever evolving. We had managed to master a funk sound with an R&B twist and were now even more appealing to a crossover audience. Artists would vibe off each other and while it created a friendly aura of competition, it was also great for the music. There was a group called The Average White Band who released their album entitled, *Soul Searching*. They stated that they were inspired by our song "Slippery When Wet."

A resurgence of whispers began amongst group members that Lionel and I were getting more songs on the album than anyone else. The group questioned if Carmichael was being fair in the decision-making process. There was also chatter that Benny Ashburn was telling Carmichael to pick the songs that Lionel and I had collaborated on. Other group members questioned if their songs were not good enough. The truth was that Lionel and I were winning. We had been cranking out so much magic musically that I truly believed that there was divine favor over our work. Lionel and I weren't complaining because who complains when they are succeeding? In retrospect, I now realize that I had not recognized the intensity of the resentment that was starting to build.

The whispers grew louder and the undertone of love amongst the brotherhood was compromised in ways that we could never have imagined. Group members began to vocalize their concerns as complaints. If we were only going to put nine songs on the album, and four of those nine were mine or Lionel's that caused a problem, but we had to keep going. We were in the midst of stardom.

During this era, artists by the name of Crosby, Stills, Nash & Young emerged and were very impactful in what was popular among other artists. Their style of harmonies inspired a song we released entitled, "Sweet Love," in which Lionel sang lead. When the Mark IV members put their touch on the song it became an innovative funky ballad with unique harmonies. I suggested that we come up with a staccato bass with accents creating a stop and go groove, with the guitar filling in the spaces between the accents. With Lionel playing the keys on top of that groove in the same manner as if it was a ballad. It was trailblazing. It violated all the rules. Another signature sound moment! As The Commodores, we were still winning with our funky, melodic songs, but in our second album we saw an emergence of substance. As our fame grew, so did our messages. We were now recognized as Motown's royalty. I can't describe the view from the top, but I'll tell you this, it was breathtaking.

The increase in opportunity required us to spend more time in Los Angeles. As a group, we decided to make our headquarters there and open an office housed in Motown. Prior to that time, we had kept our offices separate as we were skeptical and did not want the interference or to be involved in the subliminal politics. I would venture to say that as artists, we felt like they were taking control. In addition to acquiring the office, a slew of staff members was also brought on to simplify our day to day responsibilities. Our team of office superstars included our secretary, Miriam Jacobs and Jo-Ann Geffen, who dealt with public relations, Karolyn Ali, who was Benny Ashburn's assistant, and James Tarver our road manager.

Even though our focus was directed towards creating, more hands also meant more paranoia. Many of the group members were now even more curious and skeptical of Benny Ashburn's work. Our worry was that if he was working at the Motown office daily, was he still working only for us? Were any of his responsibilities with The Commodores compromised because he was acquiring new artists? No one could prove that because it was all skepticism. We would check with Benny to see what was going on with Motown, but we would simultaneously be upset about him being too close. It was a hard scenario for everyone involved and I wish that there would have been a happy compromise. Unfortunately, these are the ills of the entertainment industry that many don't speak of. The higher that you ascend, the greater the challenges that you are faced with.

I can't describe how torn my heart was when I was walking at the highest level of success and still not satisfied because I was uneasy and leery of the inner workings of the business. I wouldn't wish those feelings on anyone. How can you truly enjoy the success when your mind is constantly concerned about ill will?

No matter how much speculation occurred, everyone knew that the equation for success had been outlined — create, release, promote, tour. That sequence of events was what kept The Commodores' brand front and center. No one on the outside knew what we were dealing with internally. All the public saw was that we were a talented group of young men, who didn't get into trouble and made hit records and that was enough. We needed to get back into the studio immediately to work on our third album. It would affectionately be entitled *Moving On*.

"Sweet Love," was the single on that record and it was a hit. As with music and expression in general, a growing concern was that we were getting too pop. Many of our advisors expressed growing concerns that we were losing our black audience. Amidst that talk, we had been enlisted to embark upon another tour, this time with The O'Jays. The O'Jays and The Commodores were both headlining acts, but we chose to open for the O'Jays. During the tour, Lionel and I began to study Eddie Levert and his unprecedented charisma. His delivery of the ballads and love songs would make the ladies in the audience lose control and it was mesmerizing to watch.

As a musician, you can never touch your audience too much or too deeply. It is imperative that you find a way for your music to penetrate their minds and bodies, and truly speak to their souls.

I knew that when we prepared to record our next album, we had to create a tear jerker. *Hot on the Tracks* was our fourth studio album effort. We nailed the ballad that I had dreamed of with a song entitled "Just to Be Close to You." The calming soothing sounds of the synthesized melodies of voices played on the keyboards setting the music bed for Lionel's famous rap. Not only was it an instant classic, but it was a duet with Walter Orange and Lionel Richie. Our fans truly appreciated the song and it touched so many people in so many ways. We received a great deal of positive feedback from the song and when we went places, everyone always mentioned how it had touched them. "Just to Be Close to You," also quieted the fears of those who believed that we were losing our black audience. It not only garnered their attention, but also established us in the R&B market. It was official, The Commodores were untouchable.

Just as we had suspected, our manager Benny Ashburn began to take on the role of managing other acts. Because of this we enlisted a gentleman by the name of Cecil Willingham to come on as our second road manager and assistant to James Tarver. Steve Meyers, Lamar Williams were also hired to head our promotions and marketing. Motown's PR department was headed by Bob Jones. We didn't want to exclusively rely on Motown, but with our growth there was a need for increased media relations and as such we hired an outside PR firm.

Aside from music, developing business was still a priority. We had not come this far to only come this far. The first venture was Commodores Transportation, which was headed by Lenny Guice. This would be another entity under The Commodores empire. We acquired our own limousines and trucks. The idea was that when we were not using them, we would lease them out to others. There were also plans to expand our promotions and branding to include new promoters. From past experiences, we were still leery of promoters in general. As the music developed, Lionel began to be publicly acknowledged as the sole lead singer of The Commodores and he received accolades accordingly. The John Lennon and Paul McCartney connection between us became more than just a whisper. The rest of the guys were feeling a little precarious and seeing the differences in pay. "This is Your Life," "Sweet Love," and "Just to Be Close to You," were three powerhouse songs bringing in revenue from royalties, tours, and sales.

It appeared that Walter Orange felt as though he should have been doing more lead singing and that he should have had a more valued role in the group. He felt that Motown was starting to pull Lionel to the forefront. Lionel began receiving invitations to certain functions that Walter did not. One key factor that was not considered was that Lionel's personality was different from Walter's. You couldn't question Lionel's ability to mix and mingle with diverse groups of people, nor could you question his charisma. He became someone that everyone wanted to be around. Cohorts Suzanne de Passe, Tony Jones, and Eddie Langford were just good people to hang out with and true friendships between them, Lionel, and myself developed. Tony Jones even gave us some of his old clothes. The other group members felt like Lionel and I were getting "too Hollywood," something that we had always been warned against. The feelings of distrust couldn't be denied as it was no secret that Motown was notorious for creating groups in which lead singers emerged and went on to lead successful solo careers independent of the groups that they started with. There were countless examples, but we persisted in spite of the roar of mixed emotions.

When in discussion regarding the levels of talent, it was often vocalized that King was one of the least creative of the group. His exit and reentry into the band did not help matters because when he did return, he began complaining that Carmichael was not picking his songs and he felt those decisions were personal. He went on to complain that Lionel should not be allowed to personally and individually talk to Motown executives. "What is he up there talking to Motown for?" he would express with disdain. "Benny is the manager — when it's convenient for him — so he should be the one talking to those guys," said King. It was hard to discern why the jealousy was so prevalent. It was cancerous to the group. There had even been talk of ill will due to the color of skin. Although petty, Lionel was of a fairer complexion and Walter Orange was of a darker complexion. It was asinine that colorism would even be a part of the discussion amongst educated black men, who were climbing the ladder of success. What I did know was that these factors were not important and diluted our true reason for existence.

As time and circumstance would have it, Lionel and I grew even closer. There were times when he felt that other group members pushed him into a corner with the constant talk of favoritism and the questioning of various actions.

As individuals, we now had one foot in California and one foot in Tuskegee. Our sabbatical from school continued as work for the group was nonstop. From writing songs to appearance dates, there were no signs of The Commodores slowing down. I was willing to sacrifice anything that I could to make sure that everyone would get along and just stay together. The band was my dream that I had worked so hard to assemble and I did not want to let anyone tear it apart, including myself.

As we continued to grow as adults, more responsibilities materialized. I was now financially supporting my parents and doing so brought me great joy. I also made it a point to remain connected with my church in Eustis and the initial stages of planning to develop a school within the church began. We evolved in our professional lives and with our families, but it was our social lives that changed the most. All of the guys, including myself, now had steady girlfriends. Milan began dating a bright young woman who had an ivy league background. I was seeing a young lady from Tennessee. Lionel and William were both dating majorettes from school and Ronald's girlfriend was older and had her independence. None of us ever stopped to think that dating would be a problem, but with girlfriends came increased boundaries and the transitions of titles didn't take too long. Wedding bells were ringing everywhere and many of us found ourselves embarking upon the next steps to marriage. Lionel's girlfriend, Brenda Harvey became his wife. It is amazing how the dynamics of relationships work. As close as he and I were, it was only natural that I would become friends with his wife. She took it upon herself to find me a partner.

As a group, we wanted further success and to get there we needed to keep our eyes on the prize. My drive and determination was more apparent than ever. Each of the wives seemed to personify what their husbands believed about the group and rumors began to fly as we each spoke about others behind their backs. My wife began to talk to me about what she and Brenda spoke about. The sentiment between them was that William King's wife, a Caucasian girl out of Baltimore, was determined to be a trouble maker. King had been raised by his grandmother, after the loss of both of his parents. After he married, many said that over time he abandoned his grandmother who had truly been there for him.

King's wife was always criticizing the group and finding fault with everyone and believed that William was being overlooked a lot and she wanted something done about it. She began telling him that he needed to step up more. She could often be heard saying things like, "Are you just going to sit back and let Lionel Richie be the star? It should be more like The Beatles. You're just a wimp." While her approach seemed harsh and demeaning, it also gave him ideas about how to be more in the limelight. I began to see a cold-blooded side to William that I had not seen before. He had left the band once already and had returned because of the success of *Machine Gun*. Everyone, including myself, felt a little resentful and now, his wife and her demands added a different type of strain to the group.

THOMAS MCCLARY & ARDRE ORIE

Periodically, we assigned roles for each of us to carry out within the group. We had assigned William the role of keeping up with how many fines the group members received and owed money for. Our system was put into place to keep us focused and the professionalism intact. William didn't play games when it came to enforcing the fines. That task, led to the creation of a monster ego. "Lionel, you are late, that will be a $50 fine," he would say. It was pretty hysterical and a little scary at the same time.

There was always an unspoken dynamic of the elites versus the wannabe elites in Tuskegee. I had learned about this struggle when I lived one summer with Ronald and his mother. At the time, it was my attempt to get to know Ronald more as I had done with all of the group members to further establish the brotherhood. During that summer, I learned that Lionel and Ronald were considered to be from different sides of the tracks. Essentially, the divide was represented by the notion of the haves and the have nots and the dark skin versus the light. This divide permeated the African American race and our group was no exception. Because of the divide, there had always been an undertone of dislike between Lionel and Ronald. Sometimes you would hear, "That Motherfucker thinks that he is more than everyone else." Ronald's wife was also from the other side of the tracks and was not accepted by the elites. She had apprehensions about Lionel similar to Ronald and where he had never wanted to talk about business and group dynamics, he now had a wife who did.

Ronald was now a local hero just as Lionel was and they were both amazing representations of hope for their hometown. I found myself in the role of mediator and eventually,

I believe I lead Lionel and Ronald to a place of love, but the past and the many issues kept being resurrected through the conversations between the wives.

Due to Benny Ashburn's ties to The Commodores, his girlfriend was also considered to be a part of the wives' club. She was very pleasant and loving and often remained neutral, but observant during the wives' chatter. I'm certain that she would give Benny her synopsis of her observations in their quiet moments. No matter how much we developed into men and being The Commodores, we would all at some point experience the past, attempting to play a key role in the present. I found myself trying to be the glue that kept everyone together because quite frankly, the cohesiveness was beginning to deteriorate.

We kept pushing, creating, and touring. Lionel and I continued to discuss The Black Beatles and we also spoke about the importance of not letting our girlfriends and wives ruin the relationships that we had cultivated. As our tour dates picked up, many of the wives wanted to travel with us.

It was thought that Shirley, William's wife and Brenda, Lionel's wife would eventually bond because Lionel and William were generally roommates when we were on the road. Unfortunately, it was quite the contrary. It all started to fall apart when Lionel was on the heels of purchasing a home in Atlanta, and King went behind his back and purchased the home before Lionel could do so. Everyone was baffled and no one could understand why King would make such a move. We all started to question his ethics. A line had been crossed and the relationship between William and Lionel was strained. This was not just a musical thing that had happened in the band. That would have been one thing, but this became bigger because it affected livelihood.

The ongoing bickering and arguing, which we had not accounted for, could not be allowed to affect our music or our performances. As a group, we would eventually devise a rule to keep us sane — no wives on the road. Although the rule did not last very long, the fact that we even had to discuss finding this peace was an indicator to me that there could be bigger problems on the horizon. We chose to continue to exclude the wives in our business meetings, but we agreed that if a spouse had an opinion they were to divulge that information to their husbands. It was just too sensitive and we now had the added pressure of preparing to record our fifth album.

During this time, Milan was way out in left field. He had written a hit for our first album and we were really depending on him to keep the creative juices going. He was still writing, of course, but it wasn't with the same intensity and enthusiasm. He seemed far more interested in flying planes than making music. Lionel and I were as excited as we had always been. I found myself doing a lot of ghostwriting and I would give my ideas to whoever needed them. I just wanted to see us win and whenever I saw a weakness, I wanted to bridge the hole and fill the gap. Thankfully, Carmichael was still there every step of the way and we leaned very heavily on him and his direction. "Ok guys for this next album, we need to go to higher heights and deeper depths."

It was 1977 and we wanted to take our branding to another level. We would title our album *Commodores* and it spent an incredible eight weeks at the top of the R&B/soul albums chart. This was the second album that we had reach that level of success. It was so well received in fact, that it became our first Top 5 pop album.

We now had agents, record companies, the group, wives, promoters, families, and our manager to consider. That was a lot of extra voices to listen to while not losing your own. I felt like I was John Lennon, and that Lionel was Paul McCartney. Lionel's confidence was glaring. He had been validated by fans as well as James Carmichael and Motown. He had discovered who he was destined to become and he was beyond pleased. He was now a bona fide writer and had the ability to utilize both the gifts of song and pen like never before, but he wondered how much further he was capable of going.

I can't stress enough that there were so many unexplainable emotions in our heads. It was almost as if we were free and still trapped. Those same feelings inspired the lyrics to a song that would defy the odds entitled "Easy." The lyrics pierced your soul.

Why in the world would anybody put chains on me?
I've paid my dues to make it.
Everybody wants me to be
What they want me to be
I'm not happy when I try to fake it. No!
Ooh that's why I'm easy.

Lionel managed to put all of his heart, soul, and sadness into a song that would catapult his brand. He had the genius to make the song sound like it was about a girl so that it was easily accepted. The song was really about what was going on at the time within The Commodores. I was determined to match Lionel's level of intensity and emotion during the composition process by pouring out my heart and soul into one of the most famous guitar solos of all times. I've been told "the signature sound of "Easy" will forever be hailed as monumental for music and the legacy of the song. Shortly after the release of "Easy," Ronald LaPread's wife, Kathy was diagnosed with terminal cancer. She was a sweet woman who was always supportive and never complained. Even through the process of her illness, she still projected strength and inspiration that was unparalleled.

It was such an unusual time for everyone because even though we had many distractions and what we felt to be hardships going on, we had life through the grace of God. Kathy was fighting to survive and here we were arguing about things that could never amount to the impact of a life. We harnessed our power to come together and set aside our differences and make meaningful music with the help of James Carmichael. We now leaned on him in ways that we had never done before for support. We had no idea how deep the waters were that we were expected to tread in.

Even in the midst of his wife's illness, Ronald LaPread channeled music for strength. He and Lionel had each created a riff and they were both writing songs to encompass them. James Carmichael heard both riffs and said, "Awe man, you guys need to get together to create a song." They did and the genius that evolved was a song entitled "Zoom." "Zoom," was inspired by Kathy LaPread and remained a staple in all of our hearts. It meant the world to us to be able to honor her in a way that would never be forgotten. The immense emotion that was in the song translated to the hearts and minds of our fans. Today, it continues to reign as a classic and one of the most talked about songs in the Commodore legacy. This was our signature album and the sound was indicative of our brand. After Lionel wrote the lyrics to "Zoom" he called me and read them to me and we both cried. He said, "Tommy I didn't have anything to do with this other than being the instrument that God used. My hands couldn't stop shaking as my pen couldn't write fast enough." From that moment, until this very day, Ronald and Lionel's bond is inseparable.

There is truth in the fact that the recipe for success changes and morphs into unrecognizable ingredients at times. When your life is moving at the speed of lightening, you often miss many of the moments that simply take your breath away. In the haze of turmoil, the only place of peace was in the act of creating from our hearts and souls. That was the only way that we could escape the madness that we had all been guilty for creating. Not one of us could walk away from the responsibility of the ache that we felt deep in our hearts nor could we have prepared ourselves for it. It was the price that we paid for fame and fame is a peculiar asset. It seemed that the account that we had deposited so much of our time and resources into was becoming deficient. We often found ourselves asking, "How can we turn the tide? How can we overcome?" but there was so much uncertainty. We turned to the one series of actions that had proven successful time and again and poured every ounce of our blood, sweat, and tears into an album. Even though we couldn't find the words individually, the music told the sentiment in our hearts. I do believe that even in the midst of harrowing pain an emergence of passion was realized.

09: *Play Another Slow Jam*

As the album's success grew, we began the transition of creating our permanent lives in Los Angeles. We no longer wanted to rent and began to consider investing in property. I purchased a home in Encino, which was a few blocks from the Jackson family. It was a very nice home and a getaway from the Hollywood scene. We would record in Hollywood and spent an insane number of hours there, but it was not where I wanted to lay my head. The drive from Encino to Hollywood allowed me a priceless opportunity to gather my thoughts before and after the recordings.

The divide that we had been tiptoeing around was no longer the white elephant in the room. It became quite apparent that William King and Lionel were playing for two different teams. Milan Williams had a life away from the group as he was now a licensed pilot. Ronald LaPread and Walter Orange, who were once roommates on the road, were both busy relocating to their perfect homes in California and I was spending more time visiting other artists recording sessions. In truth, we all had other interests outside of creating music together.

As a group, we decided to do a spot date in Utah and use our bus to sleep on the way. Milan, however, decided that he was going to fly and he and Lester Morney, who was now responsible for our public relations, flew to the location. As we were riding towards the venue, we prepared mentally and vocally to do a TV show with The Osmonds. They had been so well received and we wanted to use their popularity to further ours. While riding, we turned the radio on to see if our music was being played in that market. As we approached the city, we heard the announcer come on and his voice held a level of concern. "Breaking news, there has been an emergency landing of an aircraft on the freeway," he said. Although we listened intently, I don't believe that any one of us thought much of it initially. After a little consideration, I could see everyone looking around from person to person. We couldn't help but wonder if it was Milan and we immediately tried to call and see if he had arrived at the hotel but we received no response. When we arrived at the hotel, and turned on the news and discovered that it was indeed Milan; he had crash landed. We could not believe it. Thank God that he had been trained by the brilliant pilot, Charles "Chief" Anderson of The Tuskegee Airmen. We later learned that there had been a malfunction of the engine, but Milan's quick wit and skill allowed him to land safely on the freeway.

As we prepared to depart for the appearance, we saw Milan and Lester. They were heading straight to the bar. I guess anyone in that scenario could have needed something to calm down. We rushed over to them and expressed our concern.

Milan remained calm. It was apparent that he was determined not to let that incident defeat him. We all successfully made the appearance and lived to tell the tale. Eventually, Milan would continue flying; he was many things, but a quitter was most certainly not one of them.

When we returned to LA, the studio once again became our home. We worked diligently, night and day so as not to lose the traction that we had gained and to further evolve our sounds. We were not interested in giving our fans the same thing with a new melody. We wanted to give them something new each time. Our goal was to be better than we had before as we felt excellence was the only true option. Since we first began recording, it was our tradition to keep the studio private with closed sessions. At first, it had been because we wanted to allow ourselves time and privacy to learn the ropes. Since then, it had just become the culture of The Commodores. Like many other factors within the group, that practice changed. We began to open the studio a little more and our sessions were not as closed off from new eyes and ears.

The legendary Norman Whitfield, who had been instrumental in mixing our first album, *Machine Gun* began to spend a lot of time in sessions with us, listening to our music. We were setting up our first headlining tour in the states and finishing the touches to our latest album when Carmichael said, "I think we need to have one more song on the album, a group song, but I need you all to come together and make it funky. We have enough of everything else, we just need that to complete it." We clung to Carmichael's words and yielded to his guidance.

LaPread and I were still able to channel our energy and ability to come up with grooves. We sat together and created. He came up with a baseline and I was anxious to put my guitar licks to it. I played a lick on the guitar that horns would ordinarily play with Ronald bass line. Carmichael wanted funky and that was exactly what we planned to give him. The next thing we knew, there was this groove. I mean, it was one of those that you had to poke out your mouth, squint your eyes and move your head to. During that time, we were listening to a lot from The Ohio Players. They had released a song called "Fire," and it was hot! We wanted to have our own "Fire." During the creative process, we had this track and as we started to mimic the concept of "Fire," Walter Orange said, "We've got to talk about a girl." During small breaks in the creative process, we would read whatever was nearby. As Walter was speaking, I happened to be sitting there skimming a JET Magazine. JET Magazine had a centerfold section of all of the girls in their swimwear called the "Jet Beauty of the Week." There was one featured lady in particular who was stunning. I showed the picture to Walter and he raised an eyebrow too. The article always gave the measurements of the model as an added benefit to admire the photograph. This particular lady was 34-26-36. We said, "Oh, she is a brick, shit house." There was roaring laughter in the studio. We knew that we were on to something and although we would never refer to a woman in a demeaning way, we knew that we had to find a way to speak about the beauty of her body. "Wait a minute," I said. "Brick house — she's a brick house." That was it; that was the name of the song. At that moment, "Brick House" was given life. And even though we liked the song and it had come from a fun place, we had no idea if it would be considered a throw away song or not.

Aside from the request of a funky hit from Carmichael, the rest of the album was complete. Generally, all of the guys would be involved in the mixing of their individual songs, but for the overall mixing of the album, James Carmichael, Calvin Harris and Carmichael's assistant Suzee Ikeda, and myself would be the only ones to remain and see the product completed. Jane Clark, who was an assistant engineer, joined us on this album as well. She was an understudy of Calvin Harris and after she learned the technical aspects of the studio, she went on to be responsible for mixing the single "Brick House."

During this time, some of the guys had gone back to Tuskegee, while others had stayed in LA, but everyone was leaving the mixing up to us. We spent an entire two weeks, round the clock mixing the album. We had taken over the entire studio at Motown, with Jane upstairs mixing and the rest of us downstairs. I found myself running back and forth, up and down the entire two weeks. I didn't stop until I heard an incredible mix of "Brick House." I was on my way downstairs and suddenly it was like, "Oh my God, this is a smash!" I called Carmichael and he agreed. "This song is definitely not a throw away."

"Brick House," "Easy," and "Zoom" were the biggest hits of the album. Those three songs skyrocketed our careers, and fame and fortune were ours for the taking. The tour for this album would be with The Emotions, who had a hit called "The Best of My Love." The Commodores/Emotions Tour was our first national tour in the states and it was huge. No other black act at the time had done a major tour of this magnitude, except for the Jackson Five. We were amazed at the response and the continued crossover appeal that we garnered. It was not uncommon to have other races listen to your music, but to have them attend our concerts was a tremendous source of validation and acceptance. As our audience evolved, so did our show. We had a special set that was built for the tour, and it rolled out our logo, keeping it in bright lights and at the forefront of our audience's mind. This was the beginning of the new logo and the new branding of The Commodores.

Our dear friend from Alabama, the late Bill Whitten, who was making our costumes, was determined to give us a new look. We wanted to up the ante in every part of our brand. We were inundated with love, so much so that we almost forgot about all of the quarrelling that had threatened to overtake us. From our immediate families, to fans, and friends, everyone was so happy.

The first single from the album that was released was "Brick House." The song took off like crazy. The radio promoters for Motown were beyond excited. They didn't even have to work to get radio stations to play the song. There was no arm twisting, brown nosing or bribery; all the promoters had to do was deliver it. The stations actually wanted to be the first to break the song and keep it in rotation for their respective audiences. Everything about "Brick House" proved to be a win for the group. It was Walter Orange's first hit as a lead singer and when we performed the song live, he wanted to come down off the drums in order to sing it. We all agreed that it would add another element to the performance and give our audience something that they had not yet seen. I remember thinking, we don't want to lose the uniqueness of him playing the drums and singing, but maybe for this song it would be cool.

During this time, I distinctly remember engaging in a conversation to build Walter up. I felt like it was important at the time for him to know that as he explored new territory, we would be with him every step of the way. I also wanted to establish in all of our hearts that everyone else in the industry was looking at us to set an example and that we had to soar together. We needed reminding that we could do this together and I was willing to do everything that I possibly could to ensure that we had it.

The tour was star studded. Every date, brought out all types of celebrities. For the first time in our career, we had well-known entertainers backstage to see us. That was an indication that we had "made it." Many celebrities would be provided with entrance to the backstage area to greet the ones who were performing and wish them well. This act, however was only reserved for A list celebrities. Celebrities in the making did not realize opportunities like this. For us to now have the cream of the crop coming to our backstage to greet us was surreal. Up until this point, it had been the other way around.

One of our tour stops was at Madison Square Garden and as we were preparing for our sound check, in walked Mick Jagger. I was star struck and almost at a loss for words. To know that he wanted to see us when we had been the ones to admire his work for so long, was mind blowing. I couldn't believe that in the midst of our highest success, I had the privilege to meet someone whom I had aspired to be as great as. It was a true blessing and very inspirational for me. He even told us that The Rolling Stones were playing our song, "Slippery When Wet" in their sound check. We fell out in laughter lined with disbelief. We were living our dream at the pinnacle of our accomplishments. The list of celebrities that showed their love for us continued to grow with each tour date. Even fellow label mates, Stevie Wonder, Marvin Gaye and Diana Ross made an appearance at our show in LA.

It is not possible to have experiences like that, watch your bank account grow, and truly be talented and not be a little narcissistic. I just don't believe that you can live life at that level and not at times think a little highly of yourself. On the opposite side, I also believe that it would not have been possible to reach that level of success without a stout belief in yourself. Even so, I still maintained a firm disposition in not getting caught up in the Hollywood scene. I admired it, but I did not want to become it. There is a difference between getting caught up, and using it to be more visible and grow your brand. It is my belief that our collective goal was to use our contacts and success to leverage more opportunities for success.

The year was 1977. There was a movie being filmed in Los Angeles entitled, *Thank God It's Friday*. (1) The film was labeled as an American musical comedy. A gentleman by the name of Robert Klane had been enlisted to direct the film. (2) The film was also produced by Motown Productions and Casablanca Filmworks for Columbia Pictures. (3) The disco era had taken music by storm and this was showcased in the film.

We received a request to be on the soundtrack. Even though we were still on tour, we agreed to the deal with one contingency in place. We pressured Benny to also convince the directors of the movie to give us a cameo. As always, Benny delivered. Now they were trying to figure out a scene for us. We told them the story about when we first arrived in New York and our equipment had been stolen and how the guy who stole our belongings was trying to sell them back to us. The directors loved it and added the series of events to the film as an actual scene. Talk about deja vu. We replayed this exact scene in the movie. *Thank God It's Friday*, also featured an extremely talented artist by the name of Donna Summer. In the film, she performed her song entitled "Last Dance," and would eventually win the Academy Award for Best Song. I remember her having a super sweet demeanor and an amazing sense of humor. She was the reigning Queen of Disco and I don't believe that anyone else ever realized that title. We also performed a song entitled, "Too Hot ta Trot" in this film. I wrote the music for the song on the tour bus and figuring out how to blend rock, funk, and R&B was the mission for the project. David Bowie's "Fame" influenced the rock, Sly Stone's "Higher" the funk, and Curtis Mayfield's "It's All Right" influenced the bridge to the song. When you fuse all of the elements of the song together, the combination became yet another signature sound of The Commodores.

Life for us continued to move faster and faster. We had a very strategic plan in place, but it still felt like things were spiraling out of control at times. While still on tour, we wrapped our part in the film and also began concentrating on the next album. You would think that artists wouldn't need to begin working on a new album while still on tour for their current one, but this was a necessary task that came with the territory. The truth is that you are only as good as your last hit, unless your hits are standards. We had no idea at the time, that forty years later these same songs would be around to survive all deliverable formats. As an artist, you can't remain relevant if you are not constantly putting out new music. We also felt a sense of anxiety in knowing that it would be challenging to top the album that we were currently on tour for. This meant that while we were on the road, we needed to take time to not only write, but also carve out new ideas that represented an innovative train of thought. Everyone was exhausted. Time with our families was scarce when we were on the road and our bodies were feeling the fatigue that accompanied such a gruesome schedule. We figured that we would take one month off after the tour and then immediately go back into rehearsals.

After returning from the break, we were also tasked with improving the quality and delivery of our show. There were more eyes on us now than ever and we would need to include the new songs, old songs and try to do something different so that the show would be interesting to our fans. With such a vigorous schedule, there was not much time for us to engage in bonding activities as a group. We were all focused on working and any moments that we weren't working, we tried to commit to family. The dynamics of the group continued to evolve and so did our relationships. This also meant that the dynamics of the wives evolved as well.

A series of unfortunate events painted the backdrop on the horizon. Kathy LaPread lost her battle with cancer and it impacted us all deeply. There were no words. Moments like that take your breath away and you question why good people leave so soon.

To try to make up for time that we couldn't always be with our families, we allowed the wives to come out for tour dates. Some wives chose to come for spotted dates here and there and some would stay out for multiple events. I wanted my wife to be with me and valued the time together. This was not the sentiment of everyone. Not all of the guys wanted their wives out on tour the entire time, some felt that it was a distraction.

My wife was enthusiastic and supportive of my career. She had promised that she would honor the few requests that I made of her and I did the same. When we first got married, I asked two things. The first was for her to travel with me and the second was to never ask me to make LA our home. Even though we owned a home there, it was not where I saw myself raising a family or living out our lives. She agreed to the requests prior to us getting married. Once we had exchanged vows, however, she revealed that she had neither a desire to travel nor to remain in Tuskegee. She informed me that she wanted LA to be our home. I obliged and she was the reason that I purchased the home there. How bad could it be to have your wife with you, I'd thought. After she moved to LA, she was drawn to the very thing that I wanted to avoid. Her desire to be a part of the Hollywood scene was a dead giveaway that there would be trouble in paradise for us. Now, at the pinnacle of my career, my marriage was on the rocks. Unfortunately, maintaining a family in the midst of celebrity is not for the faint of heart.

Lionel also began to experience some tumultuous times in his marriage. He was now the face of The Commodores brand. After singing the lead on songs like "Just to Be Closer to You," "Slippery When Wet," "This is Your Life," and "Easy," he was a star. In his quiet moments, he would confide in me about the many directions he was being pulled in. His wife wanted more time, the industry wanted more of him and he felt overwhelmed and understandably so.

Milan and Walter were no exception. They too were having trouble balancing the changes with wives, family and stardom. Although it is sad to say, far too often, family becomes the sacrificial offering for the price of fame. The whispering among the wives became louder and there was talk that "Old Man Motown," which was another reference of Berry Gordy, was preparing to do what they had always done. The Temptations, Smokey Robinson and so many other groups had breakout singers that had become solo acts.

The tides were also turning for Benny Ashburn, who was becoming concerned because he didn't have management contracts on us individually. I remember thinking that no matter what was shifting in the winds, we had to remain together just as The Rolling Stones had. They worked as a team and as individuals, but they always got back together. There was an undercurrent that could not be denied. Lionel was being tapped to do a solo project and it was apparent that he was torn about what to do. On the one hand, he was in a group where his light was too bright for some and he was scrutinized for having evolved into a breakout star. On the other hand, he had never been on this journey alone and felt anxious about doing so. I'm sure to some extent, he also questioned his loyalty to the group. He didn't want to abandon The Commodores in any way and that was clear to me.

Although Lionel met with resentment from the other group members, I found myself encouraging him to pursue whatever his heart desired and go wherever his talent led him. "Hey man, if you got a shot, you have to go for it. Opportunity doesn't come knocking that often," I would say. The expressed dissatisfaction was not only directed at Lionel but also at me as the guys considered me to be a traitor. They wondered how or why I would encourage him? I am certain that many believed that Lionel's pursuit of a solo project would also mean the demise of the group. In my heart, I felt that it would happen anyway. We cannot stand in the way of the gifts that God gives, nor should we ever try. It was apparent that there was a different demand for Lionel's talent, so why not encourage him? I also thought that if Lionel were able to explore other avenues, he could be instrumental in opening new doors for The Commodores. Mick Jagger would always be a Rolling Stone, and Lionel Richie would always be a Commodore. Why did a choice have to be made between the two? However, no one bought this train of thought. They knew that Lionel and I were as close as brothers and I would inevitably side with him. In this case, I wasn't siding with anyone; I truly felt like a win for one was a win for all.

I began to study other groups even more closely to see how they balanced the onset of new business ventures and remained cohesive in the midst of the undeniable changes. I would venture to say that we had hit a new low internally. The morale of the group was nowhere near where it once had been and the uncertainty of what was to come was causing everyone to feel threatened. In this unhealthy space, we returned to Tuskegee to begin preparations for our sixth studio album, which was to be entitled *Natural High*. Although we had bought a studio/rehearsal hall there, thanks to Steve Meyers who'd found the building, Carmichael approached us and said "I'm sensing competition is getting intense and it isn't healthy. I will meet you at your house and hear what you've got and then you can still present some stuff to the group, but I don't want to be influenced by negative comments for songs that you want to present." He was very in tune with the vibe of the group and was always very tactful.

The resistance to the way that the songs for the album were selected increased such that we had to revamp our strategy. Carmichael now had to come to Tuskegee to meet with each of us individually to listen to what we had created. This practice would put an end to the now roaring talk of favoritism in the selection process. We did not want for the other group members to say that we were in cahoots with Carmichael which was why Lionel and I had more songs on the album. Unfortunately, the cohesiveness of the creative process had been compromised. When you stand in truth, in both life and in the creative process, you can't deny the presence of original genius. It surpasses all barriers of ill intent and inevitably finds a way to shine through the darkness. Lionel played a ballad for Carmichael that demonstrated an anointing that I don't believe we had witnessed before within the group. When I heard the song, it was confirmation of his gifts and talents. I knew immediately that the song was a smash. Going into the process, we knew that William King, Ronald LaPread, and Walter Orange didn't want any more ballads to be selected. They even went so far as to say that they didn't care if it was a hit or not. It broke my heart that we were now in a place where we weren't all willing to choose songs for our album based on what was great music and also good for the group. The decision-making process had turned so political and poisonous that the music was often suffocated. When Lionel played the undeniable ballad for the group, they wouldn't admit to its greatness. "We're in the middle of the disco era, we don't need another sleepy song," they said.

This was confirmation that the jealousy was out of hand and I could not believe what I was witnessing. People were dying to get hit records. If it was a hit, I believed without question that it should go on the album. Carmichael began to exercise his power over the group in the face of adversity. "I don't care what y'all say. This is a hit song!" The song was "Three Times a Lady," and to date, Lionel's voice and that song reign as classic.

By this time, more and more requests began coming in through our public relations team and many of the requests were for Lionel alone as opposed to the entire group. In my mind, that was expected as he was the face of the group. The other guys were overcome with frustration. "I can't believe this," they would exclaim. They were now blaming Motown, Benny, and anyone else who could be blamed for Lionel's popularity. Lionel continued to be caught between a rock and a hard place because he had done nothing, except shine.

"Can you believe this?" Lionel would say.

"Nah man, I can't, but it is happening," I would often reply.

With Ronald and Lionel having realized major success on their collaboration on "Zoom," I thought that the competition would have been smashed, but now Walter wanted to be up front more. He even stated that he thought Lionel was getting more attention from Motown because of the complexion of his skin. It also became apparent that William King wanted more as well. He was now calling himself the leader of the group because he was responsible for collecting the money for the fines. It seemed as though he had associated some fake sense of power with the role. Even during interviews, that he was invited to, he would minimize Richie. "Everybody thinks Lionel is the total group, but really, he's not as important as you try to make him out to be." He was very insistent on the word "we."

I believed that it was "we" too, but I also believed in giving a man his dues, especially when he has earned them. Lionel had become an incredible songwriter, and he had a unique sound. There was not another voice like his. It was my thought that the guys needed to come to terms with the fact that Lionel's sound would be around and we were still a group that desperately needed to focus on creating positive vibes and music together in order to stay together. That was also my stance in interviews as well, but as usual, my actions were met with scrutiny. "There you go, boosting Richie." I was simply telling the truth. I had a reason to be proud. I had put in blood, sweat and tears into assisting Lionel in his growth while also improving my own and the groups. I knew my importance and the significance of my contribution and I wasn't about to question what I had brought to the table. The sound that we had developed musically was mine.

Let's be clear, lead vocals and the music are the two sounds that constitute the uniqueness of The Commodores. That was me and Richie.

While on a business call with Benny Ashburn, he expressed that he thought that maybe this would be a time to enjoy the fruits of our labor. He thought that doing so, might calm some of the fears. Although we had now invested in properties and business, we were still very frugal in our spending. Ashburn convinced us to release our grips, ever so slightly to indulge even if only for a moment. "I think it would be good if we caught a deal with the dealer and bought our cars at once," said Benny, and we decided to do just that. Ronald LaPread had always wanted a Porsche. In that moment, our spirits were lifted. There are only a few things that can make a man smile, and based on the grins that were on our faces, fast cars are certainly one of them. We all headed to the dealership in good spirits. All the woes and the antagonism had ceased in that moment. It felt so good, even if only temporarily. When we arrived, we were excited as we walked around the lot filled with cars. I could hear various members in laughter at the thought alone of what we were about to do. After being there for about twenty minutes, we all began to notice something peculiar. We had not been approached by a salesman. No one had even asked if they could assist us in any way. To make matters worse, the salesmen that were present were waiting on everyone except us. We were there to spend a boatload of money, and no one wanted to help us do so. We took a step back and I am certain that everyone was thinking the same thing. This was still Alabama and our money was not to be confused with an end to racism. It was still alive and well and no matter how green our money was, we were still black. We could hardly believe that we were being ignored, but after recognizing what was going on, we all made up our minds to ignore it and not allow it to rain on our parade.

Some of the guys noticed that the colors that they wanted were not on the lot or the showroom floor and would need to be ordered. We approached one salesman in particular to ask for assistance. The salesman didn't take us seriously. His actions led to us requesting to speak with his supervisor. Upon the supervisor's arrival, we explained the magnitude of the purchase that we were there to make. In the end, we made a call to Benny Ashburn, who was in New York at the time. He said, "Let me call the guy and tell him that we want to buy multiple cars." He finally got through to the owner, who fired the salesman as a result of how we had been treated. We were then able to custom order the cars and were giving each other high fives, laughing and cheering as the deals were being made and the orders put through. We left the dealership that day with a renewed sense of something. To this day, I can't quite put my finger on what it was. We just felt good and present in the moment of success. We had never put value into materialistic things and had never spent money frivolously. As a result, we were hailed for our ability to be business forward. The purchase of these cars was simply a moment where we all got to enjoy the success of our hard work and we owed no one an explanation for doing so.

When our cars were delivered, I know for certain that we felt a sense of arrival. That was our first time doing something that was impractical and fun. Prior to that moment, we had all ensured that our families were taken care of and that we had built a solid foundation financially for our futures. We all owned our own houses and now we each had a serious vehicle to park in the garage and it felt good to reward ourselves. It was a day that I would never forget and I knew that none of the guys would either.

A few days later, James Carmichael called for a meeting. He told us that it would be down in the basement of the studio. This area was down below the bottom floor. We knew that if he called for a meeting there it was serious, and that what he had to tell us would not be good. "Gentlemen, we are now entering into a phase where we have the possibility of creating songs that could be standards and around for a very long time. We need to be mindful and not let the small things redirect the attention of the group." He was always very careful to stay in his lane and spoke diplomatically so as to never show favoritism to any particular group member. In his expression, he was emphatic about not allowing any rivalry to interfere with this next album. He wanted to ensure that before we went to Los Angeles, we were on the same page.

I was able to read through his apprehension. This was his plea for us to shed the ill feelings that had brought us to this place. He recognized the tumultuous nature of our relationships and believed they would be fatal to the group's success. If we did not make some immediate changes, before going back to LA to record the next album, the creative process would suffer. Carmichael confessed in that moment how he had been forced to visit Lionel and my homes so that his judgment remained impartial. "I went to their homes to listen to their submissions, but I should never have to do something like that. Gentlemen, we've got to get this thing on page 217. Right now, it looks like we might be headed to a place that is not good." His words stuck with me and caused me great pain.

I left that meeting with a heavy heart and began to reflect back to the days when creating was simple and pure. When I played with The Matadors, we were just happy to hear the mixed melodies that so graciously arose from our instruments. There were no preconceived notions about what would be. That night, I stood in my bathroom staring at myself in the mirror. My face had changed and there was worry in my eyes. My mind drifted again to the moment when I stood in the registration line at Tuskegee, young and eager to create a group that would make history. I laughed to myself because I realized that I had been so confident, but at the same time truly unsure if I ever really believed that I could create something worthy of the history books. A single tear rolled down my cheek because I had; my dream had become my reality. The longer that I stood there, the closer I came to losing hope in my heart. Had we come this far for nothing at all? The pressure of disappointment in the direction that we were heading and the compromise of the brotherhood that we had built broke me, and that night I fell to my knees and asked God for divine guidance. I would never believe that God had brought us together and allowed us to taste the sweetness of success, only to have it leave a bitter taste in our mouths. It just was not possible.

10: *Ships in Passing*

We began our trek to LA to begin recording. Disco was still thriving and Donna Summer was now hotter than ever. The infamous A-list nightclub, Studio 54, became the backdrop for fashion, music and culture.

In true Commodore fashion, we were in the studio recording ballads. We spent three days getting the right feel for the basic track of "Three Times a Lady," which was at the top of our list. Lionel sang the lead, Walter was on drums, while Ronald and I played bass. Technically, we were playing the notes, but Carmichael insisted on discovering the feel. He knew what he was looking for and wasn't satisfied until he had it. Today, I would describe it as an aura. Carmichael's ear was in search of an emotion that could not come from words. It was very forward thinking for these times. He pushed us to be great and insisted that the music be powerful and compelling. It wasn't until he heard what he wanted that we would be able to move on to another song.

These moments of creation together ignited the start of a new era. It really took us time to understand the direction that Carmichael was pointing us in. Admittedly, we were distracted. Hands down, this was our most challenging and most emotionally demanding album to record. The most compelling part of this chapter of our lives was that we were all willing to go. When we finished recording and took the time to listen with open hearts, there was no question of Carmichael's intent. When the single came out, it did exactly what he thought it would. It was played on all of the radio stations, including the country ones. We began preparations for a tour, following the same cycle. In planning for the tour, we knew that we wanted to make a huge impact with some songs in particular. "Three Times a Lady" was one of them.

Our tour equipment had grown over the years and we were now up to several tractor trailers worth of gear. We didn't want to add any more trailers so a decision was made to collaborate with a touring company and then enlist the services of a construction company for a custom set for our tour. Our plan was such that just before we prepared to play "Three Times a Lady," the piano would roll out and be illuminated with lights and Lionel would come out to the audience's excitement. We wanted it to be a moment for our fans. The plan would position Lionel to appear as the highlight of the show and when executed it would be very dramatic. Our audience was diverse and we even had some of the Jackson Five fans and their parents that we had picked up along our earlier days of tour with them.

Our true hearts could be felt in the music, but the uncertainty within could be felt by our wives. Their actions spoke loudly about where we all stood. They were just as divided as our group, if not more.

There was further division within the group that began to steer the interactions we had inside and outside the studio. During this time, my wife and Lionel's wife continued to strengthen their friendship. Walter Orange and Ronald LaPread were still interested in using CB Radios and because of that, along with Milan Williams, they began to form a bond. Truthfully, I was very excited to witness their growing fondness for one another because it was still my hope that we would come back together and share the brotherhood that we had once known. CB Radio also brought the wives of Milan, Ronald and Walter together and gave them something to talk about. William King and his wife, however, continued to be seen by some as outcasts, due to the increased demands and push for power. William was adamant about his role as a leader and his actions seemed to be the result of needing to feel important within the group. Regardless of William's position, there was no denying that he was one of the best dancers. He and Ronald LaPread had moves and on many occasions, William would work to establish his value by choreographing routines for us. While Ronald's personality, technique, and methodology were more favorable to the group members, it was easier to appease William in order to maintain the peace and as such Ronald let William believe that he alone was the choreographer. Beyond that, he still held the position of fine collector and while we all wanted a system in place, we hadn't accounted for the fact that it would drive morale down due to the way in which it was enforced. The money collected was put into what we called the "kitty" and then it was divided amongst those who hadn't had to pay any fines. No matter who received money, the overall system was a detriment to everyone because of the spirit behind it.

We all hoped that William's roles as fine collector and acting choreographer would give him that feeling of purpose in the group and that it would defuse the accusations of favoritism and dispel some of the negative energy that went toward song selections that impacted the overall quality of the albums. Despite our best efforts, the tone of the scrutiny was so negative that we now referred to William as Adolph Hitler. "Oh, shoot, here comes Adolph", the guys would say at meetings or while in rehearsals. The negativity was disruptive to the creativity, but sadly this was only one of many distractions that kept us from being as focused as we needed to be at this crucial time in our careers.

Even with all the internal strife, the world still saw cohesiveness. The Commodores were a united front in the eyes of the public. Our stardom had reached an all-time high. We performed at the Toronto Jam in front of 500,000 people who had come to see us. It was like Woodstock and we could not believe the tremendous reception that we received. At the end of the tour, we took our month-long sabbatical like clockwork, but we all knew that those thirty or so days would fly by and that we would need to get back to work and back to business.

When we returned, we were faced with a serious time constraint as we were only granted a small window to put the next album together. Discotech was the trend and that was the vibe that many of the group members were leaning towards. Lionel and I had such a smooth dynamic when creating that we didn't want to interrupt the pattern of continuous hits, even if they were ballads and the furthest thing away from what everyone else was doing. We never backed down from a creative challenge.

Together, we began writing a song entitled, "Midnight Magic" that had a disco vibe, which was the title track of the album. Lionel also wrote a record entitled, "Still," which we believed to be one of our strongest songs for submission. Our creativity had not only proven to be well received by fans, but also profitable in many ways. The record company's goal was to sell records and ensure that we kept the momentum going. They had very little interest in the gripes of grown men. "Still" was selected as a single to be released despite the severe resistance by the other guys in the band. The struggle continued even after the song became a hit and kept us relevant while we created more music for the album. "We got too many damn slow songs," some would complain. I could not understand for the life of me why anyone would allow envy to stand in the way of the creativity that ultimately led to a paycheck for all of us. The burden of worrying about everyone's feelings when I knew without question that none of our actions were a result of spite became too heavy to carry. I placed my energy into creating and following through on the music.

"Lionel, do you have any more? If it's a hit, you've got to keep rolling," I would say.

"It's amazing, I think I have a thousand of these. When I sit down, they just seem to pop out," Lionel would say. He had reached his musical sweet spot and it was great to watch.

In 1980, Benny Ashburn received a call from Kenny Rogers requesting a song collaboration with the Commodores. By this time, we had become well versed in the fact that songwriting was a different royalty than simply singing on a song or even producing a song. There were artist royalties, publishing rights and royalties, and royalties associated with songwriting and airplay. The publishing is essentially the place where the song lives and therein lies ownership of the song. If you own publishing and writing, you have access to residuals that those not writing are not privy to.

Benny knew that Lionel and I would contribute in the writing and composition process in a more productive way and with less tension if we did it without the rest of the group. He knew that no matter who worked on the song, it was an opportunity for the whole group that could not be passed up. The group, however, did not consider it a way to increase our platform and as such we took on the collaboration alone. Lionel began writing a song that was pure and full of magic. Because of this, he decided that prior to submitting it to Kenny Rogers, we should submit the song to the group to see if they wanted to use it on the album. To my surprise, it was rejected. I was clueless as to how they couldn't recognize a hit of this magnitude. Lionel named the song "Lady," and after the group turned it down, he made the decision to submit the song to Kenny Rogers. Kenny enlisted an additional song for the album that Lionel and I wrote together to complete the project.

Even though the collaboration deal for Lionel had been facilitated by Benny Ashburn, Lionel enlisted his own lawyers outside of the attorneys that had been used for the group's affairs. The song "Lady," as it turned out, went on to sell ten million units. As seemed to be the theme, the songs popularity only further separated the group.

Though Motown released another single called, "Jesus is Love" from our upcoming album, it's success wasn't able to provide the morale boost that the group needed. What the song did was shoot up the charts and simultaneously garnered more success for Lionel, and behind the scenes, me. The levels of unbalance and disdain were surreal and it was obvious that we were on the verge of an explosion.

The guys saw me as a traitor. There was no in between or straddling the fence as they had often accused me of doing. Everyone had expected me to join in their bashing of Lionel and the number of interviews he was asked to do. They wanted me to take their side and fight the consistent production of slow songs. When I didn't join in on the criticism, they labeled me as the "kiss up" guy. I knew I wasn't because all I'd ever truly wanted was what was best for all of us.

In the middle of disco, we continued to release chart topping ballads. I had always believed that no matter what was going on, we set our own sound, and created our own trends. When people told us to be more black and R&B, we came out with "Sail On." We had served as trendsetters and created everything from a dance called the bump, to the funk of "Slippery When Wet," "I Feel Sanctified," and "Brick House." We could do it all, which in my mind gave us the creative freedom to release the music that was working for us and keeping us successful. I realized that the one area we hadn't broken into was gospel and as such we worked to compose an album entitled *Heroes*, which was a deliberate attempt to enter that market while maintaining our existing fan base. This was very challenging, but as fate would have it, "Jesus is Love" was the strongest song on the album.

As the tour rolled around, we strategized as usual to give our audience new experiences with music. We wanted the moments to be unforgettable. We decided to continue our piano bit for the performance of "Three Times a Lady," but rather than having the piano removed after the song, we would leave the piano out for the remainder of the show and end the night with "Jesus is Love." To add to the elevation of the song, we also brought out a mass choir from St. Louis. This same choir began to travel with us for the tour dates. There were about twelve members, and their presence added an aura to the moment and the music that people would leave with. To end the show while people are spiritually touched, waving, singing and holding hands was indeed a high note. There was a peace among the crowd that was unexplainable. The media that now covered our shows, would write about the way in which the audiences and fans were left feeling. And although the country was still racially tense, our show was the hallmark of tranquility.

"Jesus is Love" was a song that not only touched the audience, but both Lionel and myself. It made us connect with the music and God. I recall Lionel speaking about the song and how he knew that it was not him who had written the lyrics. "This was given to me straight from heaven," he said. We would sit and as he would read the lyrics, we would just cry. The lyrics were so heavenly inspired. That is the power of music. I couldn't live my life without music if I tried. Here we were as grown men, assembling something so beautiful that it moved us to tears. We knew that if the song had that effect on us, that others would feel the same and so it was. Not only was our fan base, a total representation of diversity, but it had grown again internationally.

Fans began to write us to speak about the way our music affected their lives. Couples let us know that they were using "Three Times a Lady" for their first dance at their weddings. Others would write that "Brick House" and "Machine Gun" were contagious songs that made them dance and that the "Easy" guitar solo would be a classic. That guitar arrangement in "Easy" is still hailed as one of the most profound arrangements in a song. It moves my heart beyond words to know that something that I created had this type of effect on people. Even our older single "This is Your Life" was impacting our fans in ways we had never imagined. We were told that it encouraged people and helped heal their hearts. "Zoom" was hailed as one of our most endearing songs, even though no one knew that it had been inspired by Kathy LaPread's fight against cancer. Our music and our sound was captivating and the positive response from our fans could not be denied.

By this time, our relationship with Marvin Gaye had developed further and we now considered him a personal friend. He had made the decision to take a sabbatical in Europe and when he returned, he spent a great deal of time with us and continued to impart his wisdom on us. I admired Marvin not only for his talent, but also for his ability to create music that mattered. He was a political activist and the undertones of his music were so melodic that people didn't even realized how much injustice he spoke out against. I felt in many ways that I had not been as active in the fight as I had been in my earlier days at Tuskegee and back at home in Eustis.

After witnessing an example of how this could be done eloquently and in a way, that was not offensive to the masses, I felt compelled to find a way to bring meaning to our music. This had always been my hope, but much of the political decisions made in the music business had prevented me from doing so. Furthermore, we had built a tremendous fan base around a musical sound, not a message. Treading those waters would prove to be challenging. My entire life, I had always wanted to stand for something and now, I began to legitimately ponder if we could make a difference politically without alienating any of our audience that had supported us over the years. Benny Ashburn and I often didn't see eye to eye on this. His stance was clear and he maintained that we would not stand for anything, political or otherwise that would deter our focus when we needed to remain steadfast in selling records.

After much thought, I decided that a better approach to my mission of activism would be to exploit the inner workings of the music industry. Over the years, the one obvious injustice was the industries disproportionate number of black executives. Why were so many the talent but not the tycoons? It was my sentiment that we should have supported more organizations who were actively fighting injustice. Our presence alone would have proven to be impactful. If there was one thing that I had learned over the years, it was that you can only be responsible for the change in your actions. No matter how hard you fight, you can only make decisions that change the trajectory of your deeds in hopes that others will take heed and follow suit, especially when your actions are intended for the greater good.

It is my belief that when you desire to put good into the world, opportunities for you to do so will appear. I was enlisted to serve as a consultant for the NAACP Image Awards, to Benjamin Hooks, CEO and Dr. William Gibson, Chairman of the Board.

The National office made the decision to take over the production of the NAACP Image Awards TV show from the local Beverly Hills Branch after then president, Willis Edwards allegedly mismanaged the finances. It was also speculated that he paid himself $25,000 to help produce the show. This event was the annual fundraiser for the local Beverly Hills Branch. Co-founder Maggie Hathaway, a member of the Beverly Hills branch was a personal friend of mine. The internal dispute became public when the Beverly Hills branch asked the entertainers to boycott the show if the National office took it away from them. Amid all the confusion, the entertainers decided to sit things out until a resolution could be reached.

With no entertainers on board, then NBC President, Brandon Tartikoff refused to renew the contract. In an effort to rectify the turmoil, we met with CBS and Fox as alternatives for the show, but both turned us down. In a plea for reconsideration, we went back to Tartikoff to negotiate. His ask was simple. "If you get the entertainers and a reputable producer/director for the show, NBC will participate." That was the only ray of hope that I needed. I was determined to reach out to my friend, entertainment executive, and industry powerhouse, Clarence Avant. He was well connected and the five degrees of separation that could turn the tide. My first request was for him to contact and connect with Earvin "Magic" Johnson, a legendary athlete and now entrepreneur to see if he would assist me in my mission. He was very receptive and quickly offered his assistance. "I'm really good friends with Janet Jackson and I will see if I can get her to commit." Janet Jackson had skyrocketed to fame and was achieving monumental success. By securing a commitment from Janet Jackson, we had a win! Once Janet committed, we received another commitment from Patti LaBelle, who clearly needs no introduction. With Janet Jackson and Patti LaBelle engaged, the names began to pour in.

My next course of action was to recommended Suzanne de Passe to produce the first show under the new NBC agreement. Suzanne had played a pivotal role in getting The Commodores signed to Motown Records and I would never forget her genius.

The televised NAACP Image Awards was saved and I had completed a mission to use my gifts and talents to fulfill more roles of advocacy.

With what was now apparent bad blood in the mix, we found ourselves on the heels of our next album, *Midnight Magic*. This point in time felt like an endless battlefield with no end in sight. Lionel and I were fighting with the group and fighting at home with our wives. We were both trying to save our marriages. Although the arguments were not related, there was a common thread — the life of an entertainer is strenuous on a relationship and you can't possibly be everywhere all of the time. The balance seemed almost impossible.

In the midst of battle, wins and losses are certain. I felt like I had been fighting a losing battle and admittedly, I was weary. I often felt engulfed with the struggles of the group. Our positions were difficult and consuming. Just when you feel that you have had enough, God always has a ram in the bush. My wife, Linda gave birth to our first child, a beaming baby girl, named Jazmyne. I will forever treasure that moment in my heart. Jazmyne's birth gave me a renewed sense of purpose and a reason to keep fighting for the group. Lionel visited me at Cedars Sinai Hospital in LA, the day that Jazmyne was born. He was the only group member that came. This spoke of the magnitude of just how far we had been distanced from each other. We had never been so separated that we didn't support each other's big life moments. As Lionel and I sat in the waiting room wearing the white scrubs that the hospital provided for us to wear, we reminisce on all that had happened over the years.

"Here we are, our first child. This is going to be our group's first child," said Lionel. "It's too bad man, that the guys couldn't be happy for me and you for the Kenny Rogers project, but hopefully we just can keep going."

"Hey, we better," I said.

Benny had opened the doors for amazing opportunities for Lionel and myself, but he remained paranoid about the next moves for the group. We still had no individual contracts in place with him, and the possibility of Lionel's solo career, as well as the uncertainty of what would happen next, was looming. It was a noticeably heavy burden for Ashburn. The prospect of the group having to find a new manager was taxing as well. This was the entertainment business and we were a sought-after brand that everyone seemed to want a piece of.

With new life, came new revelations. Even though things with the group were not pleasant, I delighted in the fact that I could still creatively contribute to records that were received well by a vast array of audiences and those that proved to be massively successful. The gift that God had given me had not been marked void, simply because others did not have the ability to believe in what we had created. I knew with certainty that God's intent was for me to walk in my purpose through music but the mounting tensions made me question if I was on the path intended for me. It would remain to be seen.

11: *Nightshift*

When it rains, it pours. By 1981, everything that had transpired, from the birth of my daughter Jazmyne, to the potential loss of Benny Ashburn as our manager, and the constant drip of gasoline that continued to fuel the flames of jealousy, and deceit among the group, had all taken a toll on me both mentally and physically.

    I found myself walking around with an undiagnosed case of double pneumonia. For almost two weeks, I napped on and off, attributing my lackluster behavior to exhaustion. We flew to England to perform and play in Manchester. After the show, I was so weak that I could barely walk. When we arrived in London, the promoters provided me with the name of a doctor who came highly recommended. The doctor's office was on Davis Avenue and upon arrival, I recall the facility being well endowed. I observed a photograph of J. Paul Getty hanging on the wall. He was one of the richest men in the world at the time and this small detail helped me to understand why the doctor was so highly recommended. He was not only well connected, but also rubbed elbows with some of society's elite. None of that mattered, however, as I was in desperate need of medical attention. When he finally came into the exam room, he said, "You are an extremely sick young man and you'll have to stay in the hospital until we can get you back on your feet. We'll get you round the clock nursing care and maybe, just maybe, in a couple of days you will feel well enough to fly back to America." I was in disbelief. Who goes to another country and gets so sick that they have to stay there? I can't say that I was frightened, but I was most certainly concerned.

My body was worn and weary. I was dehydrated, with a fever, chills and a complete loss of appetite. I remained in the hospital for four days, until I could gain my strength back and then the promoter arranged for me to take a flight back on a Concorde to the US. It was my first time on the special British jet and I remember looking out the window and seeing the curvature of the Earth. The jet flew so much higher and faster, providing a completely different experience than any other flight I'd taken. It was just an added bonus that I was home in under four hours.

I was happy to have made it safely back to the United States. No one had stayed with me when I was sick in a foreign country and when I returned, I contacted Benny Ashburn to tell him of the events that had taken place. I was frustrated and a little upset that I had allowed my body to get to this point. During our conversation, I could feel in my heart that Benny didn't have that much compassion for me. I let it go because I knew he had a great deal on his mind, we all did. We were losing our cohesiveness at every point and we all recognized it.

The mask of mistrust had been removed. No one was willing to hide their negative sentiments and feelings about each other any longer. This factor alone affected the level in which each member was devoted to the group. There were some who were more committed than others, but regardless, everyone began to pursue their own interests more proactively. I can't express the hurt that was in my heart. I continued to ask myself how we had gotten here. Moreover, I searched deep within in a desperate attempt to determine what action I could take to fix it all, as I felt responsible in so many ways because I had brought us all together. I had always been the glue that bound us, but I'll admit, it was no longer working.

I felt discredited in many ways. I had ghostwritten so many songs and received no credit for them. I had only ever operated with one goal in mind — the success of the entire group. I had often gone beyond the call of duty, staying after the actual recordings to mix the albums. I had done so much because I just wanted to keep the band together. I wanted for us to rise to the levels of success that I had envisioned. The human side of me couldn't help but question each of the guys myself. I had always taken the high road, but the subliminal maliciousness and grudges being developed and held, began to get the best of me.

I now felt that William King, was capable of stabbing me in the back. Walter Orange was more opinionated than ever after the success of the song "Brick House," in which he sang lead. I couldn't understand his lapse in humility just because he sang lead on a song. Walter's actions seemed to be the result of advice he'd been given from people that were constantly in his ear, not all of whom were in the industry. It's pretty hard for people to give advice on a walk that they have never taken. Nevertheless, Walter felt like he should have been singing more lead songs. That spot, however, wasn't available for him because Lionel was who the public demanded. Not to mention, Lionel was also the choice of the executives. Walter's resentment toward him had grown and it was evident to anyone who observed.

Milan Williams' interests began to waver, yet again. Our joke about him always being in left field was now even more of a reality. He opened a Tuskegee based nightclub and named it after his son, Jason, who had been born shortly after the release of the album. He appeared to have less and less interest in the group as he spent all of his time at his new club, or flying planes and engaging with CB Radio. What time remained, left him with low energy and little to no enthusiasm for the group.

Ronald LaPread purchased a motorcycle and began to spend a lot of time trying to immerse himself in the motorcycle gangs and lifestyle. Walter Orange eventually joined him in this effort.

Lionel's ascension to fame was now undeniable. He was feeling good about himself and what he had managed to accomplish, and I can't say that I blamed him. I couldn't blame any of the guys for pursuing their outside interests. We had grown up in the music and entertainment industry, which meant, we'd sacrificed a lot of years that others had spent enjoying life and new experiences. We had all reached a point where we could simply enjoy the fruits of our labor. I had my own developing interests with my family and in continuing to learn about the business side of music. It was just so unfortunate that all of this was happening amidst the deterioration of relationships and the standard of excellence that we worked so hard to maintain. We were now more distant than ever. Friendships had been severed and it was each man for himself — at least from my viewpoint, that is how it felt.

During a group meeting, we came to the conclusion that everyone needed a break. We were all sick of each other. We also knew that we could not stay away for too long, or we would run the risk of compromising our established pattern of releasing music. We could not afford to do that. Every year, we released an album and then we toured. That was the magic equation that worked for us. This pattern had skyrocketed us to success and we could not impede the pattern and expect that our spot in the industry would just be there, waiting for us to figure it all out. The music industry has never worked this way. You are only as good as your last hit. If you fail to keep them coming, there is always someone else working hard to fill the void. As they say, more money can bring more problems. We had grown larger than ourselves.

The break was too short for everyone's liking and when we returned, nothing had really changed, except for the fact that we all knew that we enjoyed the time away from each other. Things had become so strained between us that it became increasingly difficult to even get in contact with each other. If you called and left a message for a group member, they would get back to you when they could. If you were not a priority, you knew it. As opposed to the excitement that we had once felt in putting together music on our own to bring to the studio for the group to listen to, we now found ourselves putting together songs in the studio. This cost more time and of course, more money. Much of this part of the work would have been done back in Tuskegee, but we had remained in LA and it was obvious that it was no longer a priority for everyone to return to put in work for the group.

Prior to this time, we had always been careful with our recording budget. Many entertainers don't know or consider that the fees for studio time comes from your royalties. While it appears that there is no expense, you, the talent, pay for it on the back end. During those moments that we had to wait on someone to begin or if someone was late, it was more than just a fine imposed by the group. We were paying for it from our royalties, by the hour.

James Carmichael, loyal and true, did all that he could to preserve the chemistry in the recording environment. He often shifted the focus of our minds from the finances and redirected us towards the creativity. From past experience, he knew that there was an element of relaxation that was a part of making the music what it was. Under his guiding hand, we found ourselves playing more chess and backgammon in the studio, but even with his best efforts, the chemistry was failing and some members left to take a break and never returned.

Despite it all, we persevered. This album had a different feel to it. I couldn't quite determine if it was because of what we were all experiencing or because our sound had changed.

Lionel's career was evolving right before our eyes. We all knew that it was only a matter of time before he began to work on solo projects. After he had conquered the big hit on Kenny Rogers' album, he had also received an opportunity to work with the infamous arranger, Gene Page. None of us had worked with anyone outside of Carmichael, including Lionel until now. There were whispers about Lionel's solo career, but to the outside it looked like he was not making a concerted effort to pursue it. No one at the time knew, except me, that he was in fact positioning himself accordingly. Lionel now had a personal assistant, and separate legal counsel, having decided to no longer use the group's attorney, Lee Phillips. The changes went beyond that. During the creation of this album, Lionel began to record in a separate studio. The song that was chosen was "Oh No" and Lionel believed that it would be less stressful and less inconvenient if he recorded his song at another studio. The resentment was ever present and he had no need to deal with it. Furthermore, there was not a clear-cut path to a successful solo career and he felt a real anxiousness to see if this could be pulled off.

Suzanne de Passe, who was now hailed as a guru in the construction of solo careers, was not only Lionel's acquaintance, but they were actually friends. She was notorious for creating solo exits for musicians and her work spoke for itself. With a track record of names, including, Diana Ross, Eddie

Kendricks, lead singer of The Temptations, Smokey Robinson, and Gladys Knight & the Pips, there was no one better than her to see Lionel through this process.

Benny Ashburn recognized that losing Lionel was completely out of his control. The terms of the management agreements that we had with him would soon expire and if we were to enlist him to continue, it would have to be a decision made by all. Lionel was hesitant about resigning with Benny, and even though Benny and I had our differences, I felt without question that Benny had the fatherly guidance that we were still desperately in need of. Truth be told, he was still the one consistent factor from the beginning of our careers. We all had so many outside influences that the noise was deafening, and I still believed that Benny was the only one who possessed the ability to help us weed out some of the factors that weren't in our best interest and to make sound decisions about our future. However, there was so much distrust that everyone questioned everything. Even living arrangements were questioned. We were each responsible for paying for our living expenses while in LA, and to be more efficient, we purchased a building with condos. We kept an empty condo for any group member that might need a place to stay in the event that something happened. When Benny moved to LA, he stayed in that condo. Many saw this as opportunistic. Essentially, it was as though we were paying for Benny's living arrangements and no one liked that. This was the mindset in the midst of making the decision as to whether or not we should continue to work with Benny.

It still amazed me that all of this was unfolding before our eyes and the public didn't have a clue. We kept the music in front of the muck and that was the best thing that we could have done. I am certain that any sign of turbulence would have been detrimental to our success. We began working to assemble a tour that would follow the album and give us an even more recognized presence in the industry. That was the goal with each album. There were no limits. Even though we had fans and we were selling out shows, we were still hungry to further our impact. That may have been the one thing that we still had in common. We all wanted more from the industry, our careers, and from ourselves. We had tasted success and wanted more of it. We also recognized that we needed to show up at more events and increase our visibility. Doing so, always meant more opportunities for press and media coverage. More press and media coverage meant more exposure to existing fans and valuable opportunities to gain more. More fans meant more records and concert sales. It was like a set of dominoes, each one affects the next.

Lionel was friends with a young lady by the name of Ruth Robinson, who worked for The Hollywood Reporter. Lionel was charismatic and more outgoing than most of the guys in the group and as such he would get write ups and more exposure in the media. I was happy for him, but the sentiment wasn't shared throughout the group.

We all began to receive opportunities to do other things musically. As long as I could be back in the studio by six o'clock and perform as I always had, I was very open to the prospect of new opportunities. We made the decision to invite a few other musicians to tour with us on the road. The group was called The Mean Machine and consisted of Harold Hudson, who played trumpet and keyboard, David Cochrane, who played guitar as well as the sax and keyboard, Winston Sims who also played the sax, and Darrell Jones, who was the rhythm guitarist. They were a super talented bunch.

When they were around, nostalgia set in and I remembered the times when all we wanted to do was love the music. I enjoyed the exchange of musical energy. As a constant creator, I wanted to be around people who also loved to create and with whom I could vibe when the music hit me. My name and reputation as a ghostwriter was now resonating with new ears and more opportunities began to come my way as a result of it. I was not going to allow the creativity in me to die simply because of the constant riffs in our group.

It was my thought, that since these guys had been traveling on the road with us, it would be great to bring them into the studio to create. Harold Hudson was very interested in writing and I encouraged him to partner with William King. I had ghostwritten several songs for King in the past and I thought that this might be a way for King to score a song on the album.

Harold Hudson wrote the music and played the keys on a song that showed promise. William King presented the song to his wife Shirley and she came up with some lyrics that proved to be popular. The product of their collaboration was a song called, "Lady You Bring Me Up." This song became the first single from our ninth studio album, *In the Pocket*. The single took off right out of the box. It was a hit! This was a win for all. Much of our success had been because of ballads and now we had success with an up-tempo groove. I loved it.

Another single that performed well was "Oh No." Lionel recorded this song outside of the group and literally just put it on the album. The general public was not aware, but The Commodores did not actually play on that song. This gave ammunition to rogue behavior from many different directions.

Benny Ashburn was still our manager, but there was some dissention as Ronald LaPread did not want him to book the tour. For the life of me, I could not understand why we would want anyone other than Benny to book our tour amidst so much turbulence. This was a clear cut example of the need to exercise sound business acumen. I would have assumed that we all would have benefited from any amount of consistency that we could have achieved.

At this same time, Ken Kragen, who had been the manager for Kenny Rogers, began to woo Lionel, but his objective was not to sign The Commodores as a whole, but to sign Lionel Richie as a solo act. He assured Lionel that he could negotiate deals on his behalf. Benny Ashburn saw this as a threat to the group. He knew that if Lionel signed with Kragen, it could lead to the demise of The Commodores.

I would often speak with Lionel in depth. He was hurt by the way that things had transpired within the group. The guys kept him isolated, as if he was on his own island. "Man, I can't believe how they are treating me. This is ridiculous," he would say. Things got so bad that during the meetings, his opinion was no longer welcome and when he would bring suggestions to the table, they side eyed him and questioned his motives. They wondered if his suggestions were just to benefit him or the group as a whole? No one was certain of anything. I always had Lionel's back and I never spoke up about my true sentiments because he was my friend. I always wanted to see him win. However, I'd be lying if I said that I didn't feel some of the same things that the guys felt about Lionel leaving the group. There were many things that seemed to have been orchestrated and only in the best interest of Lionel's solo career. In my quiet moments I felt that we were being abandoned by Lionel. He was my friend, but that was also my truth.

Lionel made a move that turned the tide. He requested that all of his publishings were cleared from the welfare program. This was a huge hit to the group. Milan and William King pushed back with great resistance upon his request. Walter Orange was not a businessman and showed indifference. Ronald LaPread appeared to be playing both sides of the fence. He would say one thing to Lionel, but when he got with the rest of the group members, he would express disdain. Benny Ashburn was caught between a rock and a hard place. He wanted to keep Lionel happy, but he also didn't fully agree with his decision. With complete transparency, my position was that everyone should have their own. To hell with the Welfare Program was my sentiment. Back in 1975, we came up with a concept that we nicknamed "The Welfare Program." We had some members who emerged as writers and producers and after learning about the way that royalties worked, The Welfare Program was a way of giving guys a writer's credit for work that they really didn't do. We did this so that they could participate in the royalties, which maintained cohesiveness and helped everyone prosper financially. In retrospect, this was not fair. It meant that people were getting paid for songs that they did not write. Lionel was now fed up and I could no longer justify or merit the train of thought that had once been successful for all.

The attorneys began to negotiate the deal and the outcome was in Lionel's favor. Everyone now had their own publishing. For future accounting of the songs, Motown went back and tied up all the loose ends. For some, this meant a loss of money, but Lionel figured that it was senseless to continue to allow people to profit off of work that he had done, when he wasn't even being treated with respect from an organization that he had given so much of himself to. Whether fair or unfair, dismantling the program was a huge blow to the group. We were no longer talking about hurt feelings and mistrust, we were now talking about dollars and cents. We all know that money changes the discussion and leads people down paths that might not otherwise have been explored. The group was not a group, we were now just guys who worked together. There was no longer a bond of brotherhood. It was broken.

I now know with certainty that even in the midst of turmoil, we must find a way to treasure every moment of life and live with no regrets. Not a single day is promised. We were brought to a screeching halt when Benny Ashburn was found dead after suffering a massive heart attack at the tender age of fifty-four. No matter what had transpired over the years, Benny had given all that he had to protect us, created a path for us, and remained loyal even when we questioned his motives. The legacy of The Commodores could never be told without the mention of Benny Ashburn. I can't speak for others, but I know in my heart that I will forever be grateful for the sacrifices that he made to ensure success for each of us. And as the good word says, what profits a man to gain the whole world but lose his soul? Benny, helped us conquer the world and I pray that his soul forever rests in peace and is encapsulated with my sincere gratitude.

We were now forced to pen a new chapter and tell a new story, this one not like any of the others. The rumors were brewing and many had theories as to what brought on the stress that could have potentially attributed to Benny's demise. We cancelled a few shows in an attempt to devise a plan as to how to move forward. Benny was a part of all that we had done up to this point. It hurt and made the burden of all that was unfolding even more of a cross to bear.

I had been met with a great deal of resistance on the songs that I had submitted to the group for consideration on the album. This further continued to drive a wedge between myself and the other members. I was positioned now more than ever to welcome new opportunities and I had no intention of watching my talent go to waste. I was enlisted by George Murphy, a friend of Clarence Avant, to produce a song for a group called Klique.

Clarence Avant, was one of the most powerful executives in the music industry and my personal friend. He understood the inner workings and had seen scenarios much like ours play out before. He was also an advocate in the industry for equality. He would go to record companies and demand that they hire blacks. The proof of his actions was in his results. I admired what he'd done, as I saw it as meaningful work. I had always wanted to do more for minorities in the music industry.

Together, George Murphy and I produced a #1 song called "Stop Doggin' Me Around." It was a remake of the Jackie Wilson song. My work with Murphy compounded the jealousy that was directed towards myself and Lionel. Lionel had had enough and his exit would prove to be sooner rather than later.

Chuck Smiley, who had once been a lawyer, was enlisted to be our new manager. I can't say that he would not have been selected had Benny still been living, but now he was it. Admittedly, I thought of how things would be under Benny's guiding hand. The loss of Benny ushered in a new charge of changes.

Lionel was now preparing to make his unofficial exit and start working on his solo album. He didn't really want the publicity associated with the fact that he was leaving the group and as such, his departure was simply stated as, "He will always be a member of The Commodores." The rest of the group was coached to say that this was just a solo album. The truth was that he felt that the group was pushing him out and he was ready to go.

Creatively, I had always been there for Lionel. I had ghostwritten for him as well, on many occasions with no credit. I wanted to maintain the connection with him and although I never spoke of it, I hated to see him leave the group just as much as the other guys. I had worked so hard to bring us all together. I had toiled with everything inside of me to show the guys that we could have something different than the groups that came before us. I had dreamt of our success and touched it with my bare hands. I had heard the melodies of our music and tasted them with my soul. To have any aspect of what we had brought together, depart, was hurtful. I knew in my heart that these moments signified another end of an era for The Commodores.

Founding The Commodores had brought me so much joy in my lifetime. It was still my first love. The thought of the group now brought me great pain, as I knew that things could never be the same and the monument of brotherhood, love, and success that we had built together was crumbling before my eyes. Both Lionel and myself had proven that we could be successful in other arenas of the industry, but that night when I got home, I sat in my car with my head resting on the steering wheel feeling defeated. For the first time ever, I felt that the fate of The Commodores was no longer in my hands.

There was also another part of me that felt a sense of resentment. I had gone out of my way to support others and be there for them, but it was never returned. With the exception of Lionel, not one of the members had congratulated me on the hit with Klique. I had known for a while, but it was now a fact that I could no longer limit myself to the group as my only source of creating. If I had, my gifts would have been smothered. By staying engaged and being productive, it provided me an escape from the chaotic cocktail of turmoil. I wasn't thirsty.

The process of mourning that I felt during our downward spiral was exacerbated as my personal life was also crumbling before my eyes. The two requests that I had made to my wife was to travel with me while I was on tour, and for us to not make our permanent residence in LA. Neither request had been honored. While I did recognize that I was spending more time in LA as the popularity and growing demands of the group came about, I still wanted our true home to be in Tuskegee. She wanted to find her own way and as the time passed, the wedge between us expanded as she seemed more interested in spending time with her new LA friends, that were not mine. I was trying to save my marriage just like I was trying to save the group, but we found ourselves disagreeing on most things. We were ships passing in the night. I knew that my parents had demonstrated a long-lasting marriage spanning over fifty years. How could I not make this work? I grew up in a Christian environment and I aspired to emulate the example that my parents had set for us. They had differences, but they always worked it out.

To drown out the white noise that now existed in our home, I busied myself even more with work. I honed my skills and positioned myself as a profound ghostwriter in the industry and the calls began to flood in. I was blessed to work with the likes of Joe Jackson and James Ingram, who was an artist, producer and songwriter. I was hired to write and produce a song for Eddie Kendricks of The Temptations as well as

Levi Stubbs & the Four Tops. I had also been enlisted by the infamous Clive Davis, President of Arista Records, to help an up and coming artist who was slated to be the next best thing. Her name was Whitney Houston. I then co-wrote with Lionel on the song "Endless Love" featuring Diana Ross. I enjoyed every minute and thankfully I was good at it. It took my mind away from the troubles of the group and at home.

I was busy trying to stay true to the gift that God had given me. I didn't want to be affected by the naysaying happening within the group, but I also didn't believe that complaining was the answer, action was.

Now, I was the one who was spending less time around the group. My presence at the meetings were short lived as they tended to be ridiculously long and ended in arguments with no solutions in sight. To make matters worse, I was not fond of the management style of the group's manager. Lionel's departure had still not been made official in terms of the paperwork, but his heart and his presence had long departed. He had a single out and it was performing well. It wasn't long before he found himself rehearsing with another band and preparing to hit the road. Because of this, a conversation was started about the need to find a replacement for Lionel. I spoke out during one of the long meetings and said, "Gentleman, let's not try to find someone that looks or sounds like Lionel Richie. I think it would be to our advantage to make a clean departure from that sound and look. This is an opportunity to reinvent ourselves." I used The Doobie Brothers as an example.

A ray of light shined down on me when I was offered a solo deal with Motown as a result of getting the hit "Stop Doggin' Me Around." Yet and still, I found my fate suspended. I was trying to hang on to my wife, my friendship with Richie, the group, and my sanity. I was being spread thin.

The turnover of the team members that had created the magic with and for us was surreal. No Benny Ashburn and no Jo-Ann Geffen, as she had gone on to start her own PR Firm. There was no Karolyn Ali, who had served as Benny's Assistant. She was charting new territory as an executive in the industry at S.O.L.A.R Records. No Lenny Guise, who was Ronald LaPread's cousin and our trusted lighting technician. He became one of the most sought-after lighting technicians in the industry. No Cecil Willingham, who was now serving as the road manager for Kool & The Gang. No James Tarver, who'd gone with Laura Branigan. No Lamar Williams, who had gained massive success as a promoter. Bill Whitten was the one who had made all of our costumes. He was now enlisted to make clothes for the likes of The Jackson Five, Elton John, and Earth, Wind & Fire. There had been so much brilliance in our camp and it spoke volumes about the success that we had achieved. Would we still be able to realize the same levels without these key people in place?

The biggest blow was James Carmichael. He had been the solid foundation and backbone of our organization from the recording of our first album. I had thought that The Commodores and James Carmichael would be forever, but he had been mistreated and labeled as a traitor when he went to work with Lionel. There was no way that I, however, could feel anything other than gratitude towards Carmichael. We owed him so much, as he had been instrumental in his guidance and just leadership towards us.

The hostility of the group members would prove to be an energy that many could do without, including me. I will say that Lionel's departure was a slippery slope. There were so many aspects that could have been handled with more consideration for the group from all parties. I'm not sure what the public saw, but we all recognized that Lionel's transition was hectic and everyone felt the turbulence.

A gentleman by the name of Dennis Lambert, who was a producer and songwriter, invited us to a meeting to discuss new songs. I attended the first of what was to be many meetings. We were preparing to record another record and I had been creating some new music. I played them some of my songs, one of which revealed an innovative sound with an arrangement that was quite different. There was a sustaining bass sound that caught everyone's attention. I was trying to create something that we had not done before because I knew that the public would wonder if we had what it took to keep the hits coming in the absence of Lionel. "Wow, that is amazing. Are you going to submit that song for the record?" Lambert inquired. The next thing I knew, he invited us back to listen to a song called "Nightshift." As I listened, it was more than familiar. It was the concept that I had played for them. They had taken my concept and created a new song without adding my name to the credit. Walter Orange and Dennis Lambert had stolen my musical concept and arrangement. The spirit of collaboration had been suffocated, at least as far as collaboration with me.

The pattern of turnover continued as Jo-Ann Geffen, who had been our publicist, assumed the role of manager for a brief period in the interim. The pendulum of power swiftly swung again when Shirley King, wife of William King decided that together, they would take over the management role on behalf of the group. Their strategy consisted of a total re-branding inclusive of playing dates at nightclubs. In my opinion, this was not a strategy of ascension, it was a strategy to exit the industry altogether. This train of thought was asinine and small minded in comparison to the heights that we had reached.

The turmoil continued, but we still managed to pull together an album. No matter what occurred, somehow, the music was made. In 1983, we released our tenth studio album, *Commodore 13*. In the beginning, The Commodores were one united group, topping the charts at Motown, now we were divided as three separate acts — Lionel Richie, The Commodores, and Thomas McClary. Divided, we learned many hard lessons about the way that money dictates everything that happens, even our careers and the manifestation of our success. No one cared about the trauma that we had all experienced at the hands of show business. No one cared about the shattered relationships that had been irretrievably broken. No one cared about the tattered family units that were hanging on by a thread and struggling to survive as a result of our giving our entire lives to the business. In retrospect, every consideration, was given to the potential money that could be generated from what I viewed as the remnants of The Commodores brand. In true industry fashion, Motown releases our three records at the same time. My record had the least promotions, the least amount of money provided to support it, and had the least amount of success. I wasn't bitter because I saw it for what it was. I also recognized the series of events as an opportunity for me to grow and not be shut out of the industry, which was an all too familiar occurrence for many. We didn't tour as hard as we had for the previous albums, as the financial backing was not as plentiful.

I resolved to immerse myself further in musical endeavors outside of The Commodores brand to fill in the gaps when we were not working. My spirit was so unsettled at the prospect of how we had all been forced to choose our sides in the sand. I felt like a hostage in my mind in many ways. To the onlooker, it appeared that business was booming for all of us and that we were all growing in many different directions with the onset of new musical opportunities. I wish that had been the truth, but it wasn't. I would later learn that my heart and soul were not in sync.

One afternoon, I was at home and preparing to attend a meeting with James Ingram. I recall being tremendously exhausted but I continued to get ready as I did not want to be late. I turned on the water to prepare for my shower. As I stood under the steady stream, I was fighting to remain awake. The water ran down my face and I was startled by the sound of an audible voice. "It's time for you to come home now." It was startling and I straightened up, raising my head from the water and wiping my eyes dry. I truly thought that I was dreaming, but then I heard the voice a second time. "It's time for you to come home now." Immediately, I knew that it wasn't my wife, as we were now separated and I was in the home alone, and yet I clearly heard someone summoning me. I did everything in my power to ignore what happened, but spiritually, I knew that there was more. I knew that something was calling me to take action. I was just unsure of what that action should be.

I attended the meeting, but something was off. I was out of it. That night, I dreamed vividly, but when I awoke I couldn't recall what I had dreamt. The dreams continued over the course of a few days and each day I awoke with more clarity. I could visualize myself on top of a mountain. There was a multitude of people down in the valley, looking up and speaking in different languages simultaneously. In the dream, I was trying to understand what they were saying. Each time I dreamt, I would wake up and try to make sense of it all. As the dreams came and went, my soul was very unsettled. There was an unexplainable stirring that consumed my being.

One night, I had the same dream with the same people standing in the front, but rather than speaking various languages, they now spoke English and I could clearly hear them saying, "Man, if you could just come home, you could help all of these people out here." After that night, I knew with certainty that this was not a series of random dreams. I was in the midst of a spiritual revelation. My thoughts returned to my days in Eustis as a young boy listening intently in church. My mind raced past thoughts of how much work my parents had done to instill the fear of God in my siblings and me.

For many more nights, I lay awake in bed awaiting a clearer message from God. I knew that he was transforming something in me. As the days past, I heard neither the voice, nor dreamt the dream. I was now on heightened alert. I knew that somehow, someway, something would be revealed to me. I knew that the prayers of my mother were coming full circle. What I did not know is what they would mean for me?

After about a month of heightened spiritual awareness, I fell back into my normal routine of working to pursue new musical endeavors and hanging on to what was left of The Commodores. We were so scattered, it was hard to believe that we had music on the radio and in rotation, painting an entirely different picture of our unison and functionality as a group.

One night, I was at home alone and I began to hear someone speaking. I brushed it off thinking that I had left the radio or television on. I checked the radio, it was off. I checked the TV, it was off as well. I went downstairs to see if I had left anything else on by mistake, but everything was off — everything.

The audible voice spoke again. This time, there was no mistake. It was clearly not my imagination. I called my mom immediately back in Orlando. She was a praying woman and I knew that she could help me to make sense of it all. As soon as she picked up the phone, I began rambling. "Mom, I was in the shower and I heard a voice and it said it was 'time for me to come home' and I got out of the shower and checked to see if it was the radio and it wasn't and the voice spoke again and it said the same thing." I was out of breath by the time I finished. She paused for a brief moment and patiently began to speak.

"Well, there seems to be a calling on your life. You can either heed the calling or you can run," she said. "You've been raised as a Christian and I've been prayin for you for the last thirty years. Maybe now the prayers have caught up with you. You will have to decide what it means for you, but if you want to know what I think, I think the Lord is asking you to come home and serve him."

As I hung up the phone, I could feel my hands shivering. I walked towards the bathroom to wash my face with cool water. I wasn't myself. As I lifted my head from the sink, I could feel the water falling into my eyes. I stood there in silence, staring in the mirror. For the first time, I didn't even recognize myself. The man staring back at me was filled with pain. He had been battered and his ego had been bruised. The man staring back at me in the mirror was uncertain of who he was and in search of answers for his future. Tears began to stream down my face and I allowed the burden of every moment of my life that caused me pain to have its way. The blanket of emotion that covered me was like nothing that I had ever experienced. I couldn't stop weeping. I shed tears of sorrow for the little boy in Eustis, who was subjected to the pain of public ridicule and the piercing discomfort of oranges being thrown at him. I shed tears for the adolescent teen, who worked without ceasing to create a meager opportunity to escape financial hardship. I cried for the fog that now covered the hopes and dreams of success, once touched, but now a distant memory. Standing there in the mirror, I cried out and asked God to search my soul. I needed to hear from him. The longer that I stood there, the more the tears streamed.

Eventually, I gathered my composure and went for my now weekly meeting with James Ingram. He and I were writing songs for his new album. He had signed a new contract with Warner Brothers and they were in the process of negotiating his new deal. He wanted to create the best musical offering, and enlisted me to help him achieve this end. I wanted to honor my commitment, but on my drive into Hollywood, it was as if I was having an out of body experience. Something inside of me had been changed.

When I arrived, I sat in the parking lot, hesitating and almost too weak to go in. I needed to make a decision. I knew James was waiting for me so I left my car and walked into the building. It was then I realized that I needed to get back home to Eustis. As soon as I saw James, without even giving him a proper greeting, I said, "Man, I think I have to go home. I can't finish the project."

He was, of course, perplexed. He had no idea what was going on with me. "What do you mean, you can't finish?" He said. "I have my album that I am doing and I have my contract with Warner and this is going to be a key song as a part of my contract."

"James, I understand, I apologize, but I've got to go."

"I understand," he said. But I could tell by the look on his face that he was beyond disappointed.

Exiting the building, I felt a little lighter than when I had entered. I used the phone in my car and called Joe Jackson. He had solicited me to record and produce songs for a few of his acts.

"Hello," said Jackson.

"Joe, I've got to go home. I can't finish the project. I may be able to come back, but right now, I just have to go home," I informed him. I could tell that he heard the sense of urgency in my voice.

"I tell you what man, this must be really serious. The deposit that I gave you, don't worry, just keep it," said Jackson.

And with that, another layer of the burden had been lifted off of me.

Even still, I was still feeling bad about my marriage, the group, and my life overall. Let's just say that things did not go as planned. I made a stop by the studio and caught a few of the group members there. I told them that I was not leaving the group, but that I needed to take a sabbatical to handle some unfinished business. Not one person seemed to mind. We were all on completely different wavelengths.

That night, I drove back to Encino, packed my bags, and bought myself a ticket to Orlando, thinking that I would return once some of the negativity, confusion, and animosity subsided. The way that life had unfolded was beyond my wildest imagination. How had I gotten here? What was God calling me to do?

The Commodores were now planning for a European tour. Skyler Jett and J.D. Nicholas were brought on to replace Lionel as lead vocalists. These gentleman, plus Walter Orange, Ronald LaPread, and Milan Williams were now ready to hit the road. (2) I later learned that a guitarist by the name of Sheldon

Reynold was brought in as a hired hand. The group rode a tremendous wave of success. The single "Nightshift," became a smash hit and eventually earned the first Grammy for The Commodores. Like a thief in the night, the concept for the song and my dream had been stolen from me. It was painful, but I decided to pick up the pieces of my life. I needed to yield to the calling of my soul, and perhaps things would be different if I followed the vision God had for me instead of the one that I had orchestrated for myself. Only time would tell.

12: *A Revolution, Not A Revival*

The anguish that I felt being in sabbatical as the group received the highest recognition for a song that I knew in my heart had been conceived by me, was insurmountable. My only saving sentiment was grace. I was content in knowing that I was now on a path of obedience heading towards something greater.

Although I still owned a house in Orlando, my sister lived there and maintained it for me. As such, when I arrived in Florida, I decided to purchase an additional house in Orlando and make it my home. I began creating a new life there and as the months passed, I began to settle into the fact that Orlando could become my permanent address. I would commute back and forth between Orlando and Eustis on a daily basis. There was a small church in Eustis that I grew up going to and one day, I decided that instead of simply driving past, I would stop and pitch in wherever I saw a need. My periodic stops became a daily ritual. From working to update and repair the computers, to landscaping, I just wanted to be of service. One particular day while working, I imagined the prospect of establishing a

Christian school in Eustis. I began to conduct some research on the city, only to discover that there was no black owned and operated Christian school. This became an immediate goal for me. It was comforting to know that I could immerse myself in what felt like purpose, as I reprogrammed my mind from the entertainment industry. Thanks to the blessings of Pastor Phillip Scott, who allowed me to pursue my dream.

Every year, around the same time, a very well-known District Overseer by the name of Reverend Leon Dicks would visit and I had always offered for him to stay in my Orlando house. To me, it was the least that I could do to be hospitable, even if I was out on the road with the band. My sister, Leola, received a phone call that he would once again be visiting and she informed him that I had moved home to Florida and would be in the area to meet him.

It was truly a blessed time when he was there and I felt connected to my faith in a way that I had not experienced in quite some time. While he was there, I kept hearing that same voice, that I had heard speak to me while I was living in LA. Now, I recognized that voice as the spirit of discernment and my conscience. I embraced this new heightened level of awareness. It was like nothing that I had ever felt. The more I listened to the voice within, the less I concerned myself with the hurt from the past. That same inner voice told me that there was something so special about the District Overseer's work and his story. I witnessed the magnitude of how he positively impacted so many people in so many ways. For some reason, I felt it was my responsibility to document his story, that it might live on forever, should anything ever happen to him.

Although I am very conscious of other's privacy, I knew that this was God's calling. I contemplated how I would ask the District Overseer's permission to invade his life in this way. Prior to my request, he had never granted that type of access to anyone. He was very private about his work and obedient to his calling. I mustered up the courage to simply explain to him all that had transpired in my life over the last year. I explained to him that this was not my will but God's will.

"God is telling me to document the history of the church," I said in faith. I was shocked at his reaction.

"That's right, I believe that is of God," he said. With those words, he calmed my doubts. Little did he know, he also legitimized everything that I had been feeling. It's not easy to justify taking a sabbatical from a career in the entertainment industry at the height of success, because you heard mysterious voices summon you to return to a place that you had dreamed of leaving. In truth, I was easily misunderstood because I was no longer operating from a normal perspective. It was spiritual. I was overcome with a sea of peace and tranquility that I could not have obtained among the turmoil that engulfed every single one of us while in the group. Although, my mother and father had taught me about guidance from the Holy Spirit, up until then I'd made too much noise to hear anything but my own will for my life. The Overseer's words, reassured me that God was not finished with me.

I began to pool my resources together to direct a documentary on the history of the denomination and to show how the church had evolved. During the days that the Overseer stayed with me, he began to share things that he had not spoken of before. He went into detail about the history of the church, but also began to speak of his plans to move the churches into the next era. There was a predominately white leadership in place. He believed that the banks were taking the mortgage deeds from the black churches and putting them in the names of the national organizations. This would mean that all of the tithes would go to the national office and not back to the church where the money and other offerings had been given. I did not feel it was right. This would explain the financial deficit that was so rampant in all of the black churches. I was still a radical for equality when it came to race relations and this was another opportunity to fight injustice. As I was talking to the Overseer, he said, "I am not going to turn my church over to them because I don't think it is right either. We paid for our church and it is a historic building."

From that time spent with him, I was led to begin a process of interviewing all of the clergy that I could find that were still alive who could speak about this. I started traveling up and down the east coast conducting interviews. On this mission, I went to the Carolinas, Northern Florida, New York, and Alabama. I interviewed all of the senior staff of the churches and everyone else that I could find. They were all very old, except for the District Overseer who was in his late fifties. As soon as I had collected all of the interviews and testimonials that I needed to finalize the documentary, the District Overseer died abruptly. His death seemed to have sparked a domino effect, as one by one, all of the people who were in the video started to pass away. Most of the leaders featured were very seasoned, but their passing was not something that

I had expected. I had given this project my all, as I knew that God had requested me to complete it. With the passing of so many of the leaders who were in the video, it became highly sought after. Everyone wanted to bear witness to the words and insight from the leaders who appeared in the film. God spoke to my heart and told me to sell copies of the film and donate the proceeds back to the church. It blew my mind. I did exactly as I was asked.

During this time, I was still developing my idea for a school and raising money for the church. I was on fire and looking so forward to the path ahead. I had left the past in the past and I was now living my life for God. To be honest, I was having the time of my life. Although forever in my heart, it felt like the music business was a distant memory.

I poured my heart and soul into getting the Christian school up and running. I met with the City Manager, a man by the name of Michael Stearsman to discuss my intentions.

"Man, we couldn't believe that you had come back to Eustis. The rumor mill said that you were actually living here and I can't believe that you are actually sitting in this office. What can I do for you?"

"I want to give something back to the community that has given so much to me," I proclaimed.

"That sounds good, what are you thinking?"

I went on to explain my idea for a Christian school and the location that I had my eyes on. After my response, he slouched in his chair and put his head on the desk and stayed there for thirty seconds. "Man are you ok?" I asked. When he lifted his head, tears appeared to be streaming down his face.

"Thomas, that address can't be zoned for a school, but I'll tell you what — if you just go ahead and pursue it, every time you need to have something done, we won't put a building permit sign up. I will just give you a verbal." At the time, I didn't understand the magnitude of what I was requesting. I thought that the hardest part of what I was attempting to do would be organizing the school itself. I found myself right back in the middle of a political battle. It was familiar territory and I wasn't about to back down. It's amazing how life brings you full circle. Who would have ever believed that I would be right back in my hometown of Eustis, Florida to fight for justice.

It turned out that the NAACP had been trying to get a commercial building in that same zone for years, but to no avail. For whatever reason, there was a hidden agenda. What I did know was that I received the unofficial green light to forge ahead. I was going to ensure that this school happened come hell or high water. As I began the process in obtaining the permits, road blocks began to fall away just as the manager had promised. I would eventually move toward breaking ground.

T.H. Poole, who was the young man that had recruited me to be the consultant for the NAACP Image Awards, learned about what I was trying to accomplish. He called me to discuss the matter. "Man, how did you get this permit? We have been marching and trying to get re-zoning for that land that you are building on for years, but we could not get it."

"Man, only God," I replied.

"I understand that God did it, but who did he use to get it done?" He inquired.

"The city manager," I said. "Just go talk to him."

It was beginning to be a very interesting and exciting time for me. Of course, people would keep me in the know with bits and pieces of what was happening within the group. I'd be lying if I said that it didn't concern me, when I would learn that things were not going well. It hurt me to know that the initial vision that we created and worked so hard to realize was at times awry. Even so, after all of the years of absence, the most shocking and disappointing news I received was during a phone call from Ronald LaPread. He was distraught because the members had voted him out of the band. During our conversation, he spoke of how he and JD Nicholas had never gotten along. JD was from London and had been slated as the replacement for Lionel. I knew from our previous conversations that Ronald never thought that he was all that talented. He felt that JD was extremely demanding and had not earned enough stripes within the group to conduct himself in that manner. Ronald also felt that William King's mission to carry out his Hitler antics had worsened to the point of no return. Ronald said that King had accused him of being caught with drugs while he was out of the country and that he had been stopped by an agent. Ronald stated that none of this had ever happened. "If I had gotten stopped by an agent, don't you think it would have been national news? Come on man, I have never even done drugs," he said with conviction. In confidence, Ronald expressed to me that he felt that there was a conspiracy to vote him out of the group, now that they had been successful.

After that conversation, Ronald and I began to rekindle our friendship. We spoke in great detail of a reunion. It was 1986 and in my mind, there had been enough water under the bridge and although music with the group was no longer my priority, the prospect of a reunion also made me feel that what we once had could be possible again. Maybe now, everyone had grown up more and could treat one another with the love and respect that we began our journey together with. With nothing decided and no plans made, however, Ronald made the decision to move to New Zealand with his wife. She had business ventures there and he supported her.

I thought back over the years that I had been away from the band. In 1983, Lionel had released a song entitled, "All Night Long" and it had taken off like wildfire. His success was massive and I was so proud of him, as was Ronald. In 1984, a well-known promoter had extended a very lucrative offer for a reunion of The Commodores, but nothing had ever come of it. Although I didn't speak to Lionel on a regular basis, I knew that our friendship would be right where we left it. He had maintained that he would always be a Commodore. I had even heard him do interviews stating that he would welcome the prospect of a reunion. Shortly after 1985, a song titled "We Are the World" debuted. The song featured a host of A list celebrities including, Lionel and Michael Jackson and both were credited as writers. As far as I was concerned, it solidified Lionel's legacy as both a star and a humanitarian. In my mind, "We Are the World" also solidified the fact that Lionel had very little interest in bringing The Commodores into the fold of his budding new career as a solo artist. Although I never spoke of it, I resented the fact that he had not at least extended an invite for us to participate. There was an assembled chorus for the song. We fit the bill in every way to have participated, in my opinion. How could he have such a monumental role and not think to include the guys who were instrumental in his journey? He knew firsthand what we were up against in trying to continue to grow The Commodores brand and that opportunities like that were critical for all of us. I began to believe in my heart, that Lionel wished to distance himself from the group, even though his words spoke to the contrary. We hang on to the whispers of words, when the echos of actions speak loud and clear. Lionel was living his dreams out loud and I was proud to witness it, but I had wished that the pact that was made to maintain a sense of commitment to us had been honored.

It was in 1988 that I contemplated reaching out to Lionel to talk with him about the prospect of a reunion, but never quite got around to it. Mysteriously, I received a call from Brenda Richie, Lionel's wife, who wished to invite me to Lionel's birthday party. I had been so spiritually evolved, I wasn't sure if it would be a good choice for me to attend. The industry was a different beast of its own. I consulted with my mom as I always did and simply asked, "Can I go back out there? I mean, I'm a Christian now."

"Are you kidding me?" She exclaimed. "You have more reason to go back out there now than you ever had before. Your light is what you now need to let shine. They need to hear your testimony. Who knows? You could reach more people now because you have more of a reason to spread the gospel in a way, that perhaps, someone that has not had your background would not be able to do."

That was the reassurance that I needed. I became excited at the prospect of seeing everyone again. I had missed my dear friends Lionel and Brenda. Unlike all of the other trips to LA to visit my daughter, I knew that this one would be different.

When the limo driver arrived to pick me up from LAX, she got out and greeted me as she opened the door. "There is champagne, water, juice, and of course, plenty of libations for you to enjoy," she said. I was still very uncertain if this was the right choice. I didn't really know what to expect and had not been subjected to much temptation with my now simplified life and routine. Even though I had never been a big proponent of any of those things, something about my salvation made me feel uncomfortable in environments where anything that was not pure would be. I remained in the car until we arrived at Lionel's home.

Being at the party was a most pleasant surprise. It was such a beautiful time with nothing but good vibes in the atmosphere. I soon realized that I was the only Commodore in attendance. Regardless, Lionel had so much support from the industry. Tom Joyner, Quincy Jones, Magic Johnson, and so many of the friends that I had made while living in LA were there. It was star studded to say the least. During this same time, the media had gotten ahold of a story that Lionel had been beaten up by his wife for some reason. It shocked me a little. I had known them so well and violence was not a part of their marriage in any way. As the party started to settle, Lionel invited a group of his closest friends to come up to a private room. From out of nowhere, I heard a voice speak, "Lionel, come on man, what is this that we are reading in the media?"

"Nah man, you know I'm not going to let a lady beat me up. Come on man," he said. The room filled with laughter. It was truly good for the soul. As he was telling the story, Brenda came into the room, but Lionel's back was turned towards the door. We began motioning and trying to tell him to change the subject, vying for him to be quiet. Every husband knows that the wife is the real boss and we would have never done anything to disrespect their home. In that moment, we were just a couple of guys hanging out. It felt like old times. Everyone noticed that I wasn't drinking or smoking or engaging in anything that I felt would not be pleasing to God. One of the gentlemen there inquired, "What's up man? You good?"

"God is good," was my response.

"T-Mac, what's really going on?" Someone else asked. This single moment allowed me an opportunity to share my testimony. I began telling them a story of how I was in Vancouver, Canada and this church had never experienced the manifestation of the Holy Spirit. When I started working with the praise team and the band in the rehearsal, the manifestation of God came down and people began to praise Him and weep. The worship leader was a young Jewish man who had converted to Christianity. He confided in me that his family had abandoned him and not spoken to him in over nineteen years due to his decision to serve a different religion. He asked a favor of me. He wanted me to agree to play at a friend's house for him during a small get together. He knew that his friends would invite his sisters and brothers to the house and he hoped to sneak in the back door and reconnect with them.

On the night of the gathering, I agreed to bring my acoustic guitar. Just as he had thought, the friend invited his sisters and brothers and an additional twenty-five other people. I was literally in their living room singing old songs from The Commodores. I sang "Three Time a Lady," "Brick House," and many more. All of a sudden, the Holy Spirit led me to play "Amazing Grace." As I began to play, the power of God came in the room in such a mighty way. The gentleman who had invited me (the abandoned son) came out of the back room in the midst of the song, and his family who had not seen or interacted with him, began hugging him and asking for forgiveness. It was a surreal moment for me.

The men in the room were sitting on the edge of their seats as I told the story. That moment in Canada allowed me to be a witness of God's greatness and the moments as I retold the story afforded me another opportunity to do the same thing, only now with those whose opinions held weight in my heart. Even Lionel said, "Wow."

That day, Lionel and I had time to reflect upon our lives and careers and the jealousies that often caused the divides in the group. Legally, we were still members of The Commodores. I felt blessed to spend time with Brenda and Lionel together, as it reinforced the fact that we would always be friends. We had seen a lot of good days and bad days together, but it was comforting to know that they were still married and working every day to keep it all together.

After leaving the party and traveling back to Orlando, I discovered that it was still in my heart to orchestrate a reunion. It made me sad that more of the guys hadn't attended the party. We should have all been there to experience the same nostalgia.

Unfortunately, I continued to hear that the guys in the band were experiencing difficult times in terms of leadership. Things became less amicable when in 1989 Milan Williams was out voted regarding an offer to perform in South Africa. (1) Milan disagreed with the other members' choice to accept the offer. The racial climate in that area wasn't something Milan could ignore. The violent and oppressive Apartheid was ongoing in South Africa and Milan felt like their presence would further fuel the fire or worse, be taken as indifference to the brutal discrimination taking place. (2) The group members felt that the performance was more important that his train of thought. Not only was he out voted on the decision to do the South Africa date, but they also threatened to vote him out of the group. Taking matters into his own hands, Milan went to the press hoping the outside pressure would change the opinion of the rest of the band members. This worked and the show was cancelled, but it also cemented their move to vote him out of the group.

Milan and I had been roommates in college and roommates on the road until we began getting separate rooms. I will be the first to admit that there were times that he was out in left field, but he was still the guy who wrote our first hit, "Machine Gun." He was still the guy that would be there for you when the rubber met the road. Milan was as smart as a whip and I could not understand how something like this could happen. Then again, similar turmoil had pushed both Lionel and me away. I insisted on being there for him as this was a very trying time, and we united our friendship. He would often come to Orlando as he was a big golfer and during our time together, he persuaded me to love the game as well. It became a means for socializing and staying in touch and I enjoyed every minute of it.

The melodies in my heart never left, I just desired to play new tunes. I began to play with the church band and it eased my mind and my heart. I found the days after embarking upon my sabbatical from The Commodores to be passing with ease. Days turned into weeks and weeks turned into months. Before I knew it, I had been playing with the church band for five years. My contentment lasted longer than I expected, but now I felt the urge to impact an even larger group of people with Christian music. It was now 1991 and I set my sights on enlarging my territory and increasing my audience. I made the decision to leave my position as band leader at my church in Eustis and to look for another church where I could make a difference. I knew I was leaving the now completed school and my role as a volunteer in good hands.

I could feel my relationship with God deepening when I received, what I referred to as, my second spiritual assignment. While in prayer, God told me that I would meet a person who would be very instrumental in developing the power in my worship. I would learn from this person how to guide others through powerful worship with the gift of song. This was very similar to the story of Elijah and Elisha in the Bible. Elisha caught the spirit of Elijah by following him and being a part of his ministry.

I felt like I was moved to attend a worship seminar that I had heard a great deal about. I was somewhat hesitant because the word around town was that the minister of service was hard to work with. I decided to go anyway because I had worked with my fair share of personalities and I knew more than anyone that it was best if I made my own decision about a person.

When I arrived at the church, I sat in my car briefly and then walked towards the entrance. When I got into the building, I immediately decided to leave. It just didn't feel right. As I unlocked my car, the spirit said to me, "Go back. This is the man you are to serve to catch the spirit of music," but I denied the spirit, got in my car, and put it in reverse. Very strongly the spirit, that I now recognized as my conscience said, "If you leave, you will miss God." I pulled back into the parking space reluctantly and re-entered the church. I sat in the back and waited to speak with the minister. After the service had ended, he approached me and introduced himself as, Minister Jerry Quarterman. He then professed, "God sent you to give me a message."

I was blown away. "Uh…yeah. Uh…I…I am supposed to serve you through music. I am going to catch the spirit of music from the mantle that is upon your life."

"God had told me that someone would come, but I didn't know who it would be," he said in astonishment.

The church that I had visited was in Leesburg and in order for me to work under the minister's tutelage, I would now have to travel there daily from Orlando. For five years straight, I made the trek from Orlando to the church in Leesburg and it was an incredible experience. The pastor would host revivals and he would go into intense meetings in small towns and small churches and country churches and big churches. I was really engrossed in music, but only for the purpose of lifting God higher. My music, guitar, spirit, and soul were now in sync. There were times when I would play and people would say that the sound of the guitar was confirmation of my healing. There were times when the music would get to a zone and in a place, that was so spirit filled, that I would shake and rock just to maintain my composure. I was whole. God was so prevalent that we would have worship services with no speakers and no preaching. It became such a powerful experience that the minister would set aside one day a week just for worship. I now knew that my ability to create music in this space was even more powerful than ever before. The thought of creating a Christian album was ever present.

Because I had never been the lead singer in The Commodores, I had the advantage of not being a victim of fame. I would introduce myself and use only my first and middle name, so that they would not tie in McClary with the Commodores. I didn't want anyone to see anything except God when they looked at me. It was not the time to be using music as a mechanism for gaining advantages or self-promotion.

During those five years at the church in Leesburg, my life and the lives of my former bandmates took many twists and turns, both positive and negative. In 1993, the melodies became somber as I learned that Lionel's marriage to Brenda, was not salvageable. They remained friends, but my heart went out to both of them and I offered each of them my support.

As the years passed, the tides would turn even further and the music became more melancholy as we would experience unforeseen changes that would prove to affect us all forever. We received news that Milan was taken ill. My heart broke to learn that he had been diagnosed with terminal cancer. He went into battle and Ronald LaPread and I were the only members of The Commodores that visited him during his illness. Lionel kept in touch, calling constantly to see if there was anything he could do and in truth, he did many special deeds along the way. Lionel and I made a pact to reestablish our friendship. We agreed to never ever allow anything to come between us as friends. The blessing is that we are still friends today.

Over the years I had returned to LA consistently to visit my daughter, Jazmyne. I did everything in my power to ensure that our relationship remained intact and that she knew that she would never be without her father's love, regardless of where I lived.

Upon returning from one trip in particular, I recall checking the mailbox, and seeing a letter from an attorney by the name of Beryl Thompson. It was peculiar. I wondered who was trying to sue me. I knew that I would need to get back in touch with the attorney at some point to determine what it was regarding, but it would not be on that day. I tossed the letter on my kitchen counter and quite frankly, completely forgot about it.

The time seemed to pass by so quickly. One of my main goals was to return to enjoying the simple things in life. As a celebrity, life can move so fast that you forget to take time to hear the birds sing and enjoy the feeling of the wind blowing against your face. I had returned to a mental space where simplicity was beautiful and I took every moment possible to enjoy it.

I continued on my mission of creating a new life with new success. With a lot of prayer and deep internal thought, I decided to begin a musical career in a new genre. I knew it would take time and patience as the reception of music in the Christian world was very different from the reception of music in the secular world, but I also knew that I had what it took to be successful because I had done it before.

After returning from another trip to visit Jazmyne, I checked the mailbox as I always did. I continued with my same ritual of tossing away all of the dated circulars that I never had time to read. This time, as I prepared to throw away some of the older mail, I noticed the envelope from Attorney Thompson, that I had not opened, peeking out from the bunch. It startled me because of how much time had passed by. I immediately set the other parcels down and opened the letter. As I began to read, I realized that the letter was not from anyone who wanted to sue me. It was an invitation for me to come and speak to a youth group. Feeling bad, I picked up the phone and called the number provided. There was no answer, but that wasn't surprising as it was late in the afternoon on Friday. I left a message, hoping I'd hear back. On Monday morning, the phone rang and it was a number that I didn't recognize.

"Hello, this is the McClary residence."

"This is Attorney Beryl Thompson, returning your call."

"How dare you take two days to respond to my call," I exclaimed.

"It took you almost a year to respond to my letter," she responded. In unison, we started to laugh hysterically. It turned out that attorney Beryl Thompson was a lady with an amazing sense of humor.

"You can make it up if you come to an event that I am hosting this Tuesday. I will be speaking to some prisoners and it would be great for you to join me." I agreed to attend in hopes that I could even the score.

When I arrived, I realized I didn't know what Attorney Thompson looked like. I wanted to introduce myself and inform her that I was there to be of support, but how would I find her. As soon as I entered the room in which the event was being hosted, I look at the podium and I saw that there was only one lady present in a space filled with inmates. She was absolutely striking and I thought to myself, "Mhh, that's Beryl."

At the podium, she began speaking. "This person that I am about to introduce, some of you guys may know him. I don't really know him, know him. I know of his music, but I think that you all may recognize him." The crowd loved her charisma and I'll admit, I too was intrigued. As I walked towards the podium to address the audience, I stopped and shook her hand. She was extremely professional and even more radiant up close.

The event was meant to inspire the inmates. Everything turned out to be a success and afterwards, I asked if it would be ok if I walked her to her car to ensure that she got there safely. She accepted and as we walked to the parking lot we laughed and talked. It was almost as if I already knew her. She was smart, well educated, and very passionate about making a difference and fighting inequality. We seemed to have quite a bit in common. Our parking lot conversation lasted for over three hours. While there with her, I found a happy place that I hadn't felt in a long time. I didn't want it to end. I informed her that I would be catching a flight out to LA to visit my daughter. She volunteered to give me a ride to the airport so that I wouldn't have to park my car there. I'm not sure if she knew it or not, but I was delighted as it gave me the opportunity to spend more time with her. At the airport, we said our goodbyes and even though I was allowing her to drive away, I knew that I could not allow her to escape my life. When I returned from my trip, we continued with our courtship and ninety days later on April 10, 1994, we were married. Beryl Thompson was now Beryl McClary and our love continued to blossom and grow.

I was no longer concerned at all about what was happening in the music business. I was building the life that I had always dreamed of. The melodies were now filled with a different tempo and different sentiments from my heart. Although my ears were still tuned in, my goals were not attached to any specific levels of success because the definition had evolved. Around this same time, there was a resurgence of music from the 1970's and the world was infatuated with songs from that era. Whenever I would go to perform, I found myself singing our song, "Jesus is Love."

My mother, who had been praying for so many years for me, was overjoyed that I was happily settled and impacting lives. Lives were being changed as God was using me. The visions and recurring dreams now all made sense and I was witnessing the manifestation of it all. My father had passed away a few years prior and I found myself trying to convince my mother to not live in her home alone. Eventually, she moved into our home as we had enough space for her to have her own quarters. I was at peace.

Beryl and I continued to build our family in love. She gave her heart and soul to me and became the keeper of mine. Over the years, Beryl gifted me with five children and to watch the birth of each of them has been among my greatest joys. As the years passed, I found myself less immersed in the drama with the group and more immersed in taking my babies to piano lessons, lacrosse lessons, track, swimming lessons, soccer games, and everything else that we could sign them up for.

Beryl never abandoned her role as a driven attorney. I still wonder how she has been able to do it all over the years. Beryl was the first black female attorney to practice in Lake County, Florida, an area that was admittedly one of the most racist counties in the state.

She was so good at what she did and she was equally as successful as a loving mother. When I met Beryl, she had decided to represent a community that was located near a hospital. The hospital wanted to expand, but they did not want to compensate the residents of the community with equitable prices. Most of the residents were black and this was a grave injustice. The community could not afford adequate representation and so Beryl took the case pro bono. I was amazed that an African American female could stand there and be smart enough and tough enough to give it to the battery of lawyers that represented the city and the hospital. She won the case and though I knew it was possible and I had every faith in her, it was still incredible to witness.

Beryl was tough as an attorney, but as a mother, she was very tender and sweet. Not only did she continue to raise our children and practice law, but she also continued her advocacy work through outreach in the community. Doc Rivers, a legendary coach for the National Basketball Association (NBA) had started a fundraiser for a nonprofit called Shepherd's Hope. Their work supplemented income for senior citizens who had medical needs, but not liquid funding to cover lifesaving operations. It was an amazing organization. Prior to us getting involved, we strategized on how we could be more of service. I convinced the leadership that they could raise a lot more money if music was a part of the fundraising effort. I began performing at their events. The headline would read The Commodores Founder, Thomas McClary. For fourteen years, I performed and helped them to raise money to further promote the vision and mission. We also got involved with Celebs for Kids, an organization that raises money for children with lupus and arthritis. I never realized how severe of a problem this was for the children. We also joined efforts with the YMCA, raising money for the youth department. Between the church and community, our family was immersed in mission work to make a difference. We had discovered the key to happiness, it was love. Beryl also knew that music held a key to a compartment in my heart that could not easily be opened. She knew how to open that space and she encouraged me to never allow the music to die.

In between raising our children and staying busy with the church, I found the inspiration to create. I had done it my way. This time, I would create music God's way.

Even though I was distant from the members of The Commodores, I held the relationships that I was able to salvage in high esteem. It was because of my days on the course with Milan, that golf was my new pastime of choice. It brought a smile to my face every time I thought of all of the jokes that we had laughed hysterically at on the green. It was our haven for old memories and the cultivation of new ones. Truthfully, he gave me a gift that kept my mind at ease on so many occasions. I could never repay Milan for introducing me to the sport. I could hear his voice and those of the buddies that often joined us, even when I played alone.

On July 9, 2006 Milan departed this life at a hospital in Houston. Ronald and myself were right there with him. We wanted so much for him to know that we cared. He was the first member of The Commodores to pass away and my heart was broken. His funeral service was held in his hometown in

Mississippi and it was the first time that all of the guys were in the same place at the same time.

Lionel spoke words of encouragement during the service. I provided a prayer and Ronald LaPread also spoke, but I did not bear witness to any genuine condolences from the other guys. And while I can't say what is in someone else's heart, it seemed to me that the same undertones of disdain from the past remained. I didn't care. I only wanted to honor Milan's memory and legacy.

Milan Williams was down to earth, charismatic, and community oriented. In the beginning, Milan was the one who taught me a few guitar chords, as my knowledge came from the ukulele. To be quite honest, he was brilliant technically. Music theory showed him in a very different light than what the world ever witnessed on stage. When it came down to the group and the one for all, all for one mentality, Milan was always down for the group. He expressed it in so many ways. He was always willing to give an honest opinion, which was very commendable.

Milan was an accomplished keyboardist and he always played live. He was one of the players whose sound could be heard and felt throughout our music and will live on forever. And although quiet, his presence will never be forgotten. Milan's legacy will forever be ingrained into the fiber and culture of American music. He is a legend whose contributions to our music are priceless. Milan Williams will forever be a member of The Commodores in spirit and in truth. May he forever rest in paradise.

After Milan's passing, there was a sad cloud cast over the group. Whether we exchanged words or not, we all knew in our hearts that The Commodores group that we have built and loved would never be the same; we would never reunite as one.

Milan's death stirred my emotions. I was moved to action to complete the work that God had started in me. I finished the music that had overtaken my soul and in 2008, I recorded my first Christian rock album, *A Revolution Not a Revival*.

13: *Trial, Tribulations, and Triumphs*

I recall one evening sharing with Beryl some of the unkind words that I had been told were spoken about me by the other group members. "You have such hope," she said lovingly. I guess having been the one who assembled the group always made me feel that I had a certain level of responsibility to keep us together. I knew what was possible. I also knew that there had to be someone who was willing to put their pride aside for the greater good of the group and everyone's hearts and souls.

"Beryl, I have always felt like this was my assignment," I said and I could see the love in her eyes.

As I sat and talked with her that evening, it occurred to me that I had internalized so much. Beryl has the most unique ability to keep things light on the surface, but simultaneously really get to the matter of the heart. She has always found a way to help me see the silver lining. It is how she is wired and even in sad times, she is the guiding light of our family. I can't recall a single time that she was not there to be a pillar of strength and security. "It's all a part of God's plan," she would say, quoting her favorite phrase.

Our love story was definitely one for the books. Beryl loved me for who I was and I loved her for who she was. It wasn't something that I announced to the world, but when I met Beryl, I was actually engaged to someone else. That relationship was more so out of pressure. I was not in love. I felt that because I was getting older and time was ticking by, that I needed to settle myself after my first marriage failed.

My union to Beryl was perfectly imperfect and together our goal became to create legacy at all costs. We wanted to ensure that we were a unit from which to raise happy, healthy children who would carry our names further than we ever could.

Prior to being married to Beryl, I had one daughter, Jazmyne, from my previous wife, Linda. Jazmyne was a strong child who was very tender, loving and accommodating. Jazmyne meant the world to me as I watched her continuous display of thoughtfulness. Even though we lived in different cities, she always sent me cards and we spoke on the phone and visited each other as much and as often as we could. She was my first love.

The ink on Beryl and my marriage license had not yet dried when I found myself in a fight to gain custody of a daughter that I had fathered outside of a relationship. It became my mission to give all that I could to ensure that my beloved Julianne or Ashley, which was her nickname, had the best life possible. I knew that with Beryl's support, I could do an amazing job raising her and I wanted desperately for this to happen. As one could imagine, this was a test for our relationship, but Beryl showed that she was the true keeper of my heart. I knew how much Beryl loved me when she flew out to LA to accompany me during the court hearings. She, along with my sister, Leola, was right by my side when the courts determined that the most stable place for Ashley was with me.

With love in her heart, Beryl agreed immediately to raise Ashley as if she was her own. This was a true testament of Beryl's character. After careful evaluation of the school rankings in our home town, Beryl determined that she wanted Ashley to attend private school. She wanted the best for her and I no longer worried about how she would be raised. I knew with certainty that she was in good hands. Our biological children never even knew that Ashley was not Beryl's biological child until our youngest was in high school. This speaks volumes about Beryl as a mother. Together, Beryl and I continued to grow our brood.

Ryan McClary was our first child together and my first son. While at the hospital for his birth, I was so anxious that I could have jumped out of my shoes. Beryl, was as cool as a fan and maintained a great sense of humor during the entire delivery process. I was sweating more than she was and I began to pace the hospital hallways in angst. While doing so, I remembered that my guitar was out in the car. I needed it. When I came back, I began to play the sweetest melodies that flowed freely from my heart for Beryl and for Ryan, who had not yet arrived. This was not only soothing to them, but it also calmed me. I played old songs from The Commodores and songs of worship. I was giving them a full concert. The hospital employees began to stop by the room and even some of the patients. They would ask me to stop by their rooms to play and I was honored.

When Ryan was born, he had the most distinct facial expression. We knew that he would be special. "This can't be my baby," Beryl exclaimed. She was so proud to be a mother.

We felt so blessed when eleven months later, we found ourselves welcoming a second son, who we named Brandon McClary. He absolutely loved to eat and was a very sweet child growing up.

Ashley was an amazing big sister and she took her role very seriously. She would rock them to sleep and feed them. I don't think she realized what a tremendous help she was to Beryl and me.

Eleven months after Brandon's birth, our third son, Gabriel McClary was born. We knew immediately that he was as sharp as a tack.

Nurturing our children seemed to be second nature for both of us. Ryan had come into the world hearing the sound of my guitar and it became a tradition from then on for each of our children to enter the same way. It also came about that I was the night shift nurse for all of our children. The only help that we hired was a maid, who we desperately needed by this time as we had become a household of six.

Admittedly, I was now dealing with some unresolved feelings about the group. I had been able to move forward and leave it all behind me for a while, but suppressing such a big part of my life couldn't work forever, and as predicted things eventually resurfaced. The Commodores had been such an intricate part of my identify. God was blessing me with the desires of my heart through family, life, health, and strength, but I needed to pick up the pieces of me that were broken.

A dear friend of Beryl's by the name of Camille was a prayer warrior. She and Beryl had completed mission trips together, prior to us getting married. She would often come by the house and the three of us would pray together. We asked God for everything from peace of mind to restoration of anything that had been lost. We asked God to sustain our family and to help us be servants and position us to help others.

As a father of five, our financial posture was no laughing matter. It was not easy, but God continued to support us. I felt that He was rewarding me for my faithfulness to Him. There was a resurgence of the music that I had done with The Commodores, that resulted in a resurgence of the royalties. Music that I had already produced many years prior, would carry me through times when I did not have a traditional job. Beryl continued to work as an attorney and was truly at the height of her career. Looking back, I really can't understand her strength. All I know is that because God was with her, she could not have failed. She was a powerhouse at home and in the courtroom. There were times that I feared for her life as she prosecuted some criminal cases, but she was never one to back down from an opportunity to fight for injustice. Even in the midst of her career, we always made time for our children and our marriage.

One day, I woke up and realized that I had a house full of kids. It was almost as if it happened overnight. I jokingly said, "Who are all of these kids that I am feeding?"

Beryl laughed and said, "I'm pregnant!"

"You're pregnant again?"

We went to the doctor and discovered that we were having not one, but two babies. I fainted. I was still in disbelief that we were having any more children at all, never mind twins. The McClary's were filling up the house that had once been luxuriously spacious. We were filled to capacity.

My mom eventually decided to move in with my sister, Leola as our family continued to grow. She had taken ill and was fighting for her life. After she found out that Beryl was pregnant with twins, she was inspired to fight even harder. It was her dream to see them born. My sister Willadean had been a twin, but Virgadean, her sister, passed away shortly after birth.

We had heard that twins skip a generation, and so had no idea that we would receive the gift of twins amongst our children. We were blessed. Beryl continued to practice law right up until she went in for delivery.

On December 28, 1999, Maya and Mariah were born. The doctor said that Maya pushed Mariah out of the way to come through the birth canal first. Mariah then made her entrance. As I began to examine the personalities of the children, I realized that God had truly blessed us. I was in amazement because I knew that our legacy would live on through them.

My mother passed away shortly after their birth, having fulfilled her wish to meet them. I knew that they would be blessed in life as my mother had wished blessings upon them before she departed this life. I will never forget how far I have gotten in life on her prayers. She taught me to walk in God's illuminated path and for me to be steadfast and responsible. I can never repay my mother for the love and kindness she gave me, but I hold her close in my heart and know that I did as much for her as humanly possible all of the days that she was living. Her life and her legacy live on, through me and my children. She was the epitome of a woman.

The passing of my mother also made me realize how blessed my children were to have their mother and it made me value Beryl's contributions to our children even more than I already had. I was very grateful we were close and that we had each other.

My wife has always been my best friend and even more so after my mother's passing. My children were my best friends also. I don't think that my family ever really knew how much I leaned and depended on them. Their presence kept me on so many occasions. Jazmyne, had assumed the role of being the oldest of all of the children, which also meant that she was a mentor and safe haven for them. Even though Jazmyne was in LA, all of the children were all extremely close. They communicated regularly and still do to this day. The way that they support each other gives me unexplainable joy. As a father, I tried to ensure that they all felt loved equally. I made it a point that if I did something for one, I would do it for all. This maintained cohesiveness amongst them. Wherever Beryl and I went, all of the children went. Our family slogan was, "All or nothing."

I am certain that people wonder how Beryl and I kept it all together, but our relationship has been rooted in love and laughter. We have always been able to resolve everything. Laughter has often served as the safety net for our lives and we promised each other that no matter what happened, we would always find a way to laugh, even on our most trying days.

I feel so blessed to watch the evolution of what will be the legacy of Beryl and me. Our children have taught me so much about life and the possibilities for potential.

My oldest son Ryan has a lot of my personality. He is very creative musically and has taught me a great deal about expanding my range. At age three, he was making beats with eating utensils on the kitchen table. After enrolling all of the children in piano lessons, Ryan's ability soared. We eventually purchased him a set of drums and he was intrigued. He was making hip hop beats on his own by age five. Ryan went on to attend Berkeley school of music and became a prolific musical producer. I am so honored to call him my son.

Our second son, Brandon is very business oriented like Beryl. He is and has always been very honest. He embarked upon an educational journey to study International Business at Howard University in Washington, DC. He is very social and knows how to work a room. It would not surprise me to see him endeavor politically in the future.

Gabriel, is academically brilliant. He loves to read and is also an athlete with a passion for helping those in need. He went on a mission trip to South Africa, which stemmed from the experiences that he had as a young child.

When the children were younger, we went on a mission trip to Honduras. Beryl had a friend who was a lawyer who felt that he had been called to start a church there. It was tough to gather all of the children, but he convinced Beryl that it was imperative for her to come in support of this initiative. It was very interesting to watch our children be so helpful and loving to the children there.

As we were headed into the villages from the airport, we noticed small children playing just off the road. We asked the cab driver to stop before reaching our housing. We observed that some families didn't have housing, food, or clothing. The rainy season had just started and those who did have shelter had houses made from mud. We also found out during this time, that the village that we were staying in, had been abandoned by all of the men. One man violently disfigured the face of his wife with a machete so that she would not be desirable to other men. She was there with a two-week-old baby and three other small children. It was sad to witness, but we were told that should her husband return, he would be killed for the horrendous acts that he had committed.

Our children got out of the car and went over to the small children. In no time at all, they were able to make the local kids laugh. The Honduran families asked us to come into their homes and we were touched by their hospitality. Our children were all raised as Christians and all taught to pray. They knew the scriptures and offered prayer for the families in the village. We were proud to see their exercise of their Christianity and their love for the underprivileged.

When Gabriel graduated from high school, all of the parents came up to us to thank us for allowing him to mentor their kids. At Boston College, where he attended, they did a special on him for serving as a mentor. We didn't know of Gabriel's musical ability until he was much older. He became an incredible jazz pianist. We were told that he would use the piano as bait to attract the students on campus and then he would talk to them and mentor as he saw fit.

The twins demonstrated tremendous athletic ability. They also do a great deal of motivational speaking and they are amazing at it. It is a skill that they received from their mother.

The music that had once lived in my heart and through The Commodores, was given new life through my family. Music is and will always be a part of who the McClarys are. During family gatherings, all of the McClary's and all of the Thompsons (Beryl's family) would get together and there would be a lot of eating, singing, and playing instruments. This fulfilled the parts of me that yearned to play, create, and live in the music.

Over the years, Beryl has been so patient and kind to me. Admittedly, it is not easy to love someone who follows their passion and purpose. I can't say that there will ever be a part of me that doesn't want to play music in the same manner that I did with The Commodores. So many search aimlessly through life to discover their reason for their existence. I had discovered mine and it was hard to let it go. That is why Beryl and I have shared a love that lasted all of these years. She has always supported me in my journey. I am forever grateful to her for that. She is the embodiment of my heart and soul.

By 2007, I had put the thought of a reunion behind me. I remained focused on family, but just when you turn your back, your past has a funny way of dialing your number. That same year, I received a call from the group requesting that I play a couple gigs with them. I was elated and I agreed to do so. The reaction from the audience was amazing. The crew that worked with the group made comments like, "It sure would be great to have you out here all the time," and "There is a night and day difference when you are playing." These comments had me feeling torn. I desired to be back on the road, playing music in the same manner that had once catapulted us to success, but on the other hand, I knew that it would be an uphill battle to be amongst a group of guys who were no longer favorable to me.

I still had love for The Commodores in my heart. I had written and co-produced over half of the group's music. It hurt my heart to hear later on that their shows were not getting good reception and that ticket sales were down. To witness our name being defamed was disheartening.

In 2008, I reached out to The Commodore's manager. During our conversation, I got the impression that he too was frustrated. He stated that the members didn't want to rehearse and when they did, the backup musicians were taking over the rehearsals. I wondered how this was possible. It was apparent that they did not know how we approached our arrangements or the strategies that we used in rehearsals to increase the quality of our performances. They didn't know how to use the movements to elevate the sound, that had taken us years of practice and cohesiveness and now it appeared to be lost. He also shared the overwhelming internal struggles with me. He insisted that Walter was becoming more of a problem, particularly during the recording sessions. It is possible that some of the dismay was rooted in the fact that Walter had always wanted to do a solo album. He had worked with outsiders on his own music, but was reluctant to present it to the group. William King appeared to be in distress about everything, all of the time. I felt bad about what was continuing to unravel.

Not long after speaking with the manager, I received another request to play with the group again, as their backup guitarist would not be available. This moment for me was surreal and to my surprise, the group's response to me was warm and welcoming. Even the crew members confided in me that they noticed the difference in the energy, and a preciseness to the sound when we were all on one accord. There was no question in my mind that my presence brought about memories of the old days when we were riding high. I wondered if the guys could find the love for what we all had in their hearts?

I thought that maybe this could be an opportunity for us to get back into the studio. I had written a song called "America" and it seemed to appeal to all of the guys who listened. It was agreed upon that we would reach out to James Carmichael and get as many of the original team members back together to do an album. I could not believe that things were finally moving in a positive direction for us. We locked in a date that worked for everyone to come and work on the album. Ronald LaPread came in from New Zealand, James Carmichael came in from LA, Walter Orange, William King, JD Nicholas, and David Fish all came to my home studio to hopefully turn a new page and begin the process of resurrection. What a feeling! I began to channel the Thomas McClary who walked miles across the campus of Tuskegee, assembling a dream. I had it in me then and I was convinced that I had it in me now. I prayed without ceasing over how to approach this revival of sorts. I knew that God would not have brought us together if it were not meant for us to create harmoniously together.

By 2009, I was hopeful that I could bring us all full circle. I thought I could get the guys back together, as I had a commitment from Lionel in my back pocket that I would impel at just the right time. In the interim, Lionel had a show in New Orleans at the Superdome headlining for the Essence Festival. Lionel called me and invited me, Ronald as well as the rest of the guys to perform with him. I knew what a big stage Essence was building for their ongoing music festival and wanted very much to accept Lionel's invitation. Just like the old days, the ball was in my court to bring everyone together. Ronald LaPread was filled with excitement at the prospect. He also recognized this as a perfect time to reunite in front of an audience who loved our work. With a frenzy of emotions in my heart, I extended an invitation to the other guys.

In the back of my mind, I knew that William King and Lionel had not spoken in years, but in my heart, I believed that this opportunity was meaningful enough for the extension of an olive branch. Ronald continued my efforts to reach out to the rest of the guys on our behalf and I was dumbfounded to learn of Walter's response. Lionel and I were told that the only way William would come and play with us is if we signed documents stating that we were going to be five solo musicians during the performance and that afterwards, he and the remaining members of the group could carry on as The Commodores. This meant that he wanted for Lionel, Ronald, and myself to sign away our rights as members of The Commodores in exchange for an outward appearance of unity at the Essence Festival. When Ronald told us this, Lionel and I truly believed that he was joking. We were floored. The same repugnance that had driven a wedge between us all in the previous years, reared its ugly head once again.

Regardless of what outrageous antics William King maintained, we had not given away our rights to The Commodores and we didn't intend to. Lionel, Ronald, and I still maintained our ownership in the corporation. What in Jesus' name was he talking about?

We never really found out if any of the other members of the group wished to perform at the Essence Festival. William King shut off the lifeline on the prospect for them as well. We were now at a crossroads in determining what to do.

Lionel suggested that the three of us move forward with the performance and that was exactly what we did. The response was unimaginable. It felt so good to be back on stage with two guys that I knew had my back. We rocked that stage! You would have thought it was the Super Bowl. The media wrote articles and reviews about our performance. The headlines read something to the tune of, "Lionel Richie and three-fifth of The Commodores." It was a reunion as far as they were concerned and it felt amazing.

There was quite a feeling of accomplishment that after all those years, we were still able to come together and perform. Even more, we were delighted to know that as a band, we still could still move the crowd and entertain our fans. Shortly after the performance, we were flooded with extreme negativity from the other group members because we had moved forward with the performance. We ignored the hatred that was spewed our way at all costs. None of us were welcoming of anything that felt like the turmoil from the past. We were happy and proud of what we had managed to accomplish together. The performance in New Orleans had gone so well that we were extended an invitation for another performance in New Zealand. Nostalgia belonged to each of us and to our fans and we accepted the invitation. Although I had found true love and true happiness in my life with Beryl, being on tour again spoke to my soul in ways that many would never understand. Sadly, the negative commentary from the other group members only continued and all hopes of a reunion were dismantled.

I was weary again from the highs and lows of the group. The same energy that I no longer wanted to allow to take up time and space in my life had done so once again. More so now than ever before, I wanted my children to see who I was and what I had managed to accomplish. I wanted them to know what was possible. As I sat with Beryl one night, we talked in depth about what my legacy as the founder of The Commodores would be. I don't believe that we had ever spoken that deeply about it before. It was almost as if we were discussing my next move as a musician. I explained to her that I had not given up ownership of The Commodores name, and that in my heart, I wanted to continue performing. That night, I went to bed with the same dream that I'd had as a young, aspiring musician in Eustis. I wanted to play more than anything. I had taken time to give my all to my family and I had been obedient in taking the sabbatical from the group. I could no longer fight it. It was now time for me to sing a new song.

The next day, I was outside gardening and I began to hum a tune. I can't even recall what song it was, but I remember it being a funky groove. I stood up, looking out over my garden and my foot began to tap. I missed music so badly. It ran through my veins. About five minutes later, my son Ryan drove up. As he got out of the car, he was humming a funky tune, much like mine. It stunned me. In that moment, I realized that God had given me all that I needed to resurrect the lifeline of my career. While standing there, I made a decision to reclaim my identity and my career on my own terms. From that day forward, I had every intention of picking up where I left off. If there was one thing that I knew how to do, it was to assemble a band. I went right back into the same mode that I had been in when I created The Commodores. I examined the needs of the band musically and began to solicit the musicians needed to fill in the gaps. Ryan was a key element in the formation of my new band. It was my honor to embark upon this journey with him. I was blossoming with a newfound energy for music. The opportunity to play with Ryan by my side was a gift from God.

By 2014, my plans were in full throttle. I began to arrange rehearsals and coordinate the show's lineup. It was amazing how everything that I learned from my days with The Commodores, came back almost immediately. We decided that we would perform as "The Commodores featuring Thomas McClary." We booked a show at the Westhampton Beach Performing Arts Center.

Things just seemed to be getting worse for the band. They had made the decision to leave Motown and I would imagine that this only added to the disarray. I continued to hear through the grapevine of the turmoil within the group. The old band members were now performing at non-ticketed events. We would have never done this. Even when we played at Smalls Paradise, we had a much larger stage and tickets sold to see us perform. I was also told that the live show was so awful that they were not drawing in any fans. This hurts my heart since we had been well-known for the precision and explosiveness of our performances.

I knew that I needed to remain focused on preparing to revive what had been lost in the music. I assembled a mini tour to get the newly formed band more exposure and my excitement was at an all-time high. There were no ill feelings or distractions from jealousy. Everyone was just there to enjoy the music and the ride and we were ready to rock and roll. The first date that we booked was in New York. We sold out the performing arts center and I could feel that we were on to something. Things were looking so bright for the new band. When we arrived in New York, I felt the same way that I did when we had arrived over twenty years ago in search of Benny Ashburn to jump start our careers. It was now my responsibility to do what Benny did and keep us working. I was up for the challenge.

We settled into the dressing room and there was a true sense of nervousness mixed with adrenaline. This was what I had been waiting for. This moment was like a dream come true. I was about to show the world that Thomas McClary was a force to be reckoned with. "Showtime," said one of the promoters of the concert. The fellas and I lined up backstage and we all waiting, anxiously, feeling the heat from the stage lights. Just as we prepare to hit the stage, Beryl approached me with a very strange look on her face. In all the years that we had been married, I don't think I've seen her look that way.

"What's wrong Beryl?" I asked.

"Thomas, the guys are suing you." The words that she spoke left me flabbergasted.

"What?"

"Yes, they are suing you for infringing upon the use of the name," said Beryl. As she stood there, holding the papers, her hands were noticeably shaking. She too was in disbelief.

"You are saying that they are suing me for the name that I partially own? I have not signed away any of my rights," I exclaimed. This was a new low and another blow to my heart. There I stood, in preparation for what would be another defining moment in my career and destruction was still knocking at my door. What I knew for certain was that I had absolutely no plans on answering.

14: *Allow Me to Reintroduce Myself*

I stood in the wings of the stage preparing for a defining moment to resurrect my career with a fist full of tears. I could have lost my mind right there in that moment. I wished that everything could have just been rewound in time. I wished that Beryl could have retracted the words. I wished that the official could have rejected the offer to serve us. I wished that the men who were once my brothers rejected the malice in their hearts for me. I could feel my hand clenched so tightly with frustration and I had nowhere to send the tainted energy. In a matter of seconds, I became enraged. I could have plead temporary insanity in that very moment. I even asked God, "Why? Why now? Why here? Why me?" This was the point of no return for me. Let's be clear, I had given way more than my fair share. I had ghostwritten songs that I had never received credit for, I had allowed careers to progress off of my back, and I had always turned the other cheek. In that moment, I no longer wanted to. I became engulfed with the memories of all the work that I had done that I never even spoke of. The world had never known that I had ghostwritten "Say You, Say Me" with Lionel. The song went on to win an Oscar and I never received so much as a mention. I never asked for one. And although Lionel was not apart of The Commodores who were responsible for my being served, admittedly, he was a source of the pain for me. Standing there, made me realize that I had spent so much time fighting for people who were not willing to fight for me in return. These same sentiments would prove to be true repeatedly.

I know that the show was a major success because the reviews were through the roof. We began receiving more invitations to perform and we moved forward, full steam ahead. When we returned to Florida, Beryl and I began to examine the letter that we had been served and the allegations. The group members were seeking an injunction inclusive of punitive and monetary damages, as well as profits from work that I had done while performing as "The Commodores featuring Thomas McClary." The lawsuit had eight counts and also stated that I was guilty of trademark infringement. (1) None of it was logical to me. I had done everything well and in order. I had been responsible for founding the group. Why would I not be permitted to use the name of the group that would not have existed, if not for my blood, sweat and tears to assemble it. I was the founder of The Commodores.

Beryl and I began to conduct research into the alleged trademarks that they stated claim to. Through our research, we learned that in 2001, William King had gone to the trademark office and illegally registered The Commodores name. There were a total of four trademarks executed during this time. It was alleged that The U.S. Patent and Trademark Office, allowed him to register "The Commodores" and "Commodores" for all live performances. He did it in such a bogus and illegal way that even the information used to register the name was incorrect. We began putting the pieces of the puzzle together, as the fake trademarks were re-registered in 2010. This was all bogus. It was not possible for William King to have registered a trademark that he did not have ownership of.

The reality of the lawsuit set in when we began to receive sinister letters. They wanted us to cease and desist all future bookings that had been secured for my new band. Not only were they sending the letters to our home, but also to the venues who had booked us.

Along with our US engagements, I had also booked a European tour that we were very much looking forward to. Unfortunately, the venues and promoters in Europe began receiving written threats as well. They had every intention of cutting off my livelihood. If there had been any remnants or signs of brotherhood left, they now ceased to exist. I knew that any effort to reach out to William personally would be a mistake. This was now in the hands of the courts.

The tension continued to build and we found ourselves back on the front lines of a war. Much like before, I had no desire to fight. I had no reason to. My only goal was to defend myself and my family against the false allegations. Everything that was now transpiring was absurd, but no matter how illogical I found it to be, this lawsuit was real. I knew that I would have to enlist more counsel. Although Beryl was my attorney, we knew that we would need to hire additional lawyers from the entertainment realm for support. Moreover, Beryl was still handling a heavy caseload from her own practice.

The amount of stress that became part of our daily lives was surreal. To say that we endured some sleepless nights is an understatement. I recall one night in particular that we had remained up late, talking and exchanging, and trying to search for clarity and peace. After finally drifting off to sleep, we were awakened by the phone. Beryl answered. There was a lady on the other end who said out of the gates that we did not know her. She disclosed that she was from California and that she was a lawyer. She stated that she received regular alerts with updates regarding various cases and then went on to explain that she had come across our case and was disturbed by it. "I experienced a similar thing with my husband," she said. The husband that she spoke of was the lead singer for a wildly successful band called, The Village People. She had called because she wanted to assist us in getting the right representation to fight the case. She coached Beryl through many strategies legally and provided her with contacts that she believed could be of further assistance to us. We deemed her an angel. After speaking with her, we slept well, as we were reassured that God would not leave us to fight this battle alone and that he would send us angels on Earth to guide us along the way.

The next day, we contacted a trademark attorney from Indiana, by the name of Gregory Gatson. He immediately began to research the history of the false registration completed by William King. During one phone call, he expressed his disdain and shock. "Oh, gosh, man. This is crazy. They can't do this and get away with it." As he looked at the records, he saw that William King had signed the registrations. To add insult to injury, he was claiming that the Commodores Entertainment Corporation owned the trademark name and the actual trademark. He alleged that the group owned the logo at a time that it didn't even exist. He tried to register that the use started in 1972. The logo didn't exist until 1977. The actual branding efforts of The Commodores started in 1968, when we started performing live as The Commodores. The research proved that the case was bogus.

We continued to build our fort of legal defense. We solicited the assistance of another lawyer recommended to us by the name of Marie Merch. Marie was from San Diego, and had handled many cases similar to ours.

I was emotionally distraught and overwhelmed from the added pressure of the legal proceedings. As they say, when it rains, it pours. After receiving a call from a friend, I was notified that TMZ had printed an article that aired the dirty laundry of The Commodores. As soon as the news broke, the phone calls began to pour in. People were understandably shocked. Some of the comments were, "I can't believe this," and "Never in my wildest dreams would I imagine this would happen to you guys." I was in the same state of disbelief that they were. It was like an out-of-body experience.

Many people were asking me why I wasn't fighting back? I had never really thought of it as me fighting them. At least in the beginning I didn't. "I didn't sue them. They sued me," was always my response. In retrospect, I think that I felt like there was no reason for me to fight. Why would I fight them? The Commodores name belonged to me. I had just as much right as they did. The name belonged to all of us. The legacy of The Commodores has been just as important to me and to my family as anyone else, if not more.

My late-night talks with Beryl turned into counseling sessions. This had gotten the best of me. "You think that I can talk to them and convince them that they don't have to do this?" I pleaded.

"I know that you are looking at them as your friends and colleagues, but as your counsel and as your wife, we have to fight this. We have a certain number of days to respond or the judge will just render whatever he deems appropriate if we don't."

We had always prayed, but in the midst of this turmoil Beryl and I embarked upon an even deeper prayer life. Had I known that they would do this to me, I would have confronted them. Through it all, it was still important to me to not speak against The Commodore name. It was my beloved. All of these years, I had hoped for a reunion and now I have come to find out that during those same years, I was hated.

I could hardly comprehend what was happening. This had altered my relationship with everyone indefinitely. Ronald LaPread got the word about the lawsuit, once TMZ had it blasted everywhere. Ronald called and he had a strange demeanor. On one hand, he appeared to be sympathetic. "Oh man, how can they do this to you?"

"Not only have they done it to me, they have done it to you as well. Neither your name, Lionel's name, nor my name was on there. We didn't sign our rights away."

"Well man, you should just leave it alone. They are the bruhs. Why are you going to fight the bruhs?"

I told him that I had to defend myself. I had been sued.

"Man, you should just leave it alone."

The principle of what was happening did not rest well with my spirit. I explained that they were trying to take something that I owned and something that he owned as well. "I believe that we can stand together and fight this. I believe that we would be stronger in numbers. I understand that they have not literally sued you, but it affects you. You can stay on the sidelines or you can join the fight," I said.

Ronald decided to give a sworn affidavit explaining that he did not sign away his rights, but from that point, he wanted no further involvement. When on the battlefield, paranoia has a way of taking up space. I no longer knew who to trust. I felt like I needed to stop talking to everyone outside of my legal counsel, and of course my wife, about the case. Once again, I felt isolated.

As Marie continued to do her research, she found out that the corporation that they had claimed the rights to, had gone defunct. To prove this end, my attorney filed for the corporate charter for The Commodore Entertainment Corporation in Nevada. I own it to this day. Technically, The Commodores that William and Walter were alleging that they owned is what I rightfully own. How would they even begin to defend this?

THOMAS MCCLARY & ARDRE ORIE

I was still performing with my new band. Performances and music residuals was how I fed my family. I could never, nor will I ever, understand how anyone would want to stop someone from taking care of their families. It is my belief that there is enough for everyone to exist and do their thing. God created enough resources for all of us. After one show in particular, I learned that they were sending spies to our shows. I later learned in court, that the mole that they sent was someone whom I was also acquainted with. That person ended up having to be a witness in the court proceedings. They had written a sworn statement saying that they were at the show and we were introduced as, The Commodores Featuring Thomas McClary, and that we played all of The Commodores' songs and that I was the only Commodore up on the stage.

The weight of the case began to take over our home and affected not only me, but my entire family. My children even began to understand that things were a little abnormal. Although I continued to attend the games and activities, my lightheartedness was noticeably absent. We began to overhear the discussions of our children. They would speak about how they would be impacted. I had three children in college at the same time and two daughters in private school. The tuition was like having five children enrolled in college. There are so many decisions to make, but God's grace always kept us. Every time there was a need to pay a bill, we had the money in place to pay it. We maintained our retainer fees for our attorneys, without a misstep. This was a large sum of money for an unexpected obligation such as this.

Beryl was now balancing her practice, the children, cooking and the emotional side of the upcoming trial. We brought in domestic help to try and lighten the load, but the family really treasured Beryl's cooking. Eating out every day was not a financially sound practice and there were times that I simply wouldn't or couldn't eat. I think that I was deeply saddened and also in a state of shock. My only goal became to make sure that all of my children were sustained.

I was still receiving royalties from all of the songs that we had written, which in my mind only proved that I was still a part of the corporation. I had not signed away any of my rights, yet I was still seen as a disruption to the men who claimed to still be a part of the group. There were times when I would hear my songs on the radio and it only further confirmed what I knew — I either wrote or co-wrote the songs, I played on all of them, and I co-produced them. Would they really want me to disassociate myself from all of this? "Brick House," "Easy," "Zoom," "Sail On," "Three Times a Lady," "Lady You Bring Me Up," "Slippery When Wet," "Jesus is Love." I can go on and on. I couldn't help but feel betrayed. This fight was now not only about my legacy and body of work, but also the sustainability of my family. I would not allow this case to consume us. Financially, I had to fight back to create a means of supporting my family as I always had.

I began to really deepen my relationship with God and just immersed myself in His word. It was my hospice and shelter. In this space, I found strength, grace, and mercy. I vowed to do what I had always done in being the encourager of the group, only this time, the group was my wife and team of lawyers. The only way that I could keep my sanity was in God's word.

There were several instances where there was a continuance of the process or deadlines that we felt were impossible to meet. The pressure became almost too much to bear, but I found my joy and peace in the Lord and I shared that energy with anyone that was within my reach.

In addition to my flourishing relationship with God, I immersed myself in work at church. I also found myself working out, walking often, playing golf, and even running to keep myself physically nurtured.

Giving love to my family and children was my greatest joy. Our children were the best during these times. I was very careful to not take out my pressures on them in discipline. Beryl and I worked fervently to keep control of ourselves so that we could continue to be the positive influences that the children desired and deserved. If it were not for the Lord and continuous prayer, I would have been a grumpy father who snapped at everything and retreated often. Thankfully, I learned to turn over to God all of my pressure and all of my anxiety. We worked to stay a close-knit family.

To add to the depth of our challenges, death would visit us even in the midst of this gray cloud of legal woes. Beryl lost a sister, Priscilla Jeannette Rigby, (who we fondly called Jeannette), during the process, which was a major blow to our hearts. We had been instrumental in her care during her illness and this involvement had been therapeutic to me. We also lost my oldest sister, Claudest, whom I loved so much.

My strength was challenged because I had been positioned as the strong one and the one to rally the troops, but I must admit that I prayed on my knees so many nights in need of strength to endure. I couldn't help but wonder if my children felt that the world was somewhat closing in on the McClary's.

The days leading up to the trial sped by so quickly that I could hardly catch my breath. On the first day of the trial, my nerves were on overload as we prepared to enter the court. Even though the trial took about a week, it had taken about a year for us to prepare due to all of the various motions and appeals.

The day we entered the court, all I could think to do was to pray. I not only prayed for myself and my family, but I also prayed for the other side. I exemplified a calmness because I knew that I was no longer in control. Many of the attorneys spoke on the calmness of my demeanor. In comparison to the other guys, I appeared to be more settled. I knew for certain that I wasn't carrying my weight — God was, as it was too heavy for me.

From the moment the proceedings began, nothing seemed to be in our favor. It was almost as if the judge and the law firm that the group had hired were in bed together. I, of course, had no hard evidence to prove it, but there was a very apparent feeling of favoritism shown in the group's favor. Despite all of the erroneous occurrences and evidence disputing their claims, my legal team was being shut down from every angle.

The judge did not even allow the jury to participate in the trial. After they had sat and listened to all of the evidence presented, they never had the opportunity to engage in a discussion about the outcome of the case. There were so many discrepancies during the proceedings. My expert witness was never even allowed to testify. I had requested for Lionel to be deposed on my behalf, and he agreed but did not physically attend to support me. The court allowed parts of his sworn deposition to be read to the jury. It was vague at best. In his deposition, he stated just as I had, that he had never signed anything to relinquish his portion of the ownership of the name. I wish that he would have fought a little harder for me as I had against the other guys in the group on so many occasions. Again, I was left to fend for myself. Somehow, I always found the strength to do so, but it would have been nice for once to experience reciprocity. From the moment that we entered the courts, we were fighting a losing battle.

Initially, the judge ruled in their favor. I was grief-stricken. My family was distraught and my legal team was dumbfounded. They didn't even want me to quote the name or to have any affiliation with The Commodores. However, through the course of the legal actions, the judge officially had to come out and admit that I was the founder of the group. Thomas McClary was the founder of The Commodores. No matter what they tried to strip me of, they couldn't deny me that, not even in the court of law. It was the truth.

After the trial ended, we immediately filed an appeal. Something inside of us believed that God would not allow this injustice to prevail, but admittedly, I was drained and losing my faith. The preparation for the trial had taken so much from me. To know that all of that work had been done in vain was overwhelming for me. I was slipping into a depressed state that I could not seem to shake. I was trying to fight, but I began to experience a level of defeat that I was not sure that I could ever come back from.

Nothing seemed as if it would turn around for me, until I began to simply thank God for what had happened to me. As strange as that may seem, I literally sat at my kitchen table with my head in my hands and uttered the words "Thank you, Lord." I repeated it several times until I felt an actual shift in the atmosphere. I was home alone and I began to repeat it more. "Thank you, Lord. Thank you, Lord. Thank you, Lord." There was a mysterious weight that continued to lift from my body. I couldn't believe that after all that I had been through, I had forgotten how to channel the power of restoration. In revelation, there are opportunities for wisdom and I suddenly recognized that the lawsuit, was just another test of my obedience. I sat in power and reflected over the past two years. I had somehow allowed the trial to consume me, but at that moment, I could not deny how much God had kept me.

Although I had not recognized it then, I knew without question that God had been good to me, even in the midst of one of my most trying times. I was now beginning to open my eyes and bear witness to the miracles that had taken place while on the battlefield. As I reflected, I recognized how I was prevented from working during the trial and what a financial burden it caused my family. My hands and my feet were tied in terms of earning money, but God kept me. There were days that I would go to the mailbox only to discover checks with large sums of money. I received notices from royalties and contract negotiations at Motown that resulted in residuals. Publishing checks would just arrive unexpectedly for things that we started years past. They were always timely. There, in my home, alone at my kitchen table, I recognized that God had been sending me signs all along that he was in control and in my corner. I hadn't recognized it in the eye of the storm, but I could see clearly now. God had never allowed my children or my wife to miss a meal and we always had a roof over our heads. All that had transpired, never got in the way of my children's schooling. They remaining enrolled in school and were receiving top notch quality educations. What others meant for evil, God meant for good. He was calling me to vibrate on a higher level, in life and spiritually. I almost felt ashamed that I had not recognized it earlier, but that was the beauty of it. God wants us to remember that he is an on-time God and that he is the creator of our destiny. I thought that I had dedicated myself as much as humanly possible to my spiritual calling, but God required more. In order to fulfill our greatest purpose, we must always be willing to die to the former versions of ourselves.

Today, I am Thomas McClary, The Founder of The Commodores. I founded a world renown musical phenomenon, and produced massive hits that transformed generations, but my true identity far surpasses that. I thought that creating The Commodores was the greatest accomplishment that I had achieved. Nothing could have been further from the truth. I had made the mistake of embedding my identity and purpose into The Commodores, but there was so much more that God had in store for me. My posture changed from the enlightenment of knowing who and whose I was.

With a new perspective on life, I can't help but proclaim that through Christ, all things are possible. We have to convince ourselves to just do it. I had spent my entire life waiting for validation from others. I had sought validation from my white peers as I integrated the schools. I had waited for validation through education at Tuskegee. I had waited for validation in my first marriage. I had waited for validation from the group, and I had waited for validation from the music. Today, I recognize that you don't have to get permission from anyone to do anything that you desire to do. God has shown me that my greatest power is in the fact that he has granted me the only authority that I have ever needed. Today, I reflect on how much our need for validation hinders us from evolving into the greatest versions of ourselves. We each have the power to be whatever we aspire to be, if we just do it.

Although the appeal is still in progress as I write the pages of this book, I am no longer bound by the outcome. I am Thomas McClary. The talent that I have and my mental tenacity far surpasses anyone telling me who or what I can be. I have exemplified endurance and forward thinking my entire life, and I will continue to walk in grace. I've made up my mind that music is a gift that God gave to me to share with the world and I am not going to allow anyone to take that away from me. No one else has the control or power to do so.

I began to tell my son Ryan about my new pattern of thinking. In the middle of our conversation, he yelled out, "Just Do It."

"What?" I said.

"'Just Do It.' That's it, Dad. That's the title of our new song," he said with enthusiasm. And so, it was. Together, we began co-writing my first single as Thomas McClary, Founder of The Commodores

My message to the world today is clearer than it has ever been. We should all be walking in power. I want for the listeners of my music to know that we are not in bondage. The music that I am now writing is lyrically so different than that of my days with The Commodores. Musically, I am creating another layer of innovation for what will be my legacy.

Trendsetting has always been a part of who I am and even more so today. The music is uncomplicated, with a funky groove, yet relatable. Today, I believe that as musicians, we have a responsibility to do more than just make music that sounds good. We are also charged to give people the bread of life through our lyrics and the spirit from which the music is made. We owe it to the people to make music that is of substance. We must know that we can positively affect the lives of others and feel compelled to do so.

My assignment in life has become clearer. I now know that through music I must be the light that shines on the hill of hope to the world. I feel more excited about my career than I ever have. God ordered me to walk this new journey alone, that my children might have a lineage to stand on that did not rest in the hands of anyone else. As the founder and a lifetime member of The Commodores, I am proud to say that there is a message of love throughout all of our songs that has the ability to penetrate people's hearts around the world and transcend all languages. I will continue on in this purpose, now recognizing that I am strong enough to carry this torch with the name Thomas McClary emblazoned on it.

The ultimate sign of my evolution is living in the moment while creating music with my children. I feel replenished every time I hear the music that we have made. Together, we will release my new single "Just Do It." The song pays homage to my new take on life and the message that I so desperately want the world to hear. I want people to know that it is possible to be one nation under God. I want my music to create ambassadors of love, and peace, and truth.

I sat in awe as the collaboration evolved into an unforgettable and defining moment between my son Ryan and my daughter Mariah. Mariah came up with the melody and the hook for the song and Ryan and I came up with the music and the track itself. I couldn't be more proud. There is so much more on the horizon for Thomas McClary.

THE HUSBAND

BERYL'S EVOLUTION IS one that has continued to keep me in awe. She continues to be a pillar of excellence and it is my heart's desire to watch her thrive. She has long inspired women through her presence.

She has now set her sights on emerging as a spokesperson for women's rights and empowerment. My career would not be possible without her as she presides as an intricate part of my marketing and management team. I have no doubt that I will bear witness to her writing books filled with her experiences of over thirty years of practicing law, running for public office, and being the absolute love of my life. I know that my job is done when I can delight in her smile. It is my greatest joy.

THE FATHER

I HAVE ALWAYS BEEN and will continue to be an intricate part of creating opportunities for my children to realize their greatest potential and building their legacy. I've become both partners in business and partners in learning with my children. My hope is for them to be exactly who they have been divinely called to be and that walk boldly, and unapologetically in purpose.

THE PHILANTHROPIST

MY WIFE BERYL AND I are in the process of establishing our non-profit organization in collaboration with my commercial company, purposed to sow seeds of hope into communities. Much like the mission work that we have done in the past, I now desire to take my music on the road and utilize the trips as an opportunity to complete charitable works in each city that we visit. I believe that service, coupled with music, is a winning combination.

We have also launched our Battle of the Bands Contests. In this space, we have established a city-wide search for talented musicians, who will use their gifts to play for God. The initial launch was so successful, as we were joined by church leaders of all races, with the common vision to keep youth off of the streets and exercising their God given talents. Aretha Franklin, Little Richard, James Brown, and The Commodores of the world, all began in the church. From this platform, we will reintroduce this as an exciting place to develop talent.

Beryl and I continue to serve as ambassadors for a myriad of charitable organizations to raise money for the elderly to receive life-saving surgeries. An organization by the name of Shepard's Hope has facilitated our efforts immensely. We will also continue to raise funds and hope for children who suffer from arthritis and lupus. I often perform the hallmark songs that have been the staple of The Commodores to assist Tee-It-Up-For-The-Troops and various organizations amidst their fundraisers.

THE
ACTIVIST

NOT ONLY WAS I consistent musically, but also as an individual who stood for what was right as it related to the rights of others. I fought for the rights of those who were wronged. No one will ever know the sacrifices that were made to live this life. No one will ever be able to comprehend the magnitude of what I've given of myself to the world. I've endured so much. I only wanted to make it better, not just for myself, but for everyone. There were so many closed doors that I had to find a way to open. There were so many times that I felt lost and alone. Justice is not certain nor easily attained, especially in a world where people have been preconditioned to act from hate. There were so many times that I did not feel strong, yet I had to exemplify strength for those around me. This happened often and sometimes to my detriment. Nonetheless, I always knew that there was a greater calling that I would eventually be charged to answer to. I knew that what was required of me, would cost me more than what others might have been expected to give. I will never cease to work in the presence of injustice. I will continue to lead the charge for the betterment of people and the human race. We all deserve to thrive in a world that believes we are all of value and not because of the color of our skin, or the dollar amount that rests in our bank accounts, or because of the religion that we believe in. We all deserve a fair shot at life, because it is our birthright.

THE MUSICIAN

IF I WERE ASKED TO SELECT one word that describes my life and career as a musician, it would be tenacity. This business is extremely difficult. In no era has the music industry been easy. For me to have achieved success and power for this many years, I had to exercise tremendous endurance. Anyone who aspires to this must be built to last. This business left me no room to lose the belief in myself. I have encountered so many doubters and naysayers that I could have given up long ago, had I listened. I learned how to encourage myself in times where there was little to no encouragement from others. I worked without ceasing to develop my craft and I prayed like crazy. There were so many trials and errors, and so many doors that closed. I've endured many sleepless nights and even physical illness, but the music always came before my own health and well-being. I sacrificed my all for the love of my music. If I had the chance to do it all again, I would change nothing. The memories of my life sing the sweetest tunes that I have ever heard. I was made to create and I will do just that until there is no longer breath in my body.

THE LEGEND

EVEN THOUGH THE CASE is still pending, I don't need validation from it. I am not depending on any court of law, or any group of people, to validate my contributions to the legacy of music. All that I was ever fighting for, was a wrong to be made right. Neither are important to me today. This case has not delayed, or ever made me feel less than a man or less of who I am. I am the Founder of The Commodores. No one can deny that truth. I gave everything unselfishly to my music and I created a signature sound that has resonated around the world. Just to say that you can go to any country and that they have heard your music, is a major feat. And although it takes a tremendous number of variables, it speaks to the fact that my music has spoken to the hearts and souls of people.

Today, I have a sense of urgency in the fulfillment of this purpose. I recognize in hindsight that the trial has been just a snapshot of the pain and hurt that many experience in the world. Although it may not be legal, or the disbandment of a group, everyone experiences pain from uncertainty. What has become crystal clear to me is that I, Thomas McClary, am called to be true to the assignment given to me by God. It is my assignment, and my ability to see it through to fruition must not rest on the shoulders, or motives, or actions of anyone else. I am called and I shall answer.

As a sign of confirmation, God brought me full circle. I was invited back to a class reunion for Eustis High School. That place filled my heart with so many mixed emotions. I felt full of all of the memories of hurt and injustice that had sometimes won the battle. On the night of the reunion, my walk towards the entrance of the school was met with a different response. There were no sheriffs or lines of whites, screaming with sticks and yelling obscenities or racial slurs. Instead, I was greeted with a standing ovation. I was there, not to ask for a fair shot at life, but to share about how I had managed to transcend the obstacles that had been before me. On this evening, I was invited to serve as the keynote speaker. The specific request was that I give a speech on what it was really like integrating the school system.

"I will make this short, I don't think I even need fifteen minutes of your time today. The message in my heart is one of gratitude. I am humbled and I am grateful." I could see the perplexed looks on everyone's faces. Some were looks of confusion, some were looks of guilt, and others were looks of amazement.

"I want to thank those of you that threw oranges at me along my walks to school. The pain pierced my back. I want to thank those of you who threw rocks to harm me as I attempted to attain a better education for myself. I want to thank those of you who chanted 'Get that Nigga' as I walked through the halls in a desperate attempt to be educated. I want to thank those of you who denied me the right to shower in the locker room after having contributed towards the wins on the field that built our school records. I am humbled and grateful for every act of unkindness and denial that was meant for me. You see, I've learned over my life that the negative energy that others cast our way is filled with momentum. It is that same momentum that God uses to fuel our journey towards greatness and towards destiny. What others meant for evil, God means for our good. You motivated me in ways that I could never have dreamed of. I attribute much of the success that I have right now to your ill intent. If it weren't for that hatred, I would have never worked diligently to solve problems stemming from injustice and I would have never had a need to stand on the battlefield for justice. Today, I stand before you with only one sentiment in my heart — love. I believe with my whole heart that love conquers all. The reason that I am able to stand before you today, is because I love each of you. I am Thomas McClary, the first black student to integrate the schools in Lake County, an alumnus of Eustis High School, and I love you from the bottom of my heart. Thank you."

God had given me an opportunity to look into the eyes of those who had caused me lifelong harm and be empowered enough to tell them that I loved them. I meant every word of it. He had given me the victory. The scripture tells us that God will make your enemies your footstools in times of peril....

> *"Till I make thine enemies thy footstool."*
> **LUKE 20:43 (KING JAMES VERSION).**

As I left the stage, the same classmates that hated me, formed a line to request my autograph with their adult children bearing witness.

As I look back over my life, love has been my cross to bear. I thank God for every high and every low that has transformed me into who I am. I am ever grateful that God never left me. His hand has been upon my life since the days that my mother and father prayed for me in ways that I was not wise enough to do for myself. I am ever grateful for having been sent a best friend and a confidant in my wife Beryl, that I might never journey this life alone. I am grateful for the opportunity to witness what will be my legacy and the lineage produced in my children. Last, but not least, I am thankful for the music that lives and breathes in my heart. It is the treasure of my heart.

Allow me to reintroduce myself, my name is Thomas McClary. I am a child of God, a husband, a father, a community activist, and the founder of The Commodores. I am on a mission to change the world through music.

"What the world needs now, is love." [2]
THOMAS MCCLARY

EPILOGUE: *Soul*

"For what shall it profit a man, if he shall gain the whole world, and lose his own soul?"
MARK 8:36 (KING JAMES VERSION).

For every breath that I have taken, I have carried the weight of my calling on my back. It has been my cross to bear. There were times that I questioned God, "Why me?" Why had I been charged with the heavy laden of inequality? Sitting there in the courtroom, it occurred to me that I had received orders to take up a battle in the fight for justice in the face inequality. And while the senseless wages of war were once limited to the injustices of the world and the racial tensions that worked to conquer a people, I now saw the flames and smelled the smoke of injustice working in my own back yard. My life was in flames because of it.

In that courtroom, I wore a target on my back. I was being senselessly persecuted by those who were once closest to me. No matter how many times I had found myself in the fog of this war, today, somehow felt different. It was a far cry from the bullets of hatred that I felt from my white counterparts. On this day, the war was not in the streets, nor in an open field; we had not been forced to march or pray. There were no speeches of encouragement rendered to inspire. This war was taking place in a courtroom with people that I had once loved, whom I had once fought beside, and stood with. And while some may find fault in my doing so, I still loved them as my brothers, even in that moment.

The exercise of love throughout my life had taught me so much about who I was and who I wanted the world to remember me as. I was Thomas McClary, Founder of The Commodores. I was the original visionary that called to action a music group and a harmony that changed the way music was composed. I had assembled a monumental vision that was meticulously realized. The signature sound was birthed from the strum of the strings on my guitar. The Commodores would not have existed if it had not been for me. I had walked in purpose and in power to create something that no man could tear apart. At least that is what I thought. The lies and the mistrust, the agony of fame, the ill will, jealousy, deceit, and the desperation of better days had brought us all to this point. These were the ugly truths of why war was being waged in the court of law. Even so, I saw beauty amongst the ashes. That day, I recognized that Thomas McClary was also a son of God, a husband, a father, and a friend. These attributes were not my doing. These were roles that could have only been made possible by God and more importantly the truest measures of my soul.

I sat and reminisced over how much I had allowed The Commodores to be a part of my identity. It was not only who I was, but also who I believed that I was called to be. It had been the burden of my thoughts and the action behind the strategies that I devised that had brought us all together. I took great pride in serving and bearing the brunt of the responsibility to not only bring us together, but to keep us together. It was all smoke and mirrors now. There was no camaraderie, no exchange of jokes, and no moments to sit and reminisce over what had been. That day in the courtroom, there was only me, at battle, alone. "Thomas McClary," I heard the judge command my name.

As I stood up, I took a deep breath. I thought that my knees would buckle from the pressure. They didn't and instead I was overcome with tremendous power. I had never experienced it in this way before. That surge became the wind beneath my wings in the courtroom. I was no longer afraid of what would be. I took my first step with dignity, and then another, and another. I could hear the sound of my steps as I walked towards the stand. They reminded me that I was present in the moment and alive. I could feel the mounting tension heating the back of my neck, but had there been a flame, I was not afraid of being burned. With every step, I could hear a gentle whisper eloquently reciting the words, "No weapon formed against you shall ever prosper," and they caused me to soar like an eagle above the fray. Before ever uttering a word on the witness stand, I relinquished the agony that accompanied trying to figure out what I had done wrong and the impossible game of blame that I had played with myself on so many occasions. I knew that I too was worthy of much more than this moment. I deserved better.

"Did you ever relinquish your rights from the corporation?" The lawyer asked. "No," I rebutted. "I have worked too hard to build this group and to create the dream that we all once believed in. I will never let Commodores Entertainment Corporation separate me from the love that I have for Mr. King and Mr. Orange." From my peripheral vision, I could see the guys from the group to the right of me. I held tight to those words because I meant them. I began to cry uncontrollably. All of the pain that I had once felt was released. With a quivering voice, I continued speaking. "I never signed anything releasing any of my rights." I remained steadfast in who I was, but the moment of injustice weighed on me. The jury was noticeably moved to emotion and the war in the courtroom climaxed.

"We may need to take a break," the judge commanded.

The strike of the gavel to restore order in the court struck me in a way unimaginable to most. That old wooden chair that I sat in, tattered, and worn, bearing the remnants of the fingernail marks of those who had sat there in agony before me, sadly reminded me of the weight of my heart. It was irreparably broken. I looked out over the courtroom carefully connecting with each person whom I had shared time and exchanged turbulent energy with. In that moment, even though I saw their faces, they all appeared as souls, vapors, and mists of people I once knew. I had done nothing wrong and I had only wanted the best for us all. I was not a criminal, nor worthy of being charged. The only crime that I had committed was that of love.

My head might have been bloody, but it was unbowed. I was fighting what appeared to be a losing battle in the courtroom, but I had won and was unquestionably victorious deep down in my soul. I knew that I had done all that God had asked of me for The Commodores, for my family, and for what would become my legacy. I let out a resounding sigh of relief because I could hear a gentle whisper from the voice that had visited me on so many occasions saying, "Well done."

From that moment on, I knew that no matter how forceful the persecution in the court of law would prove to be, I had total victory through God. I silently whispered to myself, "Lord, make me over." I wanted God to remove everything from me that had allowed me to acknowledge The Commodores as the essence of who I was. I had offered so much more to the world. I was proud of what had been accomplished. My toil and sacrifice had not been in vain. My living had not been in vain. I had answered the call of God to create something larger than myself and something that would change the trajectory of life, not just for myself but for all of us. We were all better for having lived our lives as The Commodores.

When court resumed, I had gained my composure. As I prepared to step down from the stand, I lifted my head and gave God praise in the midst of the courtroom. I was not ashamed nor afraid to do so. That day was a defining moment in my life. I left the witness stand that day with the same valor that I had walked towards it with, and my dignity was intact.

And although, I was physically present for the remainder of the trial, my mind began to manifest the new things that

THOMAS McCLARY & ARDRE ORIE

God would do in my life. That day, in the courtroom, the devil tried to bury me. I guess he didn't realize that I was a seed.

Today, I delight in my willingness to always answer the call. I have never run from the truth, backed down from a challenge, or ceased to fight for equality in the face of injustice. I have walked in power, and humility, and grace. I have sung sweet melodies of peace and harmony from my heart and from the depths of my soul. I have served as a soldier in the army for music. I have changed the game. I have served as a trendsetter and a humble creator of a blueprint for excellence that others may follow. I have written the book of my life, my way. There has been nothing more liberating than the life that I have lived.

The God that rules over the heart was in search of my soul. Today, my soul is desperate to give Him all. There is a difference between living for God and living for yourself. Today, I bow down in reverence to the vision that God has for my life. I recognize that He wanted more of me. Just when I thought that I had given all that I had, I felt a tug for more. Just when I didn't think that there was more of me to give, I discovered that there was a well of love, and kindness, and discipleship that never ran dry. Today, my legacy is rooted in service.

There are two defining moments in my life that sum up my entire legacy. That day in the courtroom was one of them. It reminded me of my strength in the face of adversity. My ability to stand firmly on the truth was a testament to the little boy from Eustis who symbolized a heart of gold. The second was the day that I met my wife Beryl. God had sent me a helpmate that I might never be forced to battle alone. She had been there every step of the way. She was the vessel of my legacy and the replenisher of my soul.

Today, I am no longer on the battlefield. I have taken off my armor as I am a soldier whose leader fights battles of spiritual warfare on my behalf. I bask in the simple gift of life for I know that it is not promised. Happiness, health, strength, sound mind, and yes, even music, they are all mine.

My name is Thomas McClary and my life sings the melodies of the signature sound. Listen if you will.

AFTERWORD:
An Open Letter to the Little Boy From Eustis

Dear Thomas,

I write to remind you of your power. There will be times that lead you to forget what you've been purposed with. Within you lies greatness that is as unique as your fingerprint. You must discover the ways to harness everything inside of you for the greater good of the world. If prayer is the road paved to heaven, only faith can open the door.

You will go through fire and floods and your side will be pierced with pain. Through it all, know that you will never be faced with more than you can bear.

>You're going to have to cry sometimes.
>You're going to have to yield sometimes.
>You're going to have to sacrifice sometimes.
>You're going to have to heal sometimes.

You're going to feel the weight of the world on your shoulders, but be not dismayed.

Stand firm in your convictions. Never fear giving too much of yourself. Give the world all that you have to give. Doing anything less diminishes your divine gift.

Though all of this, rest assured that you will bear witness to the rainbow on the other side. Through all of this, you will experience life at its greatest levels. You will experience a peace that surpasses all understanding. Life will give to you more than you could ever give to it. You will be blessed in your going and coming. You will visit the mountaintops and bask in the views with the peace of companionship. You will revel in the winds of truth, and love, and acceptance. You will be crowned with righteousness for your obedience to the loudest call of your soul.

If you remember nothing else that I've told you, never forget that all the power that you will ever need has already been gifted to you. Awaken it.

Eternally,
Thomas

DISCOGRAPHY

MACHINE GUN July 1974
CAUGHT IN THE ACT February 1975
MOVING ON October 1975
HOT ON THE TRACKS June 1976
COMMODORES March 1977
NATURAL HIGH May 1978
MIDNIGHT MAGIC July 1979
IN THE POCKET June 1981
COMMODORES 13 September 1983

GREATEST HITS

December 1978
All the Great Hits July 1982

Love Songs August 1982
The Best of September 1982

Anthology May 1983
The Very Best of November 1985

The Very Best of May 1995
Twentieth Century Masters: Millennium Collection November 1999
Definitive Collection November 2003

LIVE ALBUMS

COMMODORES LIVE October 1977

HITS

MACHINE GUN (MACHINE GUN ALBUM)
I Feel Sanctified

Slippery When Wet
This is Your Life

CAUGHT IN THE ACT ALBUM

MOVING ON ALBUM
-Sweet Love

HOT ON THE TRACKS ALBUM
-Just to Be Close to You
-Fancy Dancer

ALBUM: COMMODORES
-Easy

-Brick House
-Zoom

ALBUM: COMMODORES LIVE
-Too Hot to Trot

ALBUM: NATURAL HIGH ALBUM
-Three Times a Lady
-Flying High
-Sail On

ALBUM: MIDNIGHT MAGIC
-Still
-Wondaland
-Old Fashioned Love

Album: Heroes:
-Jesus is Love

ALBUM: IN THE POCKET
-Lady You Bring Me Up
-Oh No
-Why You Wanna Try Me

ALBUM: COMMODORES 13
-Painted Picture
-Lucy
-Only You

ACKNOWLEDGEMENTS

To my heavenly Father, Jesus Christ, I thank you for your grace and your unexplainable mercy. Thank you for allowing me the opportunity to bear witness to the manifestation of my dreams with my family, my music, and my book. There is no me without God.

To my loving wife, Beryl McClary, you have been my greatest gift. I could not have made this journey that we call life, without you. To my daughters, Jazmyne, Ashley, Maya and Mariah, and sons, Ryan, Brandon, and Gabriel, your unconditional support has saved my life. You are loved and adored beyond measure. To my dog, Peaches, you have become like another one of our children, thank you for being a friend.

To my sister, Leola Williams, I humbly thank you for your love and spiritual support. To my cousin, Barbara Holt, may you continually be blessed for sharing your wonderful photos that helped to capture precious memories. To Mr. Offrey Hines and Mr. Michael Gilbert, your incredible memories of the early days of The Mystics and The Jays proved to be pure nostalgia for me. Thank you, Foy Robinson for helping me to relive those moments and the details of the infamous hostage incident my freshmen year at Tuskegee. To James Tarver, Steve Meyers, Cecil Willingham, Steward Gray, and Kent Reedy, I want you all to know that I could not have recalled all of the details of this incredible journey without your assistance.

To Jo-Ann Geffen, I thank your for the priceless photos. They were right on time. Bennavete Ashburn and Miriam Jacobs, you will always be the Commodorettes. Your thoughts and well wishes have proven to be so instrumental.

I received an amazing cover photo because of my photographer, Michael Cairns. If you can make me look good, you are a miracle worker. Rob Allen, I've got to commend you on designing my cover. Awesome job!

To my publisher, Ardre Orie and the entire team at 13th and Joan, your management of the production of my book was seamless. From design, to art direction, to editing, your watchful eye ensured that we would produce a book that not only told my story, but also solidified my legacy. Your diligence with my book made me even more excited to go on the promotional book tour that we've enlisted you to plan! Awesome job and many praises to the whole staff at 13th and Joan!

To my mentors, Berry Gordy, Suzanne de Passe, James Carmichael, The Jackson Five, Stevie Wonder, the late Norman Whitfield, Sylvia Smith, the late Marvin Gaye, Smokey Robinson, Clarence Avant, the late Skip Miller, Don Carter, Miller London, Jesus Garber, the late Bob Jones and the entire

Motown family, your words and wisdom meant so much to me. Thank you for being accessible and imparting wisdom, knowledge, and understanding, which I still benefit from today.

What can be said of a team? It is my belief that teamwork makes the dream work. To Assistant Manager, the late Karolyn Ali, world-renowned lighting director, the late Lenny Guice, stage manager, the late Rudy Rotunno, wardrobe, the late Bill Whitten and the late Teamer Washington, guitar technician, the late "Ease Up", security, Johnny Bailey, Vince Morgan, public relations, Lester Mornay, engineer, Cal Harris and Jane Clark, production assistants, and Suzee Ikeda, I humbly thank you all for giving me the real life stories.

To the original members of The Commodores, Lionel Richie, the late Milan Williams, Ronald LaPread, Walter Orange, and William King, and our manager, the late Benny Ashburn, the time that we all spent together, changed my life forever. The Commodores will always be a part of who I am.

To my late mother and father, this one's for you!

THOMAS MCCLARY

ENDNOTES

CHAPTER 1 - THIS LITTLE LIGHT OF MINE

John Hill, "A Southern Sheriff's Law and Disorder," Floridian: A Southern sheriff's law and disorder. November 28, 1999, Accessed April 24, 2017, http://www.sptimes.com/News/112899/Floridian/A_Southern_sheriff_s_.shtml.

CHAPTER 2 - AND STILL I RISE

"What Does NAACP Stand For?" NAACP, Accessed June 16, 2017, http://www.naacp.org/about-us/.

"Selma to Montgomery marches," Wikipedia. August 16, 2017, Accessed June 16, 2017, https://en.wikipedia.org/wiki/Selma_to_Montgomery_marches.

The People History -- Steve Pearson, "What Happened in 1965 Important News and Events, Key Technology and Popular Culture," What Happened in 1965 inc. Pop Culture, Prices, Significant Events, Key Technology, and Inventions, Accessed June 16, 2017, http://www.thepeoplehistory.com/1965.html.

CHAPTER 4 - MUSTARD SEED FAITH

"Tom Joyner," Black America Web, May 17, 2016, Accessed July 3, 2017, https://blackamericaweb.com/tom-joyner/.

Admin, "Lucius D. Amerson-1st Elected Black Sheriff," Blackonblackinfo.com, August 10, 2016, Accessed July 5, 2017. http://www.blackonblackinfo.com/lucius-d-amerson-1st-elected-black-sheriff/.

Associated Press, "Students Free Their Captives," The Kansas City Times, April 8, 1968, Accessed July 5, 2017, https://www.newspapers.com/clip/10591860/tuskegee_3/.

Ibid.

CHAPTER 6 - EXPERIENCE IS A PLENTIFUL TEACHER

Daily Mail Reporter, "Wife of 'American Gangster' Frank Lucas jailed for five years for plotting to sell cocaine," Daily Mail Online, February 29, 2012, Accessed July 19, 2017, http://www.dailymail.co.uk/news/article-2108022/Wife-American-Gangster-Frank-Lucas-jailed-years-plotting-sell-cocaine.html.

Gerlinda Grimes, "How Guitar Pedals Work." HowStuffWorks, March 14, 2011, Accessed July 20, 2017, http://electronics.howstuffworks.com/gadgets/audio-music/guitar-pedal.htm.

Stephen Erlewine, "Michael Jackson," Billboard.com, Accessed July 20, 2017, http://www.billboard.com/artist/310778/michael-jackson/biography.

CHAPTER 7 - FOG ON THE GLASS CEILING

"History," Classic Motown, Accessed July 11, 2017, http://classic.motown.com/history/.

Editors, "Muhammad Ali." Biography.com, June 06, 2017, Accessed July 22, 2017, https://www.biography.com/people/muhammad-ali-9181165.

CHAPTER 9 - PLAY ANOTHER SLOW JAM

United Press International, "Entertainer Crash Lands Plane on Freeway," The Town Talk (Alexandria, Louisiana), October 24, 1980, 98th ed., October 24, 1980, Accessed May 1, 2017, https://www.newspapers.com/image/?spot=10681951.

"Thank God It's Friday (1978)," IMDb. Accessed July 29, 2017, http://www.imdb.com/title/tt0078382/.

"Thank God It's Friday (film)," Wikipedia, August 16, 2017, Accessed July 29, 2017, https://en.wikipedia.org/wiki/Thank_God_It%27s_Friday_(film).

Ibid.

CHAPTER 11 - NIGHTSHIFT

Steven Overly, "The Concorde failed to change how we fly, but it still could," The Washington Post, February 13, 2017, Accessed August 14, 2017, https://www.washingtonpost.com/news/innovations/wp/2017/02/13/the-supersonic-flight-that-never-really-took-off-has-landed-for-good/?utm_term=.0a4cc70673b5.

Ben Berntson, "The Commodores," Encyclopedia of Alabama, July 3, 2012, Accessed August 17, 2017, http://www.encyclopediaofalabama.org/article/h-3274.

CHAPTER 12 - A REVOLUTION NOT A REVIVAL

Associated Press, "Commodores Dismiss Founding Member," The Index-Journal (Greenwood, South Carolina), July 28, 1989, 149th ed., sec. 1, Accessed August 18, 2017, https://www.newspapers.com/image/70112272/.

"Commodores and Apartheid," The Indianapolis Star (Indianapolis, Indiana), July 29, 1989, 87th ed., sec. 54, Accessed August 18, 2017, https://www.newspapers.com/image/?spot=13183495.

CHAPTER 14 - ALLOW ME TO REINTRODUCE MYSELF

Nathan Hale, "Commodores' TM Suit Against Guitarist To Sail On To Trial - Law360," Law360 - The Newswire for Business Lawyers, June 24, 2016, Accessed August 28, 2017, https://www.law360.com/articles/810755/commodores-tm-suit-against-guitarist-to-sail-on-to-trial

Kevin Richards, "The Story Behind The Song 'What The World Needs Now Is Love' American Songwriter," American Songwriter, December 16, 2009, Accessed August 30, 2017, http://americansongwriter.com/2009/12/chicken-soup-for-the-soul-behind-the-song-what-the-world-needs-now-is-love/.

BIBLIOGRAPHY

Admin. "Lucius D. Amerson-1st Elected Black Sheriff." Blackonblackinfo.com. August 10, 2016. Accessed July 5, 2017. http://www.blackonblackinfo.com/lucius-d-amerson-1st-elected-black-sheriff/.

Associated Press. "Commodores Dismiss Founding Member." The Index-Journal(Greenwood, South Carolina), July 28, 1989, 149th ed., sec. 1. Accessed August 18, 2017. https://www.newspapers.com/image/70112272/.

AP. "Students Free Their Captives." The Kansas City Times, April 8, 1968. Accessed July 5, 2017. https://www.newspapers.com/clip/10591860/tuskegee_3/.

Berntson, Ben. "The Commodores." Encyclopedia of Alabama. July 3, 2012. Accessed August 17, 2017. http://www.encyclopediaofalabama.org/article/h-3274.

"Commodores and Apartheid." The Indianapolis Star (Indianapolis, Indiana). July 29, 1989. 87th ed., sec. 54. Accessed August 18, 2017. https://www.newspapers.com/image/?spot=13183495.

Editors, Biography.com. "Muhammad Ali." Biography.com. June 06, 2017. Accessed July 22, 2017. https://www.biography.com/people/muhammad-ali-9181165.

Erlewine, Stephen Thomas. "Michael Jackson." Billboard.com. Accessed July 20, 2017. http://www.billboard.com/artist/310778/michael-jackson/biography.

Grimes, Gerlinda. "How Guitar Pedals Work." HowStuffWorks. March 14, 2011. Accessed July 20, 2017. http://electronics.howstuffworks.com/gadgets/audio-music/guitar-pedal.htm.

Hale, Nathan. "Commodores' TM Suit Against Guitarist To Sail On To Trial - Law360." Law360 - The Newswire for Business Lawyers. June 24, 2016. Accessed August 28, 2017. https://www.law360.com/articles/810755/commodores-tm-suit-against-guitarist-to-sail-on-to-trial.

Hill, John. "A Southern Sheriff's Law and Disorder." Floridian: A Southern sheriff's law and disorder. November 28, 1999. Accessed April 24, 2017. http://www.sptimes.com/News/112899/Floridian/A_Southern_sheriff_s_.shtml.

"History." Classic Motown. Accessed July 11, 2017. http://classic.motown.com/history/.

"How Guitar Pedals Work." HowStuffWorks. March 14, 2011. Accessed July 20, 2017. http://electronics.howstuffworks.com/gadgets/audio-music/guitar-pedal.htm.

Overly, Steven. "The Concorde failed to change how we fly, but it still could." The Washington Post. February 13, 2017. Accessed August 14, 2017. https://www.washingtonpost.com/news/innovations/wp/2017/02/13/the-supersonic-flight-that-never-really-took-off-has-landed-for-good/?utm_term=.0a4cc70673b5.

Reporter, Daily Mail. "Wife of 'American Gangster' Frank Lucas jailed for five years for plotting to sell cocaine." Daily Mail Online. February 29, 2012. Accessed July 19, 2017.

http://www.dailymail.co.uk/news/article-2108022/Wife-American-Gangster-Frank-Lucas-jailed-years-plotting-sell-cocaine.html.

Richards, Kevin. "The Story Behind The Song 'What The World Needs Now Is Love' American Songwriter." American Songwriter. December 16, 2009. Accessed August 30, 2017. http://americansongwriter.com/2009/12/chicken-soup-for-the-soul-behind-the-song-what-the-world-needs-now-is-love/.

Rogerson, Ben. "Lionel Richie reunites with Commodores bandmates." MusicRadar. July 07, 2009. Accessed August 18, 2017. http://www.musicradar.com/news/guitars/lionel-richie-reunites-with-commodores-bandmates-212129.

"Selma to Montgomery marches." Wikipedia. August 16, 2017. Accessed June 16, 2017. https://en.wikipedia.org/wiki/Selma_to_Montgomery_marches.

Spera, Keith. "Reviewing the Essence Festival's first 20 years: Kanye, Beyonce ruled, R. Kelly didn't." NOLA.com. July 01, 2014. Accessed August 18, 2017. http://www.nola.com/essencefest/index.ssf/2014/07/revisiting_essence_festivals_f.html.

"Thank God It's Friday (1978)." IMDb. Accessed July 29, 2017. http://www.imdb.com/title/tt0078382/.

The People History -- Steve Pearson. "What Happened in 1965 Important News and Events, Key Technology and Popular Culture." What Happened in 1965 inc. Pop Culture, Prices Significant Events, Key Technology and Inventions. Accessed June 16, 2017. http://www.thepeoplehistory.com/1965.html.

"Tom Joyner." Black America Web. May 17, 2016. Accessed June 3, 2017. https://blackamericaweb.com/tom-joyner/.

United Press International. "Entertainer Crash Lands Plane on Freeway." The Town Talk (Alexandria, Louisiana), October 24, 1980, 98th ed., sec. 222. October 24, 1980. Accessed May 1, 2017. https://www.newspapers.com/image/?spot=10681951.

"What Does NAACP Stand For?" NAACP. Accessed June 16, 2017. http://www.naacp.org/about-us/.

ABOUT THE AUTHOR

THOMAS MCCLARY is a singer, musician, writer, producer, and founder of the legendary funk and soul band, The Commodores. The Grammy award-winning group spent a decade at the top of the charts.

For McClary, music has always been about affecting the greater good. His music and his actions have been food for the soul. Born October 6, 1949 in Eustis, Florida, McClary was one of the first African-American students to integrate the Florida Public School System prior to the enforcement of Brown vs. Board of Education.

He continued standing up for justice while attending Tuskegee University. It was there, that he assembled The Commodores, and their bond was formed through music and social change.

McClary continues to personify musical genius, grace, and advocacy while pursuing his mission to spread love and light throughout the world. To learn more about Thomas McClary, visit www.thomasmcclary.com.

www.ingramcontent.com/pod-product-compliance
Lightning Source LLC
Chambersburg PA
CBHW040233020526
44113CB00052B/2676